Alroy: The Prince Of The Captivity

by

Benjamin Disraeli

The Echo Library 2007

Published by

The Echo Library

Echo Library
131 High St.
Teddington
Middlesex TW11 8HH

www.echo-library.com

Please report serious faults in the text to complaints@echo-library.com

ISBN 978-1-40686-130-3

AUTHOR'S PREFACE

Being at Jerusalem in the year 1831, and visiting the traditionary tombs of the Kings of Israel, my thoughts recurred to a personage whose marvellous career had, even in boyhood, attracted my attention, as one fraught with the richest materials of poetic fiction. And I then commenced these pages that should commemorate the name of Alroy. In the twelfth century, when he arose, this was the political condition of the East:

The Caliphate was in a state of rapid decay. The Seljukian Sultans, who had been called to the assistance of the Commanders of the Faithful, had become, like the Mayors of the palace in France, the real sovereigns of the Empire. Out of the dominions of the successors of the Prophet, they had carved four kingdoms, which conferred titles on four Seljukian Princes, to wit, the Sultan of Bagdad, the Sultan of Persia, the Sultan of Syria, and the Sultan of Roum, or Asia Minor.

But these warlike princes, in the relaxed discipline and doubtful conduct of their armies, began themselves to evince the natural effects of luxury and indulgence. They were no longer the same invincible and irresistible warriors who had poured forth from the shores of the Caspian over the fairest regions of the East; and although they still contrived to preserve order in their dominions, they witnessed with ill-concealed apprehension the rising power of the Kings of Karasmé, whose conquests daily made their territories more contiguous.

With regard to the Hebrew people, it should be known that, after the destruction of Jerusalem, the Eastern Jews, while they acknowledged the supremacy of their conquerors, gathered themselves together for all purposes of jurisdiction, under the control of a native ruler, a reputed descendant of David, whom they dignified with the title of 'The Prince of the Captivity.' If we are to credit the enthusiastic annalists of this imaginative people, there were periods of prosperity when the Princes of the Captivity assumed scarcely less state and enjoyed scarcely less power than the ancient Kings of Judah themselves. Certain it is that their power increased always in an exact proportion to the weakness of the Caliphate, and, without doubt, in some of the most distracted periods of the Arabian rule, the Hebrew Princes rose into some degree of local and temporary importance. Their chief residence was Bagdad, where they remained until the eleventh century, an age fatal in Oriental history, from the disasters of which the Princes of the Captivity were not exempt. They are heard of even in the twelfth century. I have ventured to place one at Hamadan, which was a favourite residence of the Hebrews, from being the burial-place of Esther and Mordecai.

With regard to the supernatural machinery of this romance, it is Cabalistical and correct. From the Spirits of the Tombs to the sceptre of Solomon, authority may be found in the traditions of the Hebrews for the introduction of all these spiritual agencies.

Grosvenor Gate: July, 1845.

CHAPTER I.

A Great Day for Israel.

THE cornets sounded a final flourish as the Prince of the Captivity dismounted from his white mule; his train shouted as if they were once more a people; and, had it not been for the contemptuous leer which played upon the countenances of the Moslem bystanders, it might have been taken for a day of triumph rather than of tribute.

'The glory has not departed!' exclaimed the venerable Bostenay, as he entered the hall of his mansion. 'It is not as the visit of Sheba unto Solomon; nevertheless the glory has not yet departed. You have done well, faithful Caleb.' The old man's courage waxed more vigorous, as each step within his own walls the more assured him against the recent causes of his fear, the audible curses and the threatened missiles of the unbelieving mob.

'It shall be a day of rejoicing and thanksgiving!' continued the Prince; 'and look, my faithful Caleb, that the trumpeters be well served. That last flourish was bravely done. It was not as the blast before Jericho; nevertheless, it told that the Lord of Hosts was for us. How the accursed Ishmaelites started! Did you mark, Caleb, that tall Turk in green upon my left? By the sceptre of Jacob, he turned pale! Oh! it shall be a day of rejoicing and thanksgiving! And spare neither the wine nor the flesh-pots for the people. Look you to this, my child, for the people shouted bravely and with a stout voice. It was not as the great shout in the camp when the ark returned; nevertheless, it was boldly done, and showed that the glory had not yet departed. So spare not the wine, my son, and drink to the desolation of Ishmael in the juice which he dare not quaff.'

'It has indeed been a great day for Israel!' exclaimed Caleb, echoing his master's exultation.

'Had the procession been forbidden,' continued Obstinacy, 'had it been reserved for me of all the princes to have dragged the accursed tribute upon foot, without trumpets and without guards, by this sceptre, my good Caleb, I really think that, sluggishly as this old blood now runs, I would—— But it is needless now to talk; the God of our fathers hath been our refuge.'

'Verily, my lord, we were as David in the wilderness of Ziph; but now we are as the Lord's anointed in the stronghold of Engedi!'

'The glory truly has not yet utterly departed,' resumed the Prince in a more subdued tone; 'yet if—— I tell you what, Caleb; praise the Lord that you are young.'

'My Prince too may yet live to see the good day.'

'Nay, my child, you misinterpret me. Your Prince has lived to see the evil day. 'Twas not of the coming that I thought when I bid you praise the Lord because you were young, the more my sin. I was thinking, Caleb, that if your hair was as mine, if you could recollect, like me, the days that are gone by, the days when it needed no bride to prove we were princes,«the glorious days when we led captivity captive; I was thinking, I say, my son, what a gainful heritage it is to be born after the joys that have passed away.'

'My father lived at Babylon,' said Caleb. 'Oh! name it not! name it not!' exclaimed the old chieftain. 'Dark was the day that we lost that second Zion! We were then also slaves to the Egyptian; but verily we ruled over the realm of Pharaoh. Why, Caleb, Caleb, you who know all, the days of toil, the nights restless as a love-sick boy's, which it has cost your Prince to gain permission to grace our tribute-day with the paltry presence of half-a-dozen guards; you who know all my difficulties, who have witnessed all my mortifications, what would you say to the purse of dirhems, surrounded by seven thousand scimitars?'

'Seven thousand scimitars!' 'Not one less; my father flourished one.' 'It was indeed a great day for Israel!' 'Nay, that is nothing. When old Alroy was prince, old David Alroy, for thirty years, good Caleb, thirty long years we paid *no* tribute to the Caliph.'

'No tribute! no tribute for thirty years! What marvel then, my Prince, that the Philistines have of late exacted interest?'

'Nay, that is nothing,' continued old Bostenay, unmindful of his servant's ejaculations. 'When Moctador was Caliph, he sent to the same Prince David, to know why the dirhems were not brought up, and David immediately called to horse, and, attended by all the chief people, rode to the palace, and told the Caliph that tribute was an acknowledgment made from the weak to the strong to insure protection and support; and, inasmuch as he and his people had garrisoned the city for ten years against the Seljuks, he held the Caliph in arrear.'

'We shall yet see an ass mount a ladder,'[1] exclaimed Caleb, with uplifted eyes of wonder.

'It is true, though,' continued the Prince; 'often have I heard my father tell the tale. He was then a child, and his mother held him up to see the procession return, and all the people shouted "The sceptre has not gone out of Jacob."'

'It was indeed a great day for Israel.'

'Nay, that is nothing. I could tell you such things! But we prattle; our business is not yet done. You to the people; the widow and the orphan are waiting. Give freely, good Caleb, give freely; the spoils of the Canaanite are no longer ours, nevertheless the Lord is still our God, and, after all, even this is a great day for Israel. And, Caleb, Caleb, bid my nephew, David Alroy, know that I would speak with him.'

'I will do all promptly, good master! We wondered that our honoured lord, your nephew, went not up with the donation this day.'

'Who bade you wonder? Begone, sir! How long are you to idle here? Away!

'They wonder he went not up with the tribute to-day. Ay! surely, a common talk. This boy will be our ruin, a prudent hand to wield our shattered sceptre. I have observed him from his infancy; he should have lived in Babylon. The old Alroy blood flows in his veins, a stiff-necked race. When I was a youth, his grandsire was my friend; I had some fancies then myself. Dreams, dreams! we have fallen on evil days, and yet we prosper. I have lived long enough to feel that a rich caravan, laden with the shawls of India and the stuffs of Samarcand, if not exactly like dancing before the ark, is still a goodly sight. And our hard-hearted rulers, with all their pride, can they subsist without us? Still we wax rich. I have lived to see the haughty Caliph sink into a slave viler far than Israel. And the victorious and voluptuous Seljuks, even now they tremble at the dim mention of the distant name of Arslan. Yet I, Bostenay, and the frail remnant of our scattered tribes, still we exist, and still, thanks to our God! we prosper. But the age of power has passed; it is by prudence now that we must flourish. The gibe and jest, the curse, perchance the blow, Israel now must bear, and with a calm or even smiling visage. What then? For every gibe and jest, for every curse, I'll have a dirhem; and for every blow, let him look to it who is my debtor, or wills to be so. But see, he comes, my nephew! His grandsire was my friend. Methinks I look upon him now: the same Alroy that was the partner of my boyish hours. And yet that fragile form and girlish face but ill consort with the dark passions and the dangerous fancies, which, I fear, lie hidden in that tender breast. Well, sir?'

'You want me, uncle?'

'What then? Uncles often want what nephews seldom offer.'

'I at least can refuse nothing; for I have naught to give.'

'You have a jewel which I greatly covet.' 'A jewel! See my chaplet! You gave it me, my uncle; it is yours.'

'I thank you. Many a blazing ruby, many a soft and shadowy pearl, and many an emerald glowing like a star in the far desert, I behold, my child. They are choice stones, and yet I miss a jewel far more precious, which, when I gave you this rich chaplet, David, I deemed you did possess.' 'How do you call it, sir?' 'Obedience.'

'A word of doubtful import; for to obey, when duty is disgrace, is not a virtue.'

'I see you read my thought. In a word, I sent for you to know, wherefore you joined me not to-day in offering our—our——'

'Tribute.'

'Be it so: tribute. Why were you absent?' 'Because it was a tribute; I pay none.' 'But that the dreary course of seventy winters has not erased the memory of my boyish follies, David, I should esteem you mad. Think you, because I am old, I am enamoured of disgrace, and love a house of bondage? If life were a mere question between freedom and slavery, glory and dishonour, all could decide. Trust me, there needs but little spirit to be a moody patriot in a sullen home, and vent your heroic spleen upon your fellow-sufferers, whose sufferings you cannot remedy. But of such stuff your race were ever made. Such deliverers ever abounded in the house of Alroy. And what has been the result? I found you and your sister orphan infants, your sceptre broken, and your tribes dispersed. The tribute, which now at least we pay like princes, was then exacted with the scourge and offered in chains. I collected our scattered people, I re-established our ancient throne, and this day, which you look upon as a day of humiliation and of mourning, is rightly considered by all a day of triumph and of feasting; for, has it not proved in the very teeth of the Ishmaelites, that the sceptre has not yet departed from Jacob?'

'I pray you, uncle, speak not of these things. I would not willingly forget you are my kinsman, and a kind one. Let there not be strife between us. What my feelings are is nothing. They are my own: I cannot change them. And for my ancestors, if they pondered much, and achieved little, why then 'twould seem our pedigree is pure, and I am their true son. At least one was a hero.'

'Ah! the great Alroy; you may well be proud of such an ancestor.'

'I am ashamed, uncle, ashamed, ashamed.'

'His sceptre still exists. At least, I have not betrayed him. And this brings me to the real purport of our interview. That sceptre I would return.'

'To whom?'

'To its right owner, to yourself.'

'Oh! no, no, no; I pray you, I pray you not. I do entreat you, sir, forget that I have a right as utterly as I disclaim it. That sceptre you have wielded it wisely and well; I beseech you keep it. Indeed, good uncle, I have no sort of talent for all the busy duties of this post.'

'You sigh for glory, yet you fly from toil.'

'Toil without glory is a menial's lot.'

'You are a boy; you may yet live to learn that the sweetest lot of life consists in tranquil duties and well-earned repose.'

'If my lot be repose, I'll find it in a lair.'

'Ah! David, David, there is a wildness in your temper, boy, that makes me often tremble. You are already too much alone, child. And for this, as well as weightier reasons, I am desirous that you should at length assume the office you inherit. What my poor experience can afford to aid you, as your counsellor, I shall ever proffer; and, for the rest, our God will not desert you, an orphan child, and born of royal blood.'

'Pr'ythee, no more, kind uncle. I have but little heart to mount a throne, which only ranks me as the first of slaves.'

'Pooh, pooh, you are young. Live we like slaves? Is this hall a servile chamber? These costly carpets, and these rich divans, in what proud harem shall we find their match? I feel not like a slave. My coffers are full of dirhems. Is that slavish? The wealthiest company of the caravan is ever Bostenay's. Is that to be a slave? Walk the bazaar of Bagdad, and you will find my name more potent than the Caliph's. Is that a badge of slavery?'

'Uncle, you toil for others.'

'So do we all, so does the bee, yet he is free and happy.'

'At least he has a sting.'

'Which he can use but once, and when he stings———'

'He dies, and like a hero. Such a death is sweeter than his honey.'

'Well, well, you are young, you are young. I once, too, had fancies. Dreams all, dreams all. I willingly would see you happy, child. Come, let that face brighten; after all, to-day is a great day. If you had seen what I have seen, David, you too would feel grateful. Come, let us feast. The Ishmaelite, the accursed child of Hagar, he does confess to-day that you are a prince; this day also you complete your eighteenth year. The custom of our people now requires that you should assume the attributes of manhood. To-day, then, your reign commences; and at our festival I will present the elders to their prince. For a while, farewell, my child. Array that face in smiles. I shall most anxiously await your presence.'

'Farewell, sir.'

He turned his head and watched his uncle as he departed: the bitter expression of his countenance gradually melted away as Bostenay disappeared: dejection succeeded to sarcasm; he sighed, he threw himself upon a couch and buried his face in his hands.

Suddenly he arose and paced the chamber with an irregular and moody step. He stopped, and leant against a column. He spoke in a tremulous and smothered voice:

'Oh! my heart is full of care, and my soul is dark with sorrow! What am I? What is all this? A cloud hangs heavy o'er my life. God of my fathers, let it burst!

'I know not what I feel, yet what I feel is madness. Thus to be is not to live, if life be what I sometimes dream, and dare to think it might be. To breathe, to feed, to sleep, to wake and breathe again, again to feel existence without hope; if this be life, why then these brooding thoughts that whisper death were better?

'Away! The demon tempts me. But to what? What nameless deed shall desecrate this hand? It must not be: the royal blood of twice two thousand years, it must not die, die like a dream. Oh! my heart is full of care, and my soul is dark with sorrow!

'Hark! the trumpets that sound our dishonour. Oh, that they but sounded to battle! Lord of Hosts, let me conquer or die! Let me conquer like David; or die, Lord, like Saul!

'Why do I live? Ah! could the thought that lurks within my secret heart but answer, not that trumpet's blast could speak as loud or clear. The votary of a false idea, I linger in this shadowy life, and feed on silent images which no eye but mine can gaze upon, till at length they are invested with all the terrible circumstance of life, and breathe, and act, and form a stirring world of fate and beauty, time, and death, and glory. And then, from out this dazzling wilderness of deeds, I wander forth and wake, and find myself in this dull house of bondage, even as I do now. Horrible! horrible!

'God, of my fathers! for indeed I dare not style thee God of their wretched sons; yet, by the memory of Sinai, let me tell thee that some of the antique blood yet beats within these pulses, and there yet is one who fain would commune with thee face to face, commune and conquer.

'And if the promise unto which we cling be not a cheat, why, let him come, come, and come quickly, for thy servant Israel, Lord, is now a slave so infamous, so woe-begone, and so contemned, that even when our fathers hung their harps by the sad waters of the Babylonian stream, why, it was paradise compared with what we suffer.

'Alas! they do not suffer; they endure and do not feel. Or by this time our shadowy cherubim would guard again the ark. It is the will that is the father to the deed, and he who broods over some long idea, however wild, will find his dream was but the prophecy of coming fate.

'And even now a vivid flash darts through the darkness of my mind. Methinks, methinks—ah! worst of woes to dream of glory in despair. No, no; I live and die a most ignoble thing; beauty and love, and fame and mighty deeds, the smile of women and the gaze of men, and the ennobling consciousness of worth, and all the fiery course of the creative passions, these are not for me, and I, Alroy, the descendant of sacred kings, and with a soul that pants for empire, I stand here extending my vain arm for my lost sceptre, a most dishonoured slave! And do I still exist? Exist! ay, merrily. Hark! Festivity holds her fair revel in these light-hearted walls. We are gay to-day; and yet, ere yon proud sun, whose mighty course was stayed before our swords that now he even does not deign to shine upon; ere yon proud sun shall, like a hero from a glorious field, enter the bright pavilion of his rest, there shall a deed be done.

'My fathers, my heroic fathers, if this feeble arm cannot redeem your heritage; if the foul boar must still wallow in thy sweet vineyard, Israel, at least I will not disgrace you. No! let me perish. The house of David is no more; no more our sacred seed shall lurk and linger, like a blighted thing, in this degenerate earth. If we cannot flourish, 'why, then, we will die!'

'Oh! say not so, my brother!'

He turns, he gazes on a face beauteous as a starry night; his heart is full, his voice is low.

'Ah, Miriam! thou queller of dark spirits! is it thou? Why art thou here?'

'Why am I here? Are you not here? and need I urge a stronger plea? Oh! brother dear, I pray you come, and mingle in our festival. Our walls are hung with flowers you love;[2] I culled them by the fountain's side; the holy lamps are trimmed and set, and you must raise their earliest flame. Without the gate, my maidens wait, to offer you a robe of state. Then, brother dear, I pray you come and mingle in our festival.'

'Why should we feast?'

'Ah! is it not in thy dear name these lamps are lit, these garlands hung? To-day to us a prince is given, to-day——'

'A prince without a kingdom.'

'But not without that which makes kingdoms precious, and which full many a royal heart has sighed for, willing subjects, David.'

'Slaves, Miriam, fellow-slaves.'

'What we are, my brother, our God has willed; and let us bow and tremble.'

'I will not bow, I cannot tremble.'

'Hush, David, hush! It was this haughty spirit that called the vengeance of the Lord upon us.'

'It was this haughty spirit that conquered Canaan.'

'Oh, my brother, my dear brother! they told me the dark spirit had fallen on thee, and I came, and hoped that Miriam might have charmed it. What we may have been, Alroy, is a bright dream; and what we may be, at least as bright a hope; and for what we are, thou art my brother. In thy love I find present felicity, and value more thy chance embraces and thy scanty smiles than all the vanished splendour of our race, our gorgeous gardens, and our glittering halls.'

'Who waits without there?'
'Caleb.'
'Caleb!'
'My lord.'
'Go tell my uncle that I will presently join the banquet. Leave me a moment, Miriam. Nay, dry those tears.'
'Oh, Alroy! they are not tears of sorrow.'
'God be with thee! Thou art the charm and consolation of my life. Farewell! farewell!

'I do observe the influence of women very potent over me. 'Tis not of such stuff that they make heroes. I know not love, save that pure affection which doth subsist between me and this girl, an orphan and my sister. We are so alike, that when, last Passover, in mimicry she twined my turban round her head, our uncle called her David.

'The daughters of my tribe, they please me not, though they are passing fair. Were our sons as brave as they are beautiful, we still might dance on Sion. Yet have I often thought that, could I pillow this moody brow upon some snowy bosom that were my own, and dwell in the wilderness, far from the sight and ken of man, and all the care and toil and wretchedness that groan and sweat and sigh about me, I might haply lose this deep sensation of overwhelming woe that broods upon by being. No matter! Life is but a dream, and mine must be a dull one.'

Without the gates of Hamadan, a short distance from the city, was an enclosed piece of elevated ground, in the centre of which rose an ancient sepulchre, the traditionary tomb of Esther and Mordecai.[3] This solemn and solitary spot was an accustomed haunt of Alroy, and thither, escaping from the banquet, about an hour before sunset, he this day repaired.

As he unlocked the massy gate of the burial-place, he heard behind him the trampling of a horse; and before he had again secured the entrance, some one shouted to him.

He looked up, and recognised the youthful and voluptuous Alschiroch, the governor of the city, and brother of the sultan of the Seljuks. He was attended only by a single running footman, an Arab, a detested favourite, and notorious minister of his pleasures.

'Dog!' exclaimed the irritated Alschiroch, 'art thou deaf, or obstinate, or both? Are we to call twice to our slaves? Unlock that gate!' 'Wherefore?' inquired Alroy.

'Wherefore! By the holy Prophet, he bandies questions with us! Unlock that gate, or thy head shall answer for it!'

'Who art thou,' inquired Alroy, 'whose voice is so loud? Art thou some holiday Turk, who hath transgressed the orders of thy Prophet, and drunken aught but water? Go to, or I will summon thee before thy Cadi;' and, so saying, he turned towards the tomb.

'By the eyes of my mother, the dog jeers us! But that we are already late, and this horse is like an untamed tiger, I would impale him on the spot. Speak to the dog, Mustapha! manage him!'

'Worthy Hebrew,' said the silky Mustapha, advancing, 'apparently you are not aware that this is our Lord Alschiroch. His highness would fain walk his horse through the burial-ground of thy excellent people, as he is obliged to repair, on urgent matters, to a holy Santon, who sojourns on the other side of the hill, and time presses.'

'If this be our Lord Alschiroch, thou doubtless art his faithful slave, Mustapha.'

'I am, indeed, his poor slave. What then, young master?'

'Deem thyself lucky that the gate is closed. It was but yesterday thou didst insult the sister of a servant of my house. I would not willingly sully my hands with such miserable blood as thine, out away, wretch, away!'

'Holy Prophet! who is this dog?' exclaimed the astonished governor.

"Tis the young Alroy,' whispered Mustapha, who had not at first recognised him; 'he they call their Prince; a most headstrong youth. My lord, we had better proceed.'

'The young Alroy! I mark him. They must have a prince too! The young Alroy! Well, let us away, and, dog!' shouted Alschiroch, rising in his stirrups, and shaking his hand with a threatening air, 'dog! remember thy tribute!'

Alroy rushed to the gate, but the massy lock was slow to open; and ere he could succeed, the fiery steed had borne Alschiroch beyond pursuit.

An expression of baffled rage remained for a moment on his countenance; for a moment he remained with his eager eye fixed on the route of his vanished enemy, and then he walked slowly towards the tomb; but his excited temper was now little in unison with the still reverie in which he had repaired to the sepulchre to indulge. He was restless and disquieted, and at length he wandered into the woods, which rose on the summit of the burial-place.

He found himself upon a brow crested with young pine-trees, in the midst of which rose a mighty cedar. He threw himself beneath its thick and shadowy branches, and looked upon a valley small and green; in the midst of which was a marble fountain, the richly-carved cupola,[4] supported by twisted columns, and banded by a broad inscription in Hebrew characters. The bases of the white pillars were covered with wild flowers, or hidden by beds of variegated gourds. The transparent sunset flung over the whole scene a soft but brilliant light.

The tranquil hour, the beauteous scene, the sweetness and the stillness blending their odour and serenity, the gentle breeze that softly rose, and summoned forth the languid birds to cool their plumage in the twilight air, and wave their radiant wings in skies as bright—— Ah! what stern spirit will not yield to the soft genius of subduing eve?

And Alroy gazed upon the silent loneliness of earth, and a tear stole down his haughty cheek.

"Tis singular! but when I am thus alone at this still hour, I ever fancy I gaze upon the Land of Promise. And often, in my dreams, some sunny spot, the bright memorial of a roving hour, will rise upon my sight, and, when I wake, I feel as if I had been in Canaan. Why am I not? The caravan that bears my uncle's goods across the Desert would bear me too. But I rest here, my miserable life running to seed in the dull misery of this wretched city, and do nothing. Why, the old captivity was empire to our inglorious bondage. We have no Esther now to share their thrones, no politic Mordecai, no purple-vested Daniel. O Jerusalem, Jerusalem! I do believe one sight of thee would nerve me to the sticking-point. And yet to gaze upon thy fallen state, my uncle tells me that of the Temple not a stone remains. 'Tis horrible. Is there no hope?'

'*The bricks are fallen, but we will rebuild with marble; the sycamores are cut down, but we will replace them with cedars.*'

'The chorus of our maidens, as they pay their evening visit to the fountain's side.[5] The burden is prophetic.

'Hark again! How beautifully, upon the soft and flowing air, their sweet and mingled voices blend and float!'

'*YET AGAIN I WILL BUILD THEE, AND THOU SHALT BE BUILT, O VIRGIN OF ISRAEL! YET AGAIN SHALT THOU DECK THYSELF WITH THY TABRETS, AND GO FORTH IN THE DANCE OF THOSE THAT MAKE MERRY. YET AGAIN SHALT THOU PLANT VINEYARDS ON THE MOUNTAINS OF SAMARIA.*'

'See! their white forms break through the sparkling foliage of the sunny shrubs as they descend, with measured step, that mild declivity. A fair society in bright procession: each one clothed in solemn drapery, veiling her shadowy face with modest hand, and bearing on her graceful head a graceful vase. Their leader is my sister.

'And now they reach the fountain's side, and dip their vases in the water, pure and beauteous as themselves. Some repose beneath the marble pillars; some, seated 'mid the flowers, gather sweets, and twine them into garlands; and that wild girl, now that the order is broken, touches with light fingers her moist vase, and showers startling drops of glittering light on her serener sisters. Hark! again they sing.'

'*O VINE OF SIBMAH! UPON THY SUMMER FRUITS, AND UPON THY VINTAGE, A SPOILER HATH FALLEN!*'

A scream, a shriek, a long wild shriek, confusion, flight, despair! Behold! from out the woods a tur-baned man rushes, and seizes the leader of the chorus. Her companions fly on all sides, Miriam alone is left in the arms of Alschiroch.

The water column wildly rising from the breast of summer ocean, in some warm tropic clime, when the sudden clouds too well discover that the holiday of heaven is over, and the shrieking sea-birds tell a time of fierce commotion, the column rising from the sea, it was not so wild as he, the young Alroy.

Pallid and mad, he swift upsprang, and he tore up a tree by its lusty roots, and down the declivity, dashing with rapid leaps, panting and wild, he struck the ravisher on the temple with the mighty pine. Alschiroch fell lifeless on the sod, and Miriam fainting into her brother's arms.

And there he stood, fixed and immovable, gazing upon his sister's deathly face, and himself exhausted by passion and his exploit, supporting her cherished but senseless body.

One of the fugitive maidens appeared reconnoitring in the distance. When she observed her mistress in the arms of one of her own people, her courage revived, and, desirous of rallying her scattered companions, she raised her voice, and sang:

'HASTE, DAUGHTERS OF JERUSALEM; O! HASTE, FOR THE LORD HAS AVENGED US, AND THE SPOILER IS SPOILED.'

And soon the verse was responded to from various quarters of the woods, and soon the virgins reassembled, singing,

'WE COME, O DAUGHTER OF JERUSALEM! WE COME; FOR THE LORD HAS AVENGED US, AND THE SPOILER IS SPOILED.'

They gathered round their mistress, and one loosened her veil, and another brought water from the fountain, and sprinkled her reviving countenance. And Miriam opened her eyes, and said, 'My brother!' And he answered, 'I am here.' And she replied in a low voice, 'Fly, David, fly; for the man you have stricken is a prince among the people.'

'He will be merciful, my sister; and, doubtless, since he first erred, by this time he has forgotten my offence.'

'Justice and mercy! Oh, my brother, what can these foul tyrants know of either! Already he has perhaps doomed you to some refined and procrastinated torture, already—— Ah! what unutterable woe is mine! fly, my brother, fly!'

'Fly, fly, fly!'

'There is no fear, my Miriam; would all his accursed race could trouble us as little as their sometime ruler. See, he sleeps soundly. But his carcass shall not defile our fresh fountain and our fragrant flowers. I'll stow it in the woods, and stroll here at night to listen to the jackals at their banquet.'

'You speak wildly, David. What! No! It is impossible! He is not dead! You have not slain him!

He sleeps, he is afraid. He mimics death that we may leave his side, and he may rise again in safety. Girls, look to him. David, you do not answer. Brother, dear brother, surely he has swooned! I thought he had fled. Bear water, maidens, to that terrible man. I dare not look upon him.'

'Away! I'll look on him, and I'll triumph. Dead! Alschiroch dead! Why, but a moment since, this clotted carcass was a prince, my tyrant! So we can rid ourselves of them, eh? If the prince fall, why not the people? Dead, absolutely dead, and I his slayer! Hah! at length I am a man. This, this indeed is life. Let me live slaying!'

'Woe! woe, our house is fallen! The wildness of his gestures frightens me. David, David, I pray thee cease. He hears me not; my voice, perchance, is thin. I am very faint. Maidens, kneel to your Prince, and soothe the madness of his passion.'

'SWEET IS THE VOICE OF A SISTER IN THE SEASON OF SORROW, AND WISE IS THE COUNSEL OF THOSE WHO LOVE US.'

'Why, this is my Goliath! a pebble or a stick, it is the same. The Lord of Hosts is with us. Rightly am I called David.'

'DELIVER US FROM OUR ENEMIES, O LORD! FROM THOSE WHO RISE UP AGAINST US, AND THOSE WHO LIE IN WAIT FOR US.'

'Were but this blow multiplied, were but the servants of my uncle's house to do the same, why, we should see again the days of Elah! The Philistine, the foul, lascivious, damnable Philistine! and he must touch my sister! Oh! that all his tribe were here, all, all! I'd tie such firebrands to their foxes' tails, the blaze should light to freedom!'

While he spoke, a maiden, who had not yet rejoined the company, came running towards them swiftly with an agitated countenance.

'Fly,' she exclaimed, 'they come, they come!'

Miriam was reclining in an attendant's arms, feeble and faint, but the moment her quick ear caught these words she sprang up, and seized her brother's arm.

'Alroy! David! brother, dear brother! I beseech thee, listen, I am thy sister, thy Miriam; they come, they come, the hard-hearted, wicked men, they come, to kill, perhaps to torture thee, my tender brother. Rouse thyself, David; rouse thyself from this wild, fierce dream: save thyself, fly!'

'Ah! is it thou, Miriam? Thou seest he sleepeth soundly. I was dreaming of noble purposes and mighty hopes. Tis over now. I am myself again. What wouldst thou?'

'They come, the fierce retainers of this fallen man; they come to seize thee. Fly, David!'

'And leave thee?'

'I and my maidens, we have yet time to escape by the private way we entered, our uncle's garden. When in his house, we are for a moment safe, as safe as our poor race can ever be. Bostenay is so rich, so wise, so prudent, so learned in man's ways, and knows so well the character and spirit of these men, all will go right; I fear nothing. But thou, if thou art here, or to be found, thy blood alone will satiate them. If they be persuaded that thou hast escaped, as I yet pray thou mayest, their late master here, whom they could scarcely love, why, give me thy arm an instant, sweet Beruna. So, that's well. I was saying, if well bribed,—and they may have all my jewels,—why, very soon, he will be as little in their memories as he is now in life. I can scarcely speak; I feel my words wander, or seem to wander; I could swoon, but will not; nay! do not fear. I will reach home. These maidens are my charge. 'Tis in these crises we should show the worth of royal blood. I'll see them safe, or die with them.'

'O! my sister, methinks I never knew I was a brother until this hour. My precious Miriam, what is life? what is revenge, or even fame and freedom without thee? I'll stay.'

'SWEET IS THE VOICE OF A SISTER IN THE SEASON OF SORROW, AND WISE IS THE COUNSEL OF THOSE WHO LOVE US.'

'Fly, David, fly!'

'Fly! whither and how?'

The neigh of a horse sounded from the thicket.

'Ah! they come!' exclaimed the distracted Miriam.

'*ALL THIS HAS COME UPON US, O LORD! YET HAVE WE NOT FORGOTTEN THEE, NEITHER HAVE WE DEALT FALSELY IN THY COVENANT.*'

'Hark! again it neighs! It is a horse that calleth to its rider. I see it. Courage, Miriam! it is no enemy, but a very present friend in time of trouble. It is Alschiroch's courser. He passed me on it by the tomb ere sunset. I marked it well, a very princely steed.'

'*BEHOLD, BEHOLD, A RAM IS CAUGHT IN THE THICKET BY HIS HORNS.*'

'Our God hath not forgotten us! Quick, maidens, bring forth the goodly steed. What! do you tremble? I'll be his groom.'

'Nay! Miriam, beware, beware. It is an untamed beast, wild as the whirlwind. Let me deal with him.'

He ran after her, dashed into the thicket, and brought forth the horse.

Short time I ween that stately steed had parted from his desert home; his haughty crest, his eye of fire, the glory of his snorting nostril, betoken well his conscious pride, and pure nobility of race. His colour was like the sable night shining with a thousand stars, and he pawed the ground with his delicate hoof, like an eagle flapping its wing.

Alroy vaulted on his back, and reined him with a master's hand.

'Hah!' he exclaimed, 'I feel more like a hero than a fugitive. Farewell, my sister; farewell, ye gentle maidens; fare ye well, and cherish my precious Miriam. One embrace, sweet sister,' and he bent down and whispered, 'Tell the good Bostenay not to spare his gold, for I have a deep persuasion that, ere a year shall roll its heavy course, I shall return and make our masters here pay for this hurried ride and bitter parting. Now for the desert!'

CHAPTER II.

The Slaying of an Ishmaelite

SPEED, fleetly speed, thou courser bold, and track the desert's trackless way. Beneath thee is the boundless earth, above thee is the boundless heaven, an iron soil and brazen sky. Speed, swiftly speed, thou courser bold, and track the desert's trackless way. Ah! dost thou deem these salty plains[6] lead to thy Yemen's happy groves, and dost thou scent on the hot breeze the spicy breath of Araby? A sweet delusion, noble steed, for this briny wilderness leads not to the happy groves of Yemen, and the breath thou scentest on the coming breeze is not the spicy breath of Araby.

The day has died, the stars have risen, with all the splendour of a desert sky, and now the Night descending brings solace on her dewy wings to the fainting form and pallid cheek of the youthful Hebrew Prince.

Still the courser onward rushes, still his mighty heart supports him. Season and space, the glowing soil, the burning ray, yield to the tempest of his frame, the thunder of his nerves, and lightning of his veins.

Food or water they have none. No genial fount, no graceful tree, rise with their pleasant company. Never a beast or bird is there, in that hoary desert bare. Nothing breaks the almighty stillness. Even the jackal's felon cry might seem a soothing melody. A grey wild rat, with snowy whiskers, out of a withered bramble stealing, with a youthful snake in its ivory teeth, in the moonlight grins with glee. This is their sole society.

Morn comes, the fresh and fragrant morn, for which even the guilty sigh. Morn comes, and all is visible. And light falls like a signet on the earth, and its face is turned like wax beneath a seal. Before them and also on their right was the sandy desert; but in the night they had approached much nearer to the mountainous chain, which bounded the desert on the left, and whither Alroy had at first guided the steed.

The mountains were a chain of the mighty Elburz; and, as the sun rose from behind a lofty peak, the horse suddenly stopped and neighed, as if asking for water. But Alroy, himself exhausted, could only soothe him with caresses. And the horse, full of courage, understood his master, and neighed again more cheerfully.

For an hour or two the Prince and his faithful companion proceeded slowly, but, as the day advanced, the heat became so oppressive, and the desire to drink so overwhelming, that Alroy again urged on the steed towards the mountains, where he knew that he should find a well. The courser dashed willingly forward, and seemed to share his master's desire to quit the arid and exhausting wilderness.

More than once the unhappy fugitive debated whether he should not allow himself to drop from his seat and die; no torture that could await him at Hamadan but seemed preferable to the prolonged and inexpressible anguish which he now endured. As he rushed along, leaning on his bearer's neck, he perceived a patch of the desert that seemed of a darker colour than the surrounding sand. Here, he believed, might perhaps be found water. He tried to check the steed, but with difficulty he succeeded, and with still greater difficulty dismounted. He knelt down, and feebly raked up the sand with his hands. It was moist. He nearly fainted over his fruitless labour. At length, when he had dug about a foot deep, there bubbled up some water. He dashed in his hand, but it was salt as the ocean. When the horse saw the water his ears rose, but, when he smelt it, he turned away his head, and neighed most piteously.

'Alas, poor beast!' exclaimed Alroy, 'I am the occasion of thy suffering, I, who would be a kind master to thee, if the world would let me. Oh, that we were once more by my own fair fountain! The thought is madness. And Miriam too! I fear I am sadly tender-hearted.' He leant against his horse's back, with a feeling of utter exhaustion, and burst into hysteric sobs.

And the steed softly moaned, and turned its head, and gently rubbed its face against his arm, as if to solace him in his suffering. And strange, but Alroy was relieved by having given way to his emotion, and, charmed with the fondness of the faithful horse, he leant down and took water, and threw it over its feet to cool them, and wiped the foam from its face, and washed it, and the horse again neighed.

And now Alroy tried to remount, but his strength failed him, and the horse immediately knelt down and received him. And the moment that the Prince was in his seat, the horse rose, and again proceeded at a rapid pace in their old direction. Towards sunset they were within a few miles of the broken and rocky ground into which the mountains descended; and afar off Alroy recognised the cupola of the long-expected well. With re-animated courage and rallied energies he patted his courser's neck, and pointed in the direction of the cupola, and the horse pricked up its ears, and increased its pace.

Just as the sun set, they reached the well. Alroy jumped off the horse, and would have led it to the fountain, but the animal would not advance. It stood shivering with a glassy eye, and then with a groan fell down and died.

Night brings rest; night brings solace; rest to the weary, solace to the sad. And to the desperate night brings despair.

The moon has sunk to early rest; but a thousand stars are in the sky. The mighty mountains rise severe in the clear and silent air. In the forest all is still. The tired wind no longer roams, but has lightly dropped on its leafy couch, and sleeps like man. Silent all but the fountain's drip. And by the fountain's side a youth is lying.

Suddenly a creature steals through the black and broken rocks. Ha, ha! the jackal smells from afar the rich corruption of the courser's clay. Suddenly and silently it steals, and stops, and smells. Brave banqueting I ween to-night for all that goodly company. Jackal, and fox, and marten-cat, haste ye now, ere morning's break shall call the vulture to his feast and rob you of your prey.

The jackal lapped the courser's blood, and moaned with exquisite delight. And in a moment, a faint bark was heard in the distance. And the jackal peeled the flesh from one of the ribs, and again burst into a shriek of mournful ecstasy.

Hark, their quick tramp! First six, and then three, galloping with ungodly glee. And a marten-cat came rushing down from the woods; but the jackals, fierce in their number, drove her away, and there she stood without the circle, panting, beautiful, and baffled, with her white teeth and glossy skin, and sparkling eyes of rabid rage.[7]

Suddenly as one of the half-gorged jackals retired from the main corpse, dragging along a stray member by some still palpitating nerves, the marten-cat made a spring at her enemy, carried off his prey, and rushed into the woods.

Her wild scream of triumph woke a lion from his lair. His mighty form, black as ebony, moved on a distant eminence, his tail flowed like a serpent. He roared, and the jackals trembled, and immediately ceased from their banquet, turning their heads in the direction of their sovereign's voice. He advanced; he stalked towards them. They retired; he bent his head, examined the carcass with condescending curiosity, and instantly quitted it with royal disdain. The jackals again collected around their garbage. The lion advanced to the fountain to drink. He beheld a man. His mane rose, his tail was wildly agitated, he bent over the sleeping Prince, he uttered an awful roar, which awoke Alroy.

He awoke; his gaze met the flaming eyes of the enormous beast fixed upon him with a blended feeling of desire and surprise. He awoke, and from a swoon; but the dreamless trance had refreshed the exhausted energies of the desolate wanderer; in an instant he collected his senses, remembered all that had passed, and comprehended his present situation. He returned the lion a glance as imperious, and fierce, and scrutinsing, as his own. For a moment, their flashing orbs vied in regal rivalry; but at length the spirit of the mere animal yielded to the genius of the man. The lion, cowed, slunk away, stalked with haughty timidity through the rocks, and then sprang into the forest.

Morn breaks; a silver light is shed over the blue and starry sky. Pleasant to feel is the breath of dawn. Night brings repose, but day brings joy.

The carol of a lonely bird singing in the wilderness! A lonely bird that sings with glee! Sunny and sweet, and light and clear, its airy notes float through the sky, and trill with innocent revelry.

The lonely youth on the lonely bird upgazes from the fountain's side. High in the air it proudly floats, balancing its crimson wings, and its snowy tail, long, delicate, and thin, shines like a sparkling meteor in the sun.

The carol of a lonely bird singing in the wilderness! Suddenly it downward dashes, and thrice with circling grace it flies around the head of the Hebrew Prince. Then by his side it gently drops a bunch of fresh and fragrant dates.

'Tis gone, 'tis gone! that cheerful stranger, gone to the palmy land it loves; gone like a bright and pleasant dream. A moment since and it was there, glancing in the sunny air, and now the sky is without a guest. Alas, alas! no more is heard the carol of that lonely bird singing in the wilderness.

'As thou didst feed Elijah, so also hast thou fed me, God of my fathers!' And Alroy arose, and he took his turban and unfolded it, and knelt and prayed. And then he ate of the dates, and drank of the fountain, and, full of confidence in the God of Israel, the descendant of David pursued his flight.

He now commenced the ascent of the mountainous chain, a wearisome and painful toil. Two hours past noon he reached the summit of the first ridge, and looked over a wild and chaotic waste full of precipices and ravines, and dark unfathomable gorges. The surrounding hills were ploughed in all directions by the courses of dried-up cataracts, and here and there a few savage goats browsed on an occasional patch of lean and sour pasture. This waste extended for many miles; the distance formed by a more elevated range of mountains, and beyond these, high in the blue sky, rose the loftiest peaks of Elburz,[8] shining with sharp glaciers of eternal snow.

It was apparent that Alroy was no stranger in the scene of his flight. He had never hesitated as to his course, and now, after having rested for a short time on the summit, he descended towards the left by a natural but intricate path, until his progress was arrested by a black ravine. Scarcely half a dozen yards divided him from the opposite precipice by which it was formed, but the gulf beneath, no one could shoot a glance at its invisible termination without drawing back with a cold shudder.

The Prince knelt down and examined the surrounding ground with great care. At length he raised a small square stone which covered a metallic plate, and, taking from his vest a carnelian talisman covered with strange characters, he knocked thrice upon the plate with the signet. A low solemn murmur sounded around. Presently the plate flew off, and Alroy pulled forth several yards of an iron chain, which he threw over to the opposite precipice. The chain fastened without difficulty to the rock, and was evidently constrained by some magnetic influence. The Prince, seizing the chain with both his hands, now swung across the ravine. As he landed, the chain parted from the rock, swiftly disappeared down the opposite aperture, and its covering closed with the same low, solemn murmur as before.

Alroy proceeded for about a hundred paces through a natural cloister of basalt until he arrived at a large uncovered court of the same formation, which a stranger might easily have been excused for believing to have been formed and smoothed by art. In its centre bubbled up a perpetual spring, icy cold; the stream had worn a channel through the pavement, and might be traced for some time wandering among the rocks, until at length it leaped from a precipice into a gorge below, in a gauzy shower of variegated spray. Crossing the court, Alroy now entered a vast cavern.

The cavern was nearly circular in form, lighted from a large aperture in the top. Yet a burning lamp, in a distant and murky corner, indicated that its inhabitant did not trust merely to this natural source of the great blessing of existence. In the centre of the cave was a circular and brazen table, sculptured with strange characters and mysterious figures: near it was a couch, on which lay several volumes.[9] Suspended from the walls were a shield, some bows and arrows, and other arms.

As the Prince of the Captivity knelt down and kissed the vacant couch, a figure advanced from the extremity of the cavern into the light. He was a man of middle age, considerably above the common height, with a remarkably athletic frame, and a strongly-marked but majestic countenance. His black beard descended to his waist, over a dark red robe, encircled by a black girdle embroidered with yellow characters, like those sculptured on the brazen table. Black also was his turban, and black his large and luminous eye.

The stranger advanced so softly, that Alroy did not perceive him, until the Prince again rose.

'Jabaster!' exclaimed the Prince.

'Sacred seed of David,' answered the Cabalist,[10] 'thou art expected. I read of thee in the stars last night. They spoke of trouble.'

'Trouble or triumph, Time must prove which it is, great master. At present I am a fugitive and exhausted. The bloodhounds track me, but methinks I have baffled them now. I have slain an Ishmaelite.'

CHAPTER III

The Hope of Israel

IT WAS midnight. Alroy slept upon the couch: his sleep was troubled. Jabaster stood by his side motionless, and gazing intently upon his slumbering guest.

'The only hope of Israel,' murmured the Cabalist,' my pupil and my prince! I have long perceived in his young mind the seed of mighty deeds, and o'er his future life have often mused with a prophetic hope. The blood of David, the sacred offspring of a solemn race. There is a magic in his flowing veins my science cannot reach.

'When, in my youth, I raised our standard by my native Tigris, and called our nation to restore their ark, why, we were numerous, wealthy, potent; we were a people then, and they flocked to it boldly. Did we lack counsel? Did we need a leader? Who can aver that Jabaster's brain or arm was ever wanting? And yet the dream dissolved, the glorious vision! Oh! when I struck down Marvan, and the Caliph's camp flung its blazing shadow over the bloody river, ah! then indeed I lived. Twenty years of vigil may gain a pardon that I then forgot we lacked the chief ingredient in the spell, the blood that sleeps beside me.

'I recall the glorious rapture of that sacred strife amid the rocks of Caucasus. A fugitive, a proscribed and outlawed wretch, whose life is common sport, and whom the vilest hind may slay without a bidding. I, who would have been Messiah!

'Burn thy books, Jabaster; break thy brazen tables; forget thy lofty science, Cabalist, and read the stars no longer.[11] But last night I stood upon the gulf which girds my dwelling: in one hand, I held my sacred talisman, that bears the name ineffable; in the other, the mystic record of our holy race. I remembered that I had evoked spirits, that I had communed with the great departed, and that the glowing heavens were to me a natural language. I recalled, as consolation to my gloomy soul, that never had my science been exercised but for a sacred or a noble purpose. And I remembered Israel, my brave, my chosen, and my antique race, slaves, wretched slaves. I was strongly tempted to fling me down this perilous abyss, and end my learning and my life together.

'But, as I gazed upon the star of David, a sudden halo rose around its rays, and ever and anon a meteor shot from out the silver veil. I read that there was trouble in the holy seed; and now comes this boy, who has done a deed which——'

'The ark, the ark! I gaze upon the ark!' 'The slumberer speaks; the words of sleep are sacred.' 'Salvation only from the house of David.' 'A mighty truth; my life too well has proved it. 'He is more calm. It is the holy hour. I'll steal into the court, and gaze upon the star that sways the fortunes of his royal house.'

The moonbeam fell upon the fountain; the pavement of the court was a flood of light; the rocks rose dark around. Jabaster, seated by the spring, and holding his talisman in his left hand, shaded his sight with the other as he gazed upon the luminous heavens.

A shriek! his name was called. Alroy, wild and panting, rushed into the court with extended arms. The Cabalist started up, seized him, and held him in his careful grasp, foaming and in convulsions.

'Jabaster, Jabaster!'

'I am here, my child.'

'The Lord hath spoken.'

'The Lord is our refuge. Calm thyself, son of David, and tell me all.'

'I have been sleeping, master; is it not so?'

'Even so, my child. Exhausted by his flight and the exciting narrative of his exploit, my Prince lay down upon the couch and slumbered; but I fear that slumber was not repose.'

'Repose and I have naught in common now. Farewell for ever to that fatal word. I am the Lord's anointed.'

'Drink of the fountain, David: it will restore thee.'

'Restore the covenant, restore the ark, restore the holy city.'

'The Spirit of the Lord hath fallen upon him. Son of David, I adjure thee tell me all that hath passed. I am a Levite; in my hand I hold the name ineffable.'

'Take thy trumpet then, summon the people, bid them swiftly raise again our temple. "The bricks have fallen, but we will rebuild with marble." Didst hear that chorus, sir?'

'Unto thy chosen ear alone it sounded.'

'Where am I? This is not our fountain. Yet thou didst say, "the fountain." Think me not wild. I know thee, I know all. Thou art not Miriam. Thou art Jabaster; I am Alroy. But thou didst say, "the fountain," and it distracted me, and called back my memory to——

'God of Israel, lo, I kneel before thee! Here, in the solitude of wildest nature, my only witness here this holy man, I kneel and vow, Lord! I will do thy bidding. I am young, O God! and weak; but thou, Lord, art all-powerful! What God is like to thee? Doubt not my courage, Lord; and fill me with thy spirit! but remember, remember her, O Lord! remember Miriam. It is the only worldly thought I have, and it is pure.'

'Still of his sister! Calm thyself, my son.'

'Holy master, thou dost remember when I was thy pupil in this cavern. Thou hast not forgotten those days of tranquil study, those sweet, long wandering nights of sacred science! I was dutiful, and hung upon each accent of thy lore with the devotion that must spring from love.'

'I cannot weep, Alroy; but were it in my power, I would yield a tear of homage to the memory of those days.'

'How calmly have we sat on some high brow, and gazed upon the stars!'

'Tis very true, sweet child.'

'And if thou e'er didst chide me, 'twas half in jest, and only for my silence.'

'What would he now infer? No matter, he grows calmer. How solemn is his visage in the moonlight! And yet not Solomon, upon his youthful throne, could look more beautiful.'

'I never told thee an untruth, Jabaster.'

'My life upon thy faith.'

'Fear not the pledge, and so believe me, on the mountain brow watching the starry heavens with thyself, I was not calmer than I feel, sir, now.'

'I do believe thee.'

'Then, Jabaster, believe as fully I am the Lord's anointed.'

'Tell me all, my child.'

'Know, then, that sleeping on the couch within, my sleep was troubled. Many dreams I had, indefinite and broken. I recall none of their images, except I feel a dim sensation 'twas my lot to live in brighter days than now rise on our race. Suddenly I stood upon a mountain tall and grey, and gazed upon the stars. And, as I gazed, a trumpet sounded. Its note thrilled through my soul. Never have I heard a sound so awful. The thunder, when it broke over the cavern here, and shivered the peak, whose ruins lie around us, was but a feeble worldly sound to this almighty music. My cheek grew pale, I panted even for breath. A flaming light spread over the sky, the stars melted away, and I beheld, advancing from the bursting radiancy, the foremost body of a mighty host.

'Oh! not when Saul led forth our fighting men against the Philistine, not when Joab numbered the warriors of my great ancestor, did human vision gaze upon a scene of so much martial splendour. Chariots and cavalry, and glittering trains of plumed warriors too robust to need a courser's solace; streams of shining spears, and banners like a sunset; reverend priests swinging their perfumed censers, and prophets hymning with their golden harps a most triumphant future.

'"Joy, joy," they say, "to Israel, for he cometh, he cometh in his splendour and his might, the great Messiah of our ancient hopes."

'And, lo! a mighty chariot now appeared, drawn by strange beasts whose forms were half obscured by the bright flames on which they seemed to float. In that glorious car a warrior stood, proud and immovable his form, his countenance. Hold my hand, Jabaster, while I speak; that chieftain was myself!'

'Proceed, proceed, my son.'

'I started in my dream, and I awoke. I found myself upsitting on my couch. The pageantry had vanished. Naught was seen but the bright moonlight and the gloomy cave. And, as I sighed to think I e'er had wakened, and mused upon the strangeness of my vision, a still small voice descended from above and called, "Alroy!" I started, but I answered not. Methought it was my fancy. Again my name was called, and now I murmured, "Lord, I am here, what wouldst thou?" Naught responded, and soon great dread came over me, and I rushed out and called to thee, my master.'

'It was "the Daughter of the Voice"[12] that spake. Since the Captivity 'tis the only mode by which the saints are summoned. Oft have I heard of it, but never in these sad degenerate days has its soft aspiration fallen upon us. These are strange times and tidings. The building of the temple is at hand. Son of David, my heart is full. Let us to prayer!'

Day dawned upon Jabaster, still musing in solitude among his rocks. Within the cavern, Alroy remained in prayer.

Often and anxiously the Cabalist shot a glance at his companion, and then again relapsed into reverie.

'The time is come that I must to this youth reveal the secrets of my early life. Much will he hear of glory, much of shame. Naught must I conceal, and naught gloss over.

'I must tell how in the plains of Tigris I upraised the sacred standard of our chosen race, and called them from their bondage; how, despairing of his recreant fathers, and inspired by human power alone, I vainly claimed the mighty office for his sacred blood alone reserved. God of my fathers, grant that future service, the humble service of a contrite soul, may in the coming glory that awaits us, atone for past presumption!

'But for him great trials are impending. Not lightly must that votary be proved, who fain would free a people. The Lord is faithful to his promise, but the Lord will choose his season and his minister. Courage, and faith, and deep humility, and strong endurance, and the watchful soul temptation cannot sully, these are the fruits we lay upon his altar, and meekly watch if some descending flame will vouchsafe to accept and brightly bless them.

'It is written in the dread volume of our mystic lore, that not alone the Saviour shall spring from out our house of princes, but that none shall rise to free us, until, alone and unassisted, he have gained the sceptre which Solomon of old wielded within his cedar palaces.

'That sceptre must he gain. This fragile youth, untried and delicate, unknowing in the ways of this strange world, where every step is danger, how much hardship, how much peril, what withering disappointment, what dull care, what long despondency, what never-ending lures, now lie in ambush for this gentle boy! O my countrymen, is this your hope? And I, with all my lore, and all my courage, and all my deep intelligence of man; unhappy Israel, why am I not thy Prince?

'I check the blasphemous thought. Did not his great ancestor, as young and as untried, a beardless stripling, with but a pebble, a small smoothed stone, level a mailed giant with the ground, and save his people?

'He is clearly summoned. The Lord is with him. Be he with the Lord, and we shall prosper.'

It was at sunset, on the third day after the arrival of Alroy at the cave of the Cabalist, that the Prince of the Captivity commenced his pilgrimage in quest of the sceptre of Solomon.

Silently the pilgrim and his master took their way to the brink of the ravine, and there they stopped to part, perhaps forever.

'It is a bitter moment, Alroy. Human feelings are not for beings like us, yet they will have their way. Remember all. Cherish the talisman as thy life: nay!

welcome death with it pressing against thy heart, rather than breathe without it. Be firm, be pious. Think of thy ancestors, think of thy God.'

'Doubt me not, dear master; if I seem not full of that proud spirit, which was perhaps too much my wont, ascribe it not to fear, Jabaster, nor even to the pain of leaving thee, dear friend. But ever since that sweet and solemn voice summoned me so thrillingly, I know not how it is, but a change has come over my temper; yet I am firm, oh! firmer far than when I struck down the Ishmaelite. Indeed, indeed, fear not for me. The Lord, that knoweth all things, knows full well I am prepared even to the death. Thy prayers, Jabaster, and——'

'Stop, stop. I do remember me. See this ring: 'tis a choice emerald. Thou mayst have wondered I should wear a bauble. Alroy, I had a brother once: still he may live. When we parted, this was the signal of his love: a love, my child, strong, though we greatly differed. Take it. The hour may come that thou mayst need his aid. It will command it. If he live, he prospers. I know his temper well. He was made for what the worldly deem prosperity. God be with thee, sacred boy: the God of our great fathers, the God of Abraham, of Isaac, and of Jacob!'

They embraced.

'We linger,' exclaimed the Cabalist, 'we linger. Oh! in vain we quell the feelings of our kind. God, God bless and be with thee! Art sure thou hast all? thy dagger and thy wallet? That staff has seen some service. I cut it on the Jordan. Ah! that I could be thy mate! 'Twould be nothing then. At the worst to die together. Such a fate seems sweeter now than parting. I'll watch thy star, my child. Thou weepest! And I too. Why! what is this? Am I indeed Jabaster? One more embrace, and so——we'll not say farewell, but only think it.'

CHAPTER IV.

Alroy Falls Among Thieves

TRADITION taught that the sceptre of Solomon could be found only in the unknown sepulchres of the ancient Hebrew monarchs, and that none might dare to touch it but one of their descendants. Armed with the cabalistic talisman, which was to guide him in his awful and difficult researches, Alroy commenced his pilgrimage to the Holy City. At this time, the love of these sacred wanderings was a reigning passion among the Jews as well as the Christians.

The Prince of the Captivity was to direct his course into the heart of those great deserts which, in his flight from Hamadan, he had only skirted. Following the track of the caravan, he was to make his way to Babylon, or Bagdad. From the capital of the caliphs, his journey to Jerusalem was one comparatively easy; but to reach Bagdad he must encounter hardship and danger, the prospect of which would have divested any one of hope, who did not conceive himself the object of an omnipotent and particular Providence.

Clothed only in a coarse black frock, common among the Kourds, girded round his waist by a cord which held his dagger, his head shaven, and covered with a large white turban, which screened him from the heat, his feet protected only by slippers, supported by his staff, and bearing on his shoulders a bag of dried meat and parched corn, and a leathern skin of water, behold, toiling over the glowing sands of Persia, a youth whose life had hitherto been a long unbroken dream of domestic luxury and innocent indulgence.

He travelled during the warm night or the early starlit morn. During the day he rested: happy if he could recline by the side of some charitable well, shaded by a palm-tree, or frighten a gazelle from its resting-place among the rough bushes of some wild rocks. Were these resources wanting, he threw himself upon the sand, and made an awning with his staff and turban.

Three weeks had elapsed since he quitted the cavern of the Cabalist. Hitherto he had met with no human being. The desert became less arid. A scanty vegetation sprang up from a more genial soil; the ground broke into gentle undulations; his senses were invigorated with the odour of wild plants, and his sight refreshed by the glancing form of some wandering bird, a pilgrim like himself, but more at ease.

Soon sprang up a grove of graceful palm-trees, with their tall thin stems, and bending feathery crowns, languid and beautiful. Around, the verdant sod gleamed like an emerald: silver streams, flowing from a bubbling parent spring, wound their white forms within the bright green turf. From the grove arose the softening song of doves, and showers of gay and sparkling butterflies, borne on their tinted wings of shifting light, danced without danger in the liquid air. A fair and fresh Oasis!

Alroy reposed in this delicious retreat for two days, feeding on the living dates, and drinking of the fresh water. Fain would he have lingered, nor indeed, until he rested, had he been sufficiently conscious of his previous exertion. But the remembrance of his great mission made him restless, and steeled him to the sufferings which yet awaited him.

At the dawn of the second day of his journey from the Oasis he beheld to his astonishment, faintly but distinctly traced on the far horizon, the walls and turrets of an extensive city.[13] Animated by this unexpected prospect, he continued his progress for several hours after sunrise. At length, utterly exhausted, he sought refuge from the overpowering heat beneath the cupola of the ruined tomb of some Moslem saint. At sunset he continued his journey, and in the morning found himself within a few miles of the city. He halted, and watched with anxiety for some evidence of its inhabitants. None was visible. No crowds or cavalcades issued from the gates. Not a single human being, not a solitary camel, moved in the vicinity.

The day was too advanced for the pilgrim to proceed, but so great was his anxiety to reach this unknown settlement, and penetrate the mystery of its silence, that ere sunset Alroy entered the gates.

A magnificent city, of an architecture with which he was unacquainted, offered to his entranced vision its gorgeous ruins and deserted splendour; long streets of palaces, with their rich line of lessening pillars, here and there broken by some fallen shaft, vast courts surrounded by ornate and solemn temples, and luxurious baths adorned with rare mosaics, and yet bright with antique gilding; now an arch of triumph, still haughty with its broken friezes; now a granite obelisk covered with strange characters, and proudly towering over a prostrate companion; sometimes a void and crumbling theatre, sometimes a long and elegant aqueduct, sometimes a porphyry column, once breathing with the heroic statue that now lies shivered at its base, all suffused with the warm twilight of an eastern eve.

He gazed with wonder and admiration upon the strange and fascinating scene. The more he beheld, the more his curiosity was excited. He breathed with difficulty; he advanced with a blended feeling of eagerness and hesitation. Fresh wonders successively unfolded themselves. Each turn developed a new scene of still and solemn splendour. The echo of his step filled him with awe. He looked around him with an amazed air, a fluttering heart, and a changing countenance. All was silent: alone the Hebrew Prince stood amid the regal creation of the Macedonian captains. Empires and dynasties flourish and pass away; the proud metropolis becomes a solitude, the conquering kingdom even a desert; but Israel still remains, still a descendant of the most ancient kings breathed amid these royal ruins, and still the eternal sun could never rise without gilding the towers of living Jerusalem. A word, a deed, a single day, a single man, and we might be a nation.

A shout! he turns, he is seized; four ferocious Kourdish bandits grapple and bind him.

The bandits hurried their captive through a street which appeared to have been the principal way of the city. Nearly at its termination, they turned by a small Ionian temple, and, clambering over some fallen pillars, entered a quarter of the city of a more ruinous aspect than that which Alroy had hitherto visited.

The path was narrow, often obstructed, and around were signs of devastation for which the exterior of the city had not prepared him.

The brilliant but brief twilight of the Orient was fast fading away; a sombre purple tint succeeded to the rosy flush; the distant towers rose black, although defined, in the clear and shadowy air; and the moon, which, when he first entered, had studded the heavens like a small white cloud, now glittered with deceptive light.

Suddenly, before them rose a huge pile. Oval in shape, and formed by tiers of arches, it was evidently much dilapidated, and one enormous, irregular, and undulating rent, extending from the top nearly to the foundation, almost separated the side to which Alroy and his companions advanced.

Clambering up the remainder of this massive wall, the robbers and their prisoner descended into an immense amphitheatre, which seemed vaster in the shadowy and streaming moonlight. In it were groups of men, horses, and camels. In the extreme distance, reclining or squatting on mats and carpets, was a large assembly, engaged in a rough but merry banquet. A fire blazed at their side, its red and uncertain flame mingling with the white and steady moonbeam, and throwing a flickering light over their ferocious countenances, their glistening armour, ample drapery, and shawled heads.

'A spy,' exclaimed the captors, as they dragged Alroy before the leader of the band.

'Hang him, then,' said the chieftain, without even looking up.

'This wine, great Scherirah, is excellent, or I am no true Moslem,' said a principal robber; 'but you are too cruel; I hate this summary punishment. Let us torture him a little, and extract some useful information.'

'As you like, Kisloch,' said Scherirah; 'it may amuse us. Fellow, where do you come from? He cannot answer. Decidedly a spy. Hang him up.'

The captors half untied the rope that bound Alroy, that it might serve him for a further purpose, when another of the gentle companions of Scherirah interfered.

'Spies always answer, captain. He is more probably a merchant in disguise.'

'And carries hidden treasure,' added Kisloch; 'these rough coats often cover jewels. We had better search him.'

'Ah! search him,' said Scherirah, with his rough brutal voice; 'do what you like, only give me the bottle. This Greek wine is choice booty. Feed the fire, men. Are you asleep? And then Kisloch, who hates cruelty, can roast him if he likes.'

The robbers prepared to strip their captive. 'Friends, friends!' exclaimed Alroy, 'for there is no reason why you should not be friends, spare me, spare me. I am poor, I am young, I am innocent. I am neither a spy nor a merchant. I have no plots, no wealth. I am a pilgrim.'

'A decided spy,' exclaimed Scherirah; 'they are ever pilgrims.'

'He speaks too well to speak truth,' exclaimed Kisloch.

'All talkers are liars,' exclaimed Scherirah.

'That is why Kisloch is the most eloquent of the band.'

'A jest at the banquet may prove a curse in the field,' replied Kisloch.

'Pooh!' exclaimed Scherirah. 'Fellows, why do you hesitate? Search the prisoner, I say!'

They advanced, they seized him. In vain he struggled.

'Captain,' exclaimed one of the band, 'he wears upon his breast a jewel!'

'I told you so,' said the third robber.

'Give it me,' said Scherirah.

But Alroy, in despair at the thought of losing the talisman, remembering the injunctions of Jabaster, and animated by supernatural courage, burst from his searchers, and, seizing a brand from the fire, held them at bay.

'The fellow has spirit,' said Scherirah, calmly. ''Tis pity it will cost him his life.'

'Bold man,' exclaimed Alroy, 'for a moment hear me! I am a pilgrim, poorer than a beggar. The jewel they talk of is a holy emblem, worthless to you, to me invaluable, and to be forfeited only with my life. You may be careless of that. Beware of your own. The first man who advances dies. I pray you humbly, chieftain, let me go.'

'Kill him,' said Scherirah.

'Stab him!' exclaimed Kisloch.

'Give me the jewel,' said the third robber.

'The God of David be my refuge, then!' exclaimed Alroy.

'He is a Hebrew, he is a Hebrew,' exclaimed Scherirah, jumping up. 'Spare him, my mother was a Jewess.'

The assailants lowered their arms, and withdrew a few paces. Alroy still remained upon his guard.

'Valiant pilgrim,' said Scherirah, advancing, with a softened voice, 'are you for the holy city?'

'The city of my fathers.'

'A perilous journey. And whence from?'

'Hamadan.'

'A dreary way. You need repose. Your name?'

'David.'

'David, you are among friends. Rest, and repose in safety. You hesitate. Fear not! The memory of my mother is a charm that always changes me!' Scherirah unsheathed his dagger, punctured his arm,[14] and, throwing away the weapon, offered the bleeding member to Alroy. The Prince of the Captivity touched the open vein with his lips.

'My troth is pledged,' said the bandit; 'I can never betray him in whose veins my own blood is flowing.' So saying, he led Alroy to his carpet.

'Eat,' David,' said Scherirah.

'I will eat bread,' answered Alroy.

'What! have you had so much meat lately that you will refuse this delicate gazelle that I brought down this morning with my own lance? 'Tis food for a caliph.'

'I pray you give me bread.'

'Oh! bread if you like. But that a man should prefer bread to meat, and such meat as this, 'tis miraculous.'

'A thousand thanks, good Scherirah; but with our people the flesh of the gazelle is forbidden. It is unclean. Its foot is *cloven*.'

'I have heard of these things,' replied Scherirah, with a thoughtful air. 'My mother was a Jewess, and my father was a Kourd. Whichever be right, I hope to be saved.'

'There is but one God, and Mahomed is his prophet!' exclaimed Kisloch; 'though I drink wine. Your health, Hebrew.'

'I will join you,' said to the third robber. 'My father was a Guebre, and sacrificed his property to his faith; and the consequence is, his son has got neither.'

'As for me,' said a fourth robber, of very dark complexion and singularly small bright eyes, 'I am an Indian, and I believe in the great golden figure with carbuncle eyes, in the temple of Delhi.'

'I have no religion,' said a tall negro in a red turban, grinning with his white teeth; 'they have none in my country; but if I had heard of your God before, Calidas, I would have believed in him.'

'I almost wish I had been a Jew,' exclaimed Scherirah, musing. 'My mother was a good woman.' 'The Jews are very rich,' said the third robber. 'When you get to Jerusalem, David, you will see the Christians,' continued Scherirah.

'The accursed Giaours,' exclaimed Kisloch, 'we are all against them.'

'With their white faces,' exclaimed the negro. 'And their blue eyes,' said the Indian. 'What can you expect of men who live in a country without a sun?' observed the Guebre.

Alroy awoke about two hours after midnight. His companions were in deep slumber. The moon had set, the fire had died away, a few red embers alone remaining; dark masses of shadow hung about the amphitheatre. He arose and cautiously stepped over the sleeping bandits. He was not in strictness a prisoner; but who could trust to the caprice of these lawless men? To-morrow might find him their slave, or their companion in some marauding expedition, which might make him almost retrace his steps to the Caucasus, or to Hamadan. The temptation to ensure his freedom was irresistible. He clambered up the ruined wall, descended into the intricate windings that led to the Ionic fane, that served him as a beacon, hurried through the silent and starry streets, gained the great portal, and rushed once more into the desert.

A vague fear of pursuit made him continue his course many hours without resting. The desert again became sandy, the heat increased. The breeze that plays about the wilderness, and in early spring is often scented with the wild fragrance of aromatic plants, sank away. A lurid brightness suffused the heavens. An appalling stillness pervaded nature; even the insects were silent. For the first time in his pilgrimage, a feeling of deep despondency fell over the soul of Alroy. His energy appeared suddenly to have deserted him. A low hot wind began to rise, and fan his cheek with pestiferous kisses, and enervate his frame with its poisonous embrace. His head and limbs ached with a dull sensation, more terrible than pain; his sight was dizzy, his tongue swollen. Vainly he looked around for aid; vainly he extended his forlorn arms, and wrung them to the remorseless heaven, almost frantic with thirst. The boundless horizon of the desert disappeared, and the unhappy victim, in the midst of his torture, found himself apparently surrounded by bright and running streams, the fleeting waters of the false mirage!

The sun became blood-red, the sky darker, the sand rose in fierce eddies, the moaning wind burst into shrieks and exhaled more ardent and still more malignant breath. The pilgrim could no longer sustain himself.[15] Faith, courage, devotion deserted him with his failing energies. He strove no longer with his destiny, he delivered himself up to despair and death. He fell upon one knee with drooping head, supporting himself by one quivering hand, and then, full of the anguish of baffled purposes and lost affections, raising his face and arm to heaven, thus to the elements he poured his passionate farewell.

'O life! once vainly deemed a gloomy toil, I feel thy sweetness now! Farewell, O life, farewell my high resolves and proud conviction of almighty fame. My days, my short unprofitable days, melt into the past; and death, with which I struggle, horrible death, arrests me in this wilderness. O my sister, could thy voice but murmur in my ear one single sigh of love; could thine eye with its soft radiance but an instant blend with my dim fading vision, the pang were nothing. Farewell, Miriam! my heart is with thee by thy fountain's side. Fatal blast, bear her my dying words, my blessing. And ye too, friends, whose too neglected love I think of now, farewell! Farewell, my uncle; farewell, pleasant home, and Hamadan's serene and shadowy bowers! Farewell, Jabaster, and the mighty lore of which thou wert the priest and I the pupil! Thy talisman throbs on my faithful heart. Green earth and golden sun, and all the beautiful and glorious sights ye fondly lavish on unthinking man, farewell, farewell! I die in the desert: 'tis bitter. No more, oh! never more for me the hopeful day shall break, and the fresh breeze rise on its cheering wings of health and joy. Heaven and earth, water and air, my chosen country and my antique creed, farewell, farewell! And thou, too, city of my soul, I cannot name thee, unseen Jerusalem———'

Amid the roar of the wind, the bosom of the earth heaved and opened, swift columns of sand sprang up to the lurid sky, and hurried towards their victim. With the clang of universal chaos, impenetrable darkness descended on the desert.

CHAPTER V.

Lord Honain Rescues Alroy

NOW our dreary way is over, now the desert's toil is past. Soon the river broadly flowing, through its green and palmy banks, to our wearied limbs shall offer baths 'which caliphs cannot buy. Allah-illah, Allah-hu. Allah-illah, Allah-hu.'

'Blessed the man who now may bear a relic from our Prophet's tomb; blessed the man who now unfolds the treasures of a distant mart, jewels of the dusky East, and silks of farthest Samarcand. Allah-illah, Allah-hu. Allah-illah, Allah-hu.'

'Him the sacred mosque shall greet with a reverence grave and low; him the busy Bezestein shall welcome with confiding smile. Holy merchant, now receive the double triumph of thy toil. Allah-illah, Allah-hu. Allah-illah, Allah-hu.'

'The camel jibs, Abdallah! See, there is something in the track.'

'By the holy stone,[16] a dead man. Poor devil! One should never make a pilgrimage on foot. I hate your humble piety. Prick the beast and he will pass the corpse.'

'The Prophet preaches charity, Abdallah. He has favoured my enterprise, and I will practise his precept. See if he be utterly dead.'

It was the Mecca caravan returning to Bagdad. The pilgrims were within a day's journey of the Euphrates, and welcomed their approach to fertile earth with a triumphant chorus. Far as the eye could reach, the long line of their straggling procession stretched across the wilderness, thousands of camels in strings, laden with bales of merchandise, and each company headed by an animal of superior size, leading with tinkling bells; groups of horsemen, clusters of litters; all the pilgrims armed to their teeth, the van formed by a strong division of Seljukian cavalry, and the rear protected by a Kourdish clan, who guaranteed the security of the pious travellers through their country.

Abdallah was the favourite slave of the charitable merchant Ali. In obedience to his master's orders, he unwillingly descended from his camel, and examined the body of the apparently lifeless Alroy.

'A Kourd, by his dress,' exclaimed Abdallah, with a sneer; 'what does he here?'

'It is not the face of a Kourd,' replied Ali; 'perchance a pilgrim from the mountains.'

'Whatever he be, he is dead,' answered the slave: 'I doubt not an accursed Giaour.'

'God is great,' exclaimed Ali; 'he breathes; the breast of his caftan heaved.'

"Twas the wind,' said Abdallah.

"Twas the sigh of a human heart,' answered Ali.

Several pilgrims who were on foot now gathered around the group.

'I am a Hakim,'[17] observed a dignified Armenian. 'I will feel his pulse; 'tis dull, but it beats.'

'There is but one God,' exclaimed Ali.

'And Mahomed is his Prophet,' responded Abdallah. 'You do not believe in him, you Armenian infidel.'

'I am a Hakim,' replied the dignified Armenian. 'Although an infidel, God has granted me skill to cure true believers. Worthy Ali, believe me, the boy may yet live.'

'Hakim, you shall count your own dirhems if he breathe in my divan in Bagdad,' answered Ali; 'I have taken a fancy to the boy. God has sent him to me. He shall carry my slippers.'

'Give me a camel, and I will save his life.'

'We have none,' said the servant.

'Walk, Abdallah,' said the master.

'Is a true believer to walk to save the life of a Kourd? Master slipper-bearer shall answer for this, if there be any sweetness in the bastinado,' murmured Abdallah.

The Armenian bled Alroy; the blood flowed slowly but surely. The Prince of the Captivity opened his eyes.

'There is but one God,' exclaimed Ali.

'The evil eye fall on him!' muttered Abdallah.

The Armenian took a cordial from his vest, and poured it down his patient's throat. The blood flowed more freely.

'He will live, worthy merchant,' said the physician.

'And Mahomed is his Prophet,' continued Ali.

'By the stone of Mecca, I believe it is a Jew,' shouted Abdallah.

'The dog!' exclaimed Ali.

'Pah!' said a negro slave, drawing back with disgust.

'He will die,' said the Christian physician, not even binding up the vein.

'And be damned,' said Abdallah, again jumping on his camel.

The party rode on, the caravan proceeded. A Kourdish horseman galloped forward. He curbed his steed as he passed Alroy bleeding to death.

'What accursed slave has wounded one of my clan?'

The Kourd leaped off his horse, stripped off a slip of his blue shirt, stanched the wound, and carried the unhappy Alroy to the rear.

The desert ceased, the caravan entered upon a vast but fruitful plain. In the extreme distance might be descried a long undulating line of palm-trees. The vanguard gave a shout, shook their tall lances in the air, and rattled their scimitars in rude chorus against their small round iron shields. All eyes sparkled, all hands were raised, all voices sounded, save those that were breathless from overpowering joy. After months wandering in the sultry wilderness, they beheld the great Euphrates.

Broad and fresh, magnificent and serene, the mighty waters rolled through the beautiful and fertile earth. A vital breeze rose from their bosom. Every being responded to their genial influence. The sick were cured, the desponding became sanguine, the healthy and light-hearted broke into shouts of laughter, jumped from their camels, and embraced the fragrant earth, or, wild in their renovated strength, galloped over the plain, and threw their wanton jerreeds in the air,[18] as if to show that suffering and labour had not deprived them of that skill and strength, without which it were vain again to enter the haunts of their less adventurous brethren.

The caravan halted on the banks of the broad river, glowing in the cool sunset. The camp was pitched, the plain glittered with tents. The camels, falling on their knees, crouched in groups, the merchandise piled up in masses by their sides. The unharnessed horses rushed neighing about the plain, tossing their glad heads, and rolling in the unaccustomed pasture. Spreading their mats, and kneeling towards Mecca, the pilgrims performed their evening orisons. Never was thanksgiving more sincere. They arose: some rushed into the river, some lighted lamps, some pounded coffee.[19] Troops of smiling villagers arrived with fresh provisions, eager to prey upon such light hearts and heavy purses. It was one of those occasions when the accustomed gravity of the Orient disappears. Long through the night the sounds of music and the shouts of laughter were heard on the banks of that starry river; long through the night you might have listened with enchantment to the wild tales of the storier, or gazed with fascination on the wilder gestures of the dancing girls.[20]

The great bazaar of Bagdad afforded an animated and sumptuous spectacle on the day after the arrival of the caravan. All the rare and costly products of the world were collected in that celebrated mart: the shawls of Cachemire and the silks of Syria, the ivory, and plumes, and gold of Afric, the jewels of Ind, the talismans of Egypt, the perfumes and manuscripts of Persia, the spices and gums of Araby, beautiful horses, more beautiful slaves, cloaks of sable, pelisses of ermine, armour alike magnificent in ornament and temper, rare animals, still rarer birds, blue apes in silver collars, white gazelles bound by a golden chain, greyhounds, peacocks, paroquets. And everywhere strange, and busy, and excited groups; men of all nations, creeds, and climes: the sumptuous and haughty Turk, the graceful and subtle Arab, the Hebrew with his black cap and anxious countenance; the Armenian Christian, with his dark flowing robes, and mild demeanour, and serene visage. Here strutted the lively, affected, and superfine Persian; and there the Circassian stalked with his long hair and chain cuirass. The fair Georgian jostled the ebony form of the merchant of Dongola or Sennaar.

Through the long, narrow, arched, and winding streets of the bazaar, lined on each side with loaded stalls, all was bustle, bargaining, and barter. A passenger approached, apparently of no common rank. Two pages preceded him, beautiful Georgian boys, clothed in crimson cloth, and caps of the same material, sitting tight to their heads, with long golden tassels. One bore a blue velvet bag, and the other a clasped and richly bound volume. Four footmen, armed, followed their master, who rode behind the pages on a milk-white mule. He was a man of middle age, eminently handsome. His ample robes concealed the only fault in his appearance, a figure which indulgence had rendered somewhat too exuberant. His eyes were large, and soft, and dark; his nose aquiline, but delicately moulded; his mouth small, and beautifully proportioned;

his lip full and red; his teeth regular and dazzling white. His ebony beard flowed, but not at too great a length, in graceful and natural curls, and was richly perfumed; a delicate mustachio shaded his upper lip, but no whisker was permitted to screen the form and shroud the lustre of his oval countenance and brilliant complexion. Altogether, the animal perhaps predominated too much in the expression of the stranger's countenance; but genius beamed from his passionate eye, and craft lay concealed in that subtle lip. The dress of the rider was sumptuous. His turban, formed by a scarlet Cachemire shawl, was of great breadth, and concealing half of his white forehead, increased by the contrast the radiant height of the other. His under-vest was of white Damascus silk, stiff with silver embroidery, and confined by a girdle formed by a Brusa scarf of gold stuff, and holding a dagger, whose hilt appeared blazing with brilliants and rubies. His loose and exterior robe was of crimson cloth. His white hands sparkled with rings, and his ears glittered with pendulous gems.

'Who is this?' asked an Egyptian merchant, in a low whisper, of the dealer whose stuffs he was examining.

"Tis the Lord Honain,' replied the dealer. 'And who may he be?' continued the Egyptian. 'Is he the Caliph's son?'

'A much greater man; his physician.' The white mule stopped at the very stall where this conversation was taking place. The pages halted, and stood on each side of their master, the footmen kept off the crowd.

'Merchant,' said Honain, with a gracious smile of condescension, and with a voice musical as a flute, 'Merchant, did you obtain me my wish?'

'There is but one God,' replied the dealer, who was the charitable Ali, 'and Mahomed is his Prophet. I succeeded, please your highness, in seeing at Aleppo the accursed Giaour, of whom I spoke, and behold, that which you desired is here.' So saying, Ali produced several Greek manuscripts, and offered them to his visitor.

'Hah!' said Honain, with a sparkling eye, "tis well; their cost?'

'The infidel would not part with them under five hundred dirhems,' replied Ali.

'Ibrahim, see that this worthy merchant receive a thousand.'

'As many thanks, my Lord Honain.'

The Caliph's physician bowed gracefully.

'Advance, pages,' continued Honain; 'why this stoppage? Ibrahim, see that our way be cleared. What is all this?'

A crowd of men advanced, pulling along a youth, who, almost exhausted, still singly struggled with his ungenerous adversaries.

'The Cadi, the Cadi,' cried the foremost of them, who was Abdallah, 'drag him to the Cadi.'

'Noble lord,' cried the youth, extricating himself by a sudden struggle from the grasp of his captors, and seizing the robe of Honain, 'I am innocent and injured. I pray thy help.'

'The Cadi, the Cadi,' exclaimed Abdallah; 'the knave has stolen my ring, the ring given me by my faithful Fatima on our marriage-day, and which I would not part with for my master's stores.'

The youth still clung to the robe of Honain, and, mute from exhaustion, fixed upon him his beautiful and imploring eye.

'Silence,' proclaimed Honain, 'I will judge this cause.'

'The Lord Honain, the Lord Honain, listen to the Lord Honain!'

'Speak, thou brawler; of what hast thou to complain?' said Honain to Abdallah.

'May it please your highness,' said Abdallah, in a whining voice, 'I am the slave of your faithful servant, Ali: often have I had the honour of waiting on your highness. This young knave here, a beggar, has robbed me, while slumbering in a coffee-house, of a ring; I have my witnesses to prove my slumbering. 'Tis a fine emerald, may it please your highness, and doubly valuable to me as a love-token from my Fatima. No consideration in the world could induce me to part with it; and so, being asleep, here are three honest men who will prove the sleep, comes this little vagabond, may it please your highness, who while he pretends to offer me my coffee, takes him my finger, and slips off this precious ring, which he now wears upon his beggarly paw, and will not restore to me without the bastinado.'

'Abdallah is a faithful slave, may it please your highness, and a Hadgee,' said Ali, his master.

'And what sayest thou, boy?' inquired Honain.

'That this is a false knave, who lies as slaves ever will.'

'Pithy, and perhaps true,' said Honain.

'You call me a slave, you young scoundrel?' exclaimed Abdallah; 'shall I tell you what you are? Why, your highness, do not listen to him a moment. It is a shame to bring such a creature into your presence; for, by the holy stone, and I am a Hadgee, I doubt little he is a Jew.'

Honain grew somewhat pale, and bit his lip. He was perhaps annoyed that he had interfered so publicly in behalf of so unpopular a character as a Hebrew, but he was unwilling to desert one whom a moment before he had resolved to befriend, and he inquired of the youth where he had obtained the ring.

'The ring was given to me by my dearest friend when I first set out upon an arduous pilgrimage not yet completed. There is but one person in the world, except the donor, to whom I would part with it, and with that person I am unacquainted. All this may seem improbable, but all this is true. I have truth alone to support me. I am destitute and friendless; but I am not a beggar, nor will any suffering induce me to become one. Feeling, from various circumstances, utterly exhausted, I entered a coffee-house and lay down, it may have been to die. I could not sleep, although my eyes were shut, and nothing would have roused me from a tremulous trance, which I thought was dying, but this plunderer here, who would not wait until death had permitted him quietly to possess himself of a jewel I value more than life.'

'Show me the jewel.'

The youth held up his hand to Honain, who felt his pulse, and then took off the ring.

'O, my Fatima!' exclaimed Abdallah.

'Silence, sir!' said Honain. 'Page, call a jeweller.'

Honain examined the ring attentively. Whether he were near-sighted, or whether the deceptive light of the covered bazaar prevented him from examining it with ease, he certainly raised his hand to his brow, and for some moments his countenance was invisible.

The jeweller arrived, and, pressing his hand to his heart, bowed before Honain.

'Value this ring,' said Honain, in a low voice.

The jeweller took the ring, viewed it in all directions with a scrutinising glance, held it to the light, pressed it to his tongue, turned it over and over, and finally declared that he could not sell such a ring under a thousand dirhems.

'Whatever be the justice of the case,' said Honain to Abdallah, 'art thou ready to part with this ring for a thousand dirhems?'

'Most certainly,' said Abdallah. 'And thou, lad, if the decision be in thy favour, wilt thou take for the ring double the worth at which the jeweller prizes it?'

'My lord, I have spoken the truth. I cannot part with that ring for the palace of the Caliph.'

'The truth for once is triumphant,' said Honain. 'Boy, the ring is thine; and for thee, thou knave,' turning to Abdallah, 'liar, thief, and slanderer!—for thee the bastinado,[21] which thou destinedst for this innocent youth. Ibrahim, see that he receives five hundred. Young pilgrim, thou art no longer destitute or friendless. Follow me to my palace.'

The arched chamber was of great size and beautiful proportion. The ceiling, encrusted with green fretwork, and studded with silver stars, rested upon clustered columns of white and green marble. In the centre of a variegated pavement of the same material, a fountain rose and fell into a green porphyry basin, and by the side of the fountain, upon a couch of silver, reposed Honain.

He raised his eyes from the illuminated volume on which he had been long intent; he clapped his hands, and a Nubian slave advanced, and, folding his arms upon his breast, bowed in silence before his lord. 'How fares the Hebrew boy, Analschar?'

'Master, the fever has not returned. We gave him the potion; he slumbered for many hours, and has now awakened, weak but well.'

'Let him rise and attend me.'

The Nubian disappeared.

'There is nothing stranger than sympathy,' soliloquised the physician of the Caliph, with a meditative air; 'all resolves itself into this principle, and I confess this learned doctor treats it deeply and well. An erudite spirit truly, and an eloquent pen; yet he refines too much. 'Tis too scholastic. Observation will teach us more than dogma. Meditating upon my passionate youth, I gathered wisdom. I have seen so much that I have ceased to wonder. However we doubt, there is a mystery beyond our penetration. And yet 'tis near our grasp. I sometimes deem a step, a single step, would launch us into light. Here comes my patient. The rose has left his cheek, and his deep brow is wan and melancholy. Yet 'tis a glorious visage, Meditation's throne; and Passion lingers in that languid eye. I know not why, a strong attraction draws me to this lone child.

'Gentle stranger, how fares it with thee?'

'Very well, my lord. I come to thank thee for all thy goodness. My only thanks are words, and those too weak; and yet the orphan's blessing is a treasure.'

'You are an orphan, then'

'I have no parent but my father's God.'

'And that God is———'

'The God of Israel.'

'So I deemed. He is a Deity we all must honour; if he be the great Creator whom we all allow.'

'He is what he is, and we are what we are, a fallen people, but faithful still.'

'Fidelity is strength.'

'Thy words are truth, and strength must triumph.'

'A prophecy!'

'Many a prophet is little honoured, till the future proves his inspiration.'

'You are young and sanguine.'

'So was my ancestor within the vale of Elah. But I speak unto a Moslem, and this is foolishness.'

'I have read something, and can take your drift. As for my faith, I believe in truth, and wish all men to do the same. By-the-bye, might I inquire the name of him who is the inmate of my house?'

'They call me David.'

'David, you have a ring, an emerald cut with curious characters, Hebrew, I believe.'

''Tis here.'

'A fine stone, and this inscription means———'

'A simple legend, "*Parted, but one*," the kind memorial of a brother's love.'

'Your brother?'

'I never had a brother.'

'I have a silly fancy for this ring: you hesitate. Search my palace, and choose the treasure you deem its match.'

'Noble sir, the gem is little worth; but were it such might deck a Caliph's brow, 'twere a poor recompense for all thy goodness. This ring is a trust rather than a possession, and strange to say, although I cannot offer it to thee who mayst command, as thou hast saved, the life of its unhappy wearer, some stranger may cross my path to-morrow, and almost claim it as his own.'

'And that stranger is———'

'The brother of the donor.'

'The brother of Jabaster?'

'Jabaster!'

'Even so. I am that parted brother.'

'Great is the God of Israel! Take the ring. But what is this? the brother of Jabaster a turbaned chieftain! a Moslem! Say, but say, that thou hast not assumed their base belief; say, but say, that thou hast not become a traitor to our covenant, and I will bless the fortunes of this hour.'

'I am false to no God. Calm thyself, sweet youth. These are higher questions than thy faint strength can master now. Another time we'll talk of this, my boy; at present of my brother and thyself. He lives and prospers?'

'He lives in faith; the pious ever prosper.'

'A glorious dreamer! Though our moods are different, I ever loved him. And thyself? Thou art not what thou seemest. Tell me all. Jabaster's friend can be no common mind. Thy form has heralded thy fame. Trust me.'

'I am Alroy.'

'What! the Prince of our Captivity?'

'Even so.'

'The slayer of Alschiroch?'

'Ay!'

'My sympathy was prophetic. I loved thee from the first. And what dost thou here? A price is set upon thy head: thou knowest it?'

'For the first time; but I am neither astonished nor alarmed. I am upon the Lord's business.'

'What wouldst thou?'

'Free his people.'

'The pupil of Jabaster: I see it all. Another victim to his reveries. I'll save this boy. David,—for thy name must not be sounded within this city,—the sun is dying. Let us to the terrace, and seek the solace of the twilight breeze.'

'What is the hour, David?'

'Near to midnight. I marvel if thy brother may read in the stars our happy meeting.'

'Men read that which they wish. He is a learned Cabalist.'

'But what we wish comes from above.'

'So they say. We make our fortunes, and we call them Fate.'

'Yet the Voice sounded, the Daughter of the Voice that summoned Samuel.'

'You have told me strange things; I have heard stranger solved.'

'My faith is a rock.'

'On which you may split.'

'Art thou a Sadducee?'

'I am a man who knows men.'

'You are learned, but different from Jabaster.'

'We are the same, though different. Day and Night are both portions of Time.'

'And thy portion is——'

'Truth.'

'That is, light.'

'Yes; so dazzling that it sometimes seems dark.'

'Like thy meaning.'
'You are young.'
'Is youth a defect?'
'No, the reverse. But we cannot eat the fruit while the tree is in blossom.'
'What fruit?'
'Knowledge.'
'I have studied.'
'What?'
'All sacred things.'
'How know you that they are sacred?'
'They come from God.'
'So does everything. Is everything sacred?'
'They are the deep expression of his will.'
'According to Jabaster. Ask the man who prays in yonder mosque, and he will tell you that Jabaster's wrong.'
'After all, thou art a Moslem?'
'No.'
'What then?'
'I have told you, a man.'
'But what dost thou worship?'
'What is worship?'
'Adoration due from the creature to the Creator.'
'Which is he?'
'Our God.'
'The God of Israel?'
'Even so.'
'A frail minority, then, burn incense to him.'
'We are the chosen people.'
'Chosen for scoffs, and scorns, and contumelies. Commend me to such choice.'
'We forgot Him, before He chastened us.'
'Why did we?'
'Thou knowest the records of our holy race.'
'Yes, I know them; like all records, annals of blood.'
'Annals of victory, that will dawn again.'
'If redemption be but another name for carnage, I envy no Messiah.'
'Art thou Jabaster's brother?' 'So our mother was wont to say: a meek and blessed woman.'

'Lord Honain, thou art rich, and wise, and powerful. Thy fellow-men speak of thee only with praise or fear, and both are cheering. Thou hast quitted our antique ark; why, no matter. We'll not discuss it. 'Tis something; if a stranger, at least thou art not a renegade. The world goes well with thee, my Lord Honain. But if, instead of bows and blessings, thou, like thy brethren, wert greeted only with the cuff and curse; if thou didst rise each morning only to feel existence to be dishonour, and to find thyself marked out among surrounding men as something foul and fatal; if it were thy lot, like theirs, at best to drag on a mean and dull career, hopeless and aimless, or with no other hope or aim but that which is degrading, and all this, too, with a keen sense of thy intrinsic worth, and a deep conviction of superior race; why, then, perchance, Honain might even discover 'twere worth a struggle to be free and honoured.' 'I pray your pardon, sir; I thought you were Jabaster's pupil, a dreaming student. I see you have a deep ambition.'

'I am a prince; and I fain would be a prince without my fetters.'

'Listen to me, Alroy,' said Honain in a low voice, and he placed his arm around him, 'I am your friend. Our acquaintance is very brief: no matter, I love you; I rescued you in injury, I tended you in sickness, even now your life is in my power, I would protect it with my own. You cannot doubt me. Our affections are not under our own control; and mine are yours. The sympathy between us is entire. You see me, you see what I am; a Hebrew, though unknown; one of that despised, rejected, persecuted people, of whom you are the chief. I too would be free and honoured. Freedom and honour are mine, but I was my own messiah. I quitted in good time our desperate cause, but I gave it a trial. Ask Jabaster how I fought. Youth could be my only excuse for such indiscretion. I left this country; I studied and resided among the Greeks. I returned from Constantinople, with all their learning, some of their craft. No one knew me. I assumed their turban, and I am the Lord Honain. Take my experience, child, and save yourself much sorrow. Turn your late adventure to good account. No one can recognise you here. I will introduce you amongst the highest as my child by some fair Greek. The world is before you. You may fight, you may love, you may revel. War, and Women, and luxury are all at your command. With your person and talents you may be grand vizir. Clear your head of nonsense. In the present disordered state of the empire, you may even carve yourself out a kingdom, infinitely more delightful than the barren land of milk and honey. I have seen it, child; a rocky wilderness, where I would not let my courser graze.'

He bent down, and fixed his eyes upon his companion with a scrutinising glance. The moonlight fell upon the resolved visage of the Prince of the Captivity.

'Honain,' he replied, pressing his hand, 'I thank thee. Thou knowest not me, but still I thank thee.'

'You are resolved, then, on destruction.'

'On glory, eternal glory.'

'Is it possible to succeed?'

'Is it possible to fail?'

'You are mad.'

'I am a believer.'

'Enough. You have yet one chance. My brother has saddled your enterprise with a condition, and an impossible one. Gain the sceptre of Solomon, and I will agree to be your subject. You will waste a year in this frolic. You are young, and can afford it. I trust you will experience nothing worse than a loss of time, which is, however, valuable. My duty will be, after all your sufferings, to send you forth on your adventures in good condition, and to provide you means for a less toilsome pilgrimage than has hitherto been your lot. Trust me, you will return to Bagdad to accept my offers. At present, the dews are descending, and we will return to our divan, and take some coffee.'

Some few days after this conversation on the terrace, as Alroy was reclining in a bower, in the beautiful garden of his host, meditating on the future, some one touched him on the back. He looked up. It was Honain.

'Follow me,' said the brother of Jabaster.

The Prince rose, and followed him in silence. They entered the house, and, passing through the saloon already described, they proceeded down a long gallery, which terminated in an arched flight of broad steps leading to the river. A boat was fastened to the end of the stairs, floating on the blue line of the Tigris, bright in the sun.

Honain now gave to Alroy a velvet bag, which he requested him to carry, and then they descended the steps and entered the covered boat; and, without any directions to the rower, they were soon skimming over the water. By the sound of passing vessels, and the occasional shouts of the boatmen, Alroy, although he could observe nothing, was conscious that for some time their course lay through a principal thoroughfare of the city; but by degrees the sounds became less frequent, and in time entirely died away, and all that caught his ear was the regular and monotonous stroke of their own oar.

At length, after the lapse of nearly an hour from their entrance, the boat stopped, and was moored against a quay. The curtains were withdrawn, and Honain and his companion debarked.

A low but extensive building, painted in white and gold arabesque, and irregular but picturesque in form, with many small domes, and tall thin towers, rose amid groves of cypress on the bank of the broad and silent river. The rapid stream had carried them far from the city, which was visible but distant. Around was no habitation, no human being. The opposite bank was occupied by enclosed gardens. Not even a boat passed.

Honain, beckoning to Alroy to accompany him, but still silent, advanced to a small portal, and knocked. It was instantly opened by a single Nubian, who bowed reverently as the visitors passed him. They proceeded along a low and gloomy passage, covered with arches of fretwork, until they arrived at a door of tortoise-shell and mother-of-pearl.[22] Here Honain, who was in advance, turned round to Alroy, and said, 'Whatever happen, and whoever may address you, as you value your life and mine, do not speak.'

The door opened, and they found themselves in a vast and gorgeous hall. Pillars of many-coloured marbles rose from a red and blue pavement of the same material, and supported a vaulted, circular, and highly-embossed roof of purple, scarlet, and gold.[23] Around a fountain, which rose fifty feet in height from an immense basin of lapis-lazuli, and reclining on small yellow Barbary mats, was a group of Nubian eunuchs, dressed in rich habits of scarlet and gold,[24] and armed with ivory battle-axes, the white handles worked in precious arabesque finely contrasting with the blue and brilliant blades.

The commander of the eunuch-guard rose on seeing Honain, and pressing his hand to his head, mouth, and heart, saluted him. The physician of the Caliph, motioning Alroy to remain, advanced some paces in front of him, and entered into a whispering conversation with the eunuch. After a few minutes, this officer resumed his seat, and Honain, beckoning to Alroy to rejoin him, crossed the hall.

Passing through an open arch, they entered a quadrangular court of roses,[25] each bed of flowers surrounded by a stream of sparkling water, and floating like an enchanted islet upon a fairy ocean. The sound of the water and the sweetness of the flowers blended together, and produced a lulling sensation, which nothing but his strong and strange curiosity might have enabled Alroy to resist. Proceeding along a cloister of light airy workmanship which connected the hall with the remainder of the buildings, they stood before a lofty and sumptuous portal.

It was a monolith gate, thirty feet in height, formed of one block of green and red jasper, and cut into the fanciful undulating arch of the Saracens. The consummate artist had seized the advantage afforded to him by the ruddy veins of the precious stone, and had formed them in bold relief into two vast and sinuous serpents, which shot forth their crested heads and glittering eyes at Honain and his companion.

The physician of the Caliph, taking his dagger from his girdle, struck the head of one of the serpents thrice. The massy portal opened with a whirl and a roar, and before them stood an Abyssinian giant,[26] holding in his leash a roaring lion.

'Hush, Haroun!' said Honain to the animal, raising at the same time his arm; and the beast crouched in silence. 'Worthy Morgargon, I bring you a remembrance.' The Abyssinian showed his tusks, larger and whiter than the lion's, as he grinningly received the tribute of the courtly Honain; and he uttered a few uncouth sounds, but he could not speak, for he was a mute.

The jasper portal introduced the companions to a long and lofty and arched chamber, lighted by high windows of stained glass, hung with tapestry of silk and silver, covered with prodigious carpets, and surrounded by immense couches. And thus through similar chambers they proceeded, in some of which were signs of recent habitation, until they arrived at another quadrangle nearly filled by a most singular fountain which rose from a basin of gold encrusted with pearls, and which was surrounded by figures of every rare quadruped[27] in the most costly materials. Here a golden tiger, with flaming eyes of ruby and flowing stripes of opal, stole, after some bloody banquet, to the refreshing brink; a camelopard raised its slender neck of silver from the centre of a group of every inhabitant of the forest; and brilliant bands of monkeys, glittering with precious stones, rested, in every variety of fantastic posture, on the margin of the basin.

The fountain itself was a tree of gold and silver[28] spreading into innumerable branches, covered with every variety of curious birds, their plumage appropriately imitated by the corresponding tints of precious stones, which warbled in beautiful melody as they poured forth from their bills the musical and refreshing element.

It was with difficulty that Alroy could refrain from an admiring exclamation, but Honain, ever quick, turned to him, with his finger pressed on his mouth, and quitting the quadrangle, they entered the gardens.

Lofty terraces, dark masses of cypress, winding walks of acacia, in the distance an interminable paradise, and here and there a glittering pavilion and bright kiosk! Its appearance on the river had not prepared Alroy for the extent of the palace itself. It seemed infinite, and it was evident that he had only viewed a small portion of it. While they were moving on, there suddenly rose a sound of trumpets. The sound grew nearer and nearer, louder and louder: soon was heard the tramp of an approaching troop. Honain drew Alroy aside. A procession appeared advancing from a dark grove of cypress. Four hundred men led as many white bloodhounds with collars of gold and rubies.[29] Then came one hundred men, each with a hooded hawk; then six horsemen in rich dresses; after them a single horseman, mounted on a steed, marked on its forehead with a star.[30] The rider was middle-aged, handsome, and dignified. He was plainly dressed, but the staff of his hunting-spear was entirely of diamonds and the blade of gold.

He was followed by a company of Nubian eunuchs, with their scarlet dresses and ivory battle-axes, and the procession closed.

'The Caliph,' whispered Honain, when they had passed, placing at the same time his finger on his lip to prevent any inquiry. This was the first intimation that had reached Alroy of what he had already suspected, that he was a visitor to the palace of the Commander of the Faithful.

The companions turned down a wild and winding walk, which, after some time, brought them to a small and gently sloping lawn, surrounded by cedar-trees of great size. Upon the lawn was a kiosk, a long and many-windowed building, covered with blinds, and further screened by an overhanging roof. The kiosk was built of white and green marble, the ascent to it was by a flight of steps the length of the building, alternately of white and green marble, and nearly covered with rose-trees. Honain went up these steps alone, and entered the kiosk. After a few minutes he looked out from the blinds and beckoned to Alroy. David advanced, but Honain, fearful of some indiscretion, met him, and said to him in a low whisper between his teeth, 'Remember you are deaf, a mute, and a eunuch.' Alroy could scarcely refrain from smiling, and the Prince of the Captivity and the physician of the Caliph entered the kiosk together. Two women, veiled, and two eunuchs of the guard, received them in an antechamber. And then they passed into a room which ran nearly the whole length of the kiosk, opening on one side to the gardens, and on the other supported by an ivory wall, with niches painted in green fresco, and in each niche a rose-tree. Each niche, also, was covered with an almost invisible golden grate, which confined a nightingale, and made him constant to the rose he loved. At the foot of each niche was a fountain, but, instead of water, each basin was replenished with the purest quicksilver.[31] The roof of the kiosk was of mother-of-pearl inlaid with tortoise-shell; the pavement, a mosaic of rare marbles and precious stones, representing the most delicious fruits and the most beautiful flowers. Over this pavement, a Georgian page flung at intervals refreshing perfumes. At the end of this elegant chamber was a divan of light green silk, embroidered with pearls, and covered with cushions of white satin and gold. Upon one of these cushions, in the middle of the divan, sat a lady, her eyes fixed in abstraction upon a volume of Persian poetry lying on her knees, one hand playing with a rosary of pearls and emeralds,[32] and the other holding a long gold chain, which imprisoned a white gazelle.

The lady looked up as Honain and his companion entered. She was very young, as youthful as Alroy. Her long light brown hair, drawn off a high white forehead covered with blue veins, fell braided with pearls over each shoulder. Her eyes were large and deeply blue; her nose small, but high and aquiline. The fairness of her face was dazzling, and, when she looked up and greeted Honain, her lustrous cheeks broke into dimples, the more fascinating from their contrast with the general expression of her countenance, which was haughty and derisive. The lady was dressed in a robe of crimson silk girded round her waist by a green shawl, from which peeped forth the diamond hilt of a small poniard.[33] Her round white arms looked infinitely small, as they occasionally flashed forth from their large loose hanging sleeves. One was covered with jewels, and the right arm was quite bare.

Honain advanced, and, bending, kissed the lady's proffered hand. Alroy fell into the background.

'They told me that the Rose of the World drooped this morning,' said the physician, bending again as he smiled, 'and her slave hastened at her command to tend her.'

'It was a south wind. The wind has changed, and the Rose of the World is better,' replied the lady laughing.

Honain touched her pulse.

'Irregular,' said the physician.

'Like myself,' said the lady. 'Is that a new slave?'

'A recent purchase, and a great bargain. He is good-looking, has the advantage of being deaf and dumb, and is harmless in every respect.'

"Tis a pity,' replied the lady; 'it seems that all good-looking people are born to be useless. I, for instance.'

'Yet rumour whispers the reverse,' remarked the physician.

'How so?' inquired the lady.

'The young King of Karasmé.'

'Poh! I have made up my mind to detest him. A barbarian!'

'A hero!'

'Have you ever seen him?'

'I have.'

'Handsome?'

'An archangel.'

'And sumptuous?'

'Is he not a conqueror? All the plunder of the world will be yours.'

'I am tired of magnificence. I built this kiosk to forget it.'

'It is not in the least degree splendid,' said Honain, looking round with a smile.

'No,' answered the lady, with a self-satisfied air: 'here, at least, one can forget one has the misfortune to be a princess.'

'It is certainly a great misfortune,' said the physician.

'And yet it must be the only tolerable lot,' replied the lady.

'Assuredly,' replied Honain.

'For our unhappy sex, at least.'

'Very unhappy.'

'If I were only a man!'

'What a hero you would be!'

'I should like to live in endless confusion.'

'I have not the least doubt of it.'

'Have you got me the books?' eagerly inquired the Princess.

'My slave bears them,' replied Honain.

'Let me see them directly.'

Honain took the bag from Alroy, and unfolded its contents; the very volumes of Greek romances which Ali, the merchant, had obtained for him.

'I am tired of poetry,' said the Princess, glancing over the costly volumes, and tossing them away; 'I long to see the world.'

'You would soon be tired of that,' replied the physician.

'I suppose common people are never tired.' said the Princess.

'Except with labour;' said the physician; 'care keeps them alive.'

'What is care?' asked the Princess, with a smile.

'It is a god,' replied the physician, 'invisible, but omnipotent. It steals the bloom from the cheek and lightness from the pulse; it takes away the appetite, and turns the hair grey.'

'It is no true divinity, then,' replied the Princess, 'but an idol we make ourselves. I am a sincere Moslem, and will not worship it. Tell me some news, Honain.'

'The young King of Karasmé——'

'Again! the barbarian! You are in his pay. I'll none of him. To leave one prison, and to be shut up in another,—why do you remind me of it? No, my dear Hakim, if I marry at all, I will marry to be free.'

'An impossibility,' said Honain.

'My mother was free till she was a queen and a slave. I intend to end as she began. You know what she was.'

Honain knew well, but he was too politic not to affect ignorance.

'The daughter of a bandit,' continued the Princess, 'who fought by the side of her father. That is existence! I must be a robber. 'Tis in the blood. I want my fate foretold, Honain. You are an astrologer; do it.'

'I have already cast your nativity. Your star is à comet.'

'That augurs well; brilliant confusion and erratic splendour. I wish I were a star,' added the Princess in a deep rich voice, and with a pensive air; 'a star in the clear blue sky, beautiful and free. Honain, Honain, the gazelle has broken her chain, and is eating my roses.'

Alroy rushed forward and seized the graceful truant. Honain shot him an anxious look; the Princess received the chain from the hand of Alroy, and cast at him a scrutinising glance.

'What splendid eyes the poor beast has got!' exclaimed the Princess.

'The gazelle?' inquired the physician.

'No, your slave,' replied the Princess. 'Why, he blushes. Were he not deaf as well as dumb, I could almost believe he understood me.'

'He is modest,' replied Honain, rather alarmed; 'and is frightened at the liberty he has taken.'

'I like modesty,' said the Princess; 'it is interesting. I am modest; you think so?'

'Certainly,' said Honain.

'And interesting?'

'Very.'

'I detest an interesting person. After all, there is nothing like plain dulness.'

'Nothing,' said Honain.

'The day flows on so serenely in such society.'

'It does,' said Honain.

'No confusion; no scenes.'

'None.'

'I make it a rule only to have ugly slaves.'

'You are quite right.'

'Honain, will you ever contradict me? You know very well I have the handsomest slaves in the world.'

'Every one knows it.'

'And, do you know, I have taken a great fancy to your new purchase, who, according to your account, is eminently qualified for the post. Why, do you not agree with me?'

'Why, yes; I doubt not your Highness would find him eminently qualified, and certainly few things would give me greater pleasure than offering him for your acceptance; but I got into such disgrace by that late affair of the Circassian, that——'

'Oh! leave it to me,' said the Princess.

'Certainly,' said the physician, turning the conversation; 'and when the young King of Karasmé arrives at Bagdad, you can offer him to his majesty as a present.'

'Delightful! and the king is really handsome and young as well as brave; but has he any taste?'

'You have enough for both.'

'If he would but make war against the Greeks!'

'Why so violent against the poor Greeks?'

'You know they are Giaours. Besides, they might beat him, and then I should have the pleasure of being taken prisoner.'

'Delightful!'

'Charming! to see Constantinople, and marry the Emperor.'

'Marry the Emperor!'

'To be sure. Of course he would fall in love with me.'

'Of course.'

'And then, and then, I might conquer Paris!'

'Paris!'

'You have been at Paris?'[34]

'Yes.'

'The men are shut up there,' said the Princess with a smile, 'are they not? and the women do what they like?'

'You will always do what you like,' said Honain, rising.

'You are going?'

'My visits must not be too long.'

'Farewell, dear Honain!' said the Princess, with a melancholy air. 'You are the only person who has an idea in all Bagdad, and you leave me. A miserable lot is mine, to feel everything, and be nothing. These books and flowers, these sweet birds, and this fair gazelle: ah! poets may feign as they please, but how cheerfully would I resign all these elegant consolations of a captive life for one hour of freedom! I wrote some verses on myself yesterday; take them, and get them blazoned for me by the finest scribe in the city; letters of silver on a violet ground with a fine flowing border; I leave the design to you. Adieu! Come hither, mute.' Alroy advanced to her beckon, and knelt. 'There, take that rosary for thy master's sake, and those dark eyes of thine.'

The companions withdrew, and reached their boat in silence. It was sunset. The musical and sonorous voice of the Muezzin resounded from the innumerable minarets of the splendid city. Honain threw back the curtains of the barque. Bagdad rose before them in huge masses of sumptuous dwellings, seated amid groves and gardens. An infinite population, summoned by the invigorating twilight, poured forth in all directions. The glowing river was covered with sparkling caiques, the glittering terraces with showy groups. Splendour, and power, and luxury, and beauty were arrayed before them in their most captivating forms, and the heart of Alroy responded to their magnificence. 'A glorious vision!' said the Prince of the Captivity.

'Very different from Hamadan,' said the physician of the Caliph.

'To-day I have seen wonders,' said Alroy.

'The world is opening to you,' said Honain.

Alroy did not reply; but after some minutes he said, in a hesitating voice, 'Who was that lady?'

'The Princess Schirene,' replied Honain, 'the favourite daughter of the Caliph. Her mother was a Georgian and a Giaour.'

The moonlight fell upon the figure of Alroy lying on a couch; his face was hidden by his arm. He was motionless, but did not sleep.

He rose and paced the chamber with agitated steps; sometimes he stopped, and gazed on the pavement, fixed in abstraction. He advanced to the window, and cooled his feverish brow in the midnight air.

An hour passed away, and the young Prince of the Captivity remained fixed in the same position. Suddenly he turned to a tripod of porphyry, and, seizing a rosary of jewels, pressed it to his lips.

'The Spirit of my dreams, she comes at last; the form for which I have sighed and wept; the form which rose upon my radiant vision when I shut my eyes against the jarring shadows of this gloomy world.

'Schirene! Schirene! here in this solitude I pour to thee the passion long stored up: the passion of my life, no common life, a life full of deep feeling and creative thought. O beautiful! O more than beautiful! for thou to me art as a dream unbroken: why art thou not mine? why lose a moment in our glorious lives, and balk our destiny of half its bliss?

'Fool, fool, hast thou forgotten? The rapture of a prisoner in his cell, whose wild fancy for a moment belies his fetters! The daughter of the Caliph and a Jew!

'Give me my fathers' sceptre.

'A plague on talismans! Oh! I need no inspiration but her memory, no magic but her name. By heavens! I will enter this glorious city a conqueror, or die.

'Why, what is Life? for meditation mingles ever with my passion: why, what is Life? Throw accidents to the dogs, and tear off the painted mask of false society! Here am I a hero; with a mind that can devise all things, and a heart of superhuman daring, with youth, with vigour, with a glorious lineage, with a form that has made full many a lovely maiden of our tribe droop her fair head by Hamadan's sweet fount, and I am—nothing!

'Out on Society! 'twas not made for me. I'll form my own, and be the deity I sometimes feel.

'We make our fortunes, and we call them Fate. Thou saidst well, Honain. Most subtle Sadducee! The saintly blood flowed in my fathers' veins, and they did nothing; but I have an arm formed to wield a sceptre, and I will win one.

'I cannot doubt my triumph. Triumph is a part of my existence. I am born for glory, as a tree is born to bear its fruit, or to expand its flowers. The deed is done. 'Tis thought of, and 'tis done. I will confront the greatest of my diademed ancestors, and in his tomb. Mighty Solomon! he wedded Pharaoh's daughter. Hah! what a future dawns upon my hope. An omen, a choice omen!

'Heaven and earth are mingling to form my fortunes. My mournful youth, which I have so often cursed, I hail thee: thou wert a glorious preparation; and when feeling no sympathy with the life around me, I deemed myself a fool, I find that I was a most peculiar being. By heavens, I am joyful; for the first time in my life I am joyful. I could laugh, and fight, and drink. I am new-born; I am another being; I am mad!

'O Time, great Time! the world belies thy fame. It calls thee swift. Methinks thou art wondrous slow. Fly on, great Time, and on thy coming wings bear me my sceptre!

'All is to be. It is a lowering thought. My fancy, like a bright and wearied bird, will sometimes flag and fall, and then I am lost. The young King of Karasmé, a youthful hero! Would he had been Alschiroch! My heart is sick even at the very name. Alas! my trials have not yet begun. Jabaster warned me: good, sincere Jabaster! His talisman presses on my frantic heart, and seems to warn me. I am in danger. Braggart to stand here, filling the careless air with idle words, while all is unaccomplished. I grow dull. The young King of Karasmé! Why, what am I compared to this same prince? Nothing, but in my thoughts. In the full bazaar, they would not deem me worthy even to hold his stirrup or his slipper—— Oh! this contest, this constant, bitter, never-ending contest between my fortune and my fancy! Why do I exist? or, if existing, why am I not recognised as I would be?

'Sweet voice, that in Jabaster's distant cave de-scendedst from thy holy home above, and whispered consolation, breathe again! Again breathe thy still summons to my lonely ear, and chase away the thoughts that hover round me; thoughts dark and doubtful, like fell birds of prey hovering around a hero in expectation of his fall, and gloating on their triumph over the brave. There is something fatal in these crowded cities. Faith flourishes in solitude.'

He threw himself upon the couch, and, leaning down his head, seemed lost in meditation. He started up, and, seizing his tablets, wrote upon them these words:

'Honain, I have been the whole night like David in the wilderness of Ziph; but, by the aid of the Lord, I have conquered. I fly from this dangerous city upon his business, which I have too much neglected. Attempt not to discover me, and accept my gratitude.'

CHAPTER VI.

The Learned Rabbi Zimri.

A SCORCHING sun, a blue and burning sky, on every side lofty ranges of black and barren mountains, dark ravines, deep caverns, unfathomable gorges! A solitary being moved in the distance. Faint and toiling, a pilgrim slowly clambered up the steep and stony track.

The sultry hours moved on; the pilgrim at length gained the summit of the mountain, a small and rugged table-land, strewn with huge masses of loose and heated, rock. All around was desolation: no spring, no herbage; the bird and the insect were alike mute. Still it was the summit: no loftier peaks frowned in the distance; the pilgrim stopped, and breathed with more facility, and a faint smile played over his languid and solemn countenance.

He rested a few minutes; he took from his wallet some locusts and wild honey, and a small skin of water. His meal was short as well as simple. An ardent desire to reach his place of destination before nightfall urged him to proceed. He soon passed over the table-land, and commenced the descent of the mountain. A straggling olive-tree occasionally appeared, and then a group, and soon the groups swelled into a grove. His way wound through the grateful and unaccustomed shade. He emerged from the grove, and found that he had proceeded down more than half the side of the mountain. It ended precipitously in a dark and narrow ravine, formed on the other side by an opposite mountain, the lofty steep of which was crested by a city gently rising on a gradual slope.

Nothing could be conceived more barren, wild, and terrible than the surrounding scenery, unillumined by a single trace of culture. The city stood like the last gladiator in an amphitheatre of desolation.

It was surrounded by a lofty turreted wall, of an architecture to which the pilgrim was unaccustomed: gates with drawbridge and portcullis, square towers, and loopholes for the archer. Sentinels, clothed in steel and shining in the sunset, paced, at regular intervals, the cautious wall, and on a lofty tower a standard waved, a snowy standard, with a red, red cross!

The Prince of the Captivity at length beheld the lost capital of his fathers.[35]

A few months back, and such a spectacle would have called forth all the latent passion of Alroy; but time and suffering, and sharp experience, had already somewhat curbed the fiery spirit of the Hebrew Prince. He gazed upon Jerusalem, he beheld the City of David garrisoned by the puissant warriors of Christendom, and threatened by the innumerable armies of the Crescent. The two great divisions of the world seemed contending for a prize, which he, a lonely wanderer, had crossed the desert to rescue.

If his faith restrained him from doubting the possibility of his enterprise, he was at least deeply conscious that the world was a very different existence from what he had fancied amid the gardens of Hamadan and the rocks of Caucasus, and that if his purpose could be accomplished, it could only be effected by one means. Calm, perhaps somewhat depressed, but full of pious humiliation, and not deserted by holy hope, he descended into the Valley of Jehoshaphat, and so, slaking his thirst at Siloah, and mounting the opposite height, David Alroy entered Jerusalem by the gate of Zion.[36]

He had been instructed that the quarter allotted to his people was near this entrance. He inquired the direction of the sentinel, who did not condescend to answer him. An old man, in shabby robes, who was passing, beckoned to him.

'What want you, friend?' inquired Alroy.

'You were asking for the quarter of our people. You must be à stranger, indeed, in Jerusalem, to suppose that a Frank would speak to a Jew. You were lucky to get neither kicked nor cursed.'

'Kicked and cursed! Why, these dogs——'

'Hush! hush! for the love of God,' said his new companion, much alarmed. 'Have you lent money to their captain that you speak thus? In Jerusalem our people speak only in a whisper.'

'No matter: the cure is not by words. Where is our quarter?'

'Was the like ever seen! Why, he speaks as if he were a Frank. I save him from having his head broken by a gauntlet, and——'

'My friend, I am tired. Our quarter?'

'Whom may you want?'

'The Chief Rabbi.'

'You bear letters to him?'

'What is that to you?'

'Hush! hush! You do not know what Jerusalem is, young man. You must not think of going on in this way. Where do you come from?'

'Bagdad.'

'Bagdad! Jerusalem is not Bagdad. A Turk is a brute, but a Christian is a demon.'

'But our quarter, our quarter?'

'Hush! you want the Chief Rabbi?'

'Ay! ay!'

'Rabbi Zimri?'

'It may be so. I neither know nor care.'

'Neither knows nor cares! This will never do; you must not go on in this way at Jerusalem. You must not think of it.'

'Fellow, I see thou art a miserable prattler. Show me our quarter, and I will pay thee well, or be off.'

'Be off! Art thou a Hebrew? to say "be off" to any one. You come from Bagdad! I tell you what, go back to Bagdad. You will never do for Jerusalem.'

'Your grizzled beard protects you. Old fool, I am a pilgrim just arrived, wearied beyond expression, and you keep me here listening to your flat talk!'

'Flat talk! Why! what would you?'

'Lead me to the Rabbi Zimri, if that be his name.'

'If that be his name! Why, every one knows Rabbi Zimri, the Chief Rabbi of Jerusalem, the successor of Aaron. We have our temple yet, say what they like. A very learned doctor is Rabbi Zimri.'

'Wretched driveller. I am ashamed to lose my patience with such a dotard.'

'Driveller! dotard! Why, who are you?'

'One you cannot comprehend. Without another word, lead me to your chief.'

'Chief! you have not far to go. I know no one of the nation who holds his head higher than I do here, and they call me Zimri.'

'What, the Chief Rabbi, that very learned doctor?'

'No less; I thought you had heard of him.'

'Let us forget the past, good Zimri. When great men play the incognito, they must sometimes hear rough phrases. It is the Caliph's lot as well as yours. I am glad to make the acquaintance of so great a doctor. Though young, and roughly habited, I have seen the world a little, and may offer next Sabbath in the synagogue more dirhems than you would perhaps suppose. Good and learned Zimri, I would be your guest.'

'A very worshipful young man! And he speaks low and soft now! But it was lucky I was at hand. Good, what's your name?'

'David.'

'A very honest name, good David. It was lucky I was at hand when you spoke to the sentinel, though. A Jew speak to a Frank, and a sentinel too! Hah! hah! hah! that is good. How Rabbi Maimon will laugh! Faith it was very lucky, now, was not it?'

'Indeed, most fortunate.'

'Well that is candid! Here! this way. 'Tis not far. We number few, sir, of our brethren here, but a better time will come, a better time will come.'

'I think so. This is your door?'

'An humble one. Jerusalem is not Bagdad, but you are welcome.'

'King Pirgandicus[37] entered them,' said Rabbi Maimon, 'but no one since.'

'And when did he live?' inquired Alroy. 'His reign is recorded in the Talmud,' answered Rabbi Zimri, 'but in the Talmud there are no dates.' 'A long while ago?' asked Alroy. 'Since the Captivity,' answered Rabbi Maimon. 'I doubt that,' said Rabbi Zimri, 'or why should he be called king?'

'Was he of the house of David?' said Alroy.

'Without doubt,' said Rabbi Maimon; 'he was one of our greatest kings, and conquered Julius Caesar.'[38]

'His kingdom was in the northernmost parts of Africa,' said Rabbi Zimri, 'and exists to this day, if we could but find it.'

'Ay, truly,' added Rabbi Maimon, 'the sceptre has never departed out of Judah; and he rode always upon a white elephant.'

'Covered with cloth of gold,' added Rabbi Zimri. 'And he visited the Tombs of the Kings?'[39] inquired Alroy.

'Without doubt,' said Rabbi Maimon. 'The whole account is in the Talmud.'

'And no one can now find them?' 'No one,' replied Rabbi Zimri: 'but, according to that learned doctor, Moses Hallevy, they are in a valley in the mountains of Lebanon, which was sealed up by the Archangel Michael.'

'The illustrious Doctor Abarbanel, of Babylon,' said Rabbi Maimon, 'gives one hundred and twenty reasons in his commentary on the Gemara to prove that they sunk under the earth at the taking of the Temple.'

'No one reasons like Abarbanel of Babylon,' said Rabbi Zimri.

'The great Rabbi Akiba, of Pundebita, has answered them all,' said Rabbi Maimon, 'and holds that they were taken up to heaven.'

'And which is right?' inquired Rabbi Zimri.

'Neither,' said Rabbi Maimon.

'One hundred and twenty reasons are strong proof,' said Rabbi Zimri.

'The most learned and illustrious Doctor Aaron Mendola, of Granada,' said Rabbi Maimon, 'has shown that we must look for the Tombs of the Kings in the south of Spain.'

'All that Mendola writes is worth attention,' said Rabbi Zimri.

'Rabbi Hillel,[40] of Samaria, is worth two Mendolas any day,' said Rabbi Maimon.

"Tis a most learned doctor,' said Rabbi Zimri; 'and what thinks he?'

'Hillel proves that there are two Tombs of the Kings,' said Rabbi Maimon, 'and that neither of them are the right ones.'

'What a learned doctor!' exclaimed Rabbi Zimri.

'And very satisfactory,' remarked Alroy.

'These are high subjects,' continued Maimon, his blear eyes twinkling with complacency. 'Your guest, Rabbi Zimri, must read the treatise of the learned Shimei, of Damascus, on "Effecting Impossibilities."'

'That is a work!' exclaimed Zimri.

'I never slept for three nights after reading that work,' said Rabbi Maimon. 'It contains twelve thousand five hundred and thirty-seven quotations from the Pentateuch, and not a single original observation.'

'There were giants in those days,' said Rabbi Zimri; 'we are children now.'

'The first chapter makes equal sense, read backward or forward,' continued Rabbi Maimon. 'Ichabod!' exclaimed Rabbi Zimri. 'And the initial letter of every section is a cabalistical type of a king of Judah.'

'The temple will yet be built,' said Rabbi Zimri. 'Ay, ay! that is learning!' exclaimed Rabbi Maimon; 'but what is the great treatise on "Effecting Impossibilities" to that profound, admirable, and———'

'Holy Rabbi!' said a youthful reader of the synagogue, who now entered, 'the hour is at hand.'

'You don't say so! Learned Miamon, I must to the synagogue. I could sit here all day listening to you. Come, David, the people await us.'

Zimri and Alroy quitted the house, and proceeded along the narrow hilly streets to the chief temple of the Hebrews.

'It grieves the venerable Maimon much that he cannot join us,' said Rabbi Zimri. 'You have doubtless heard of him at Bagdad; a most learned doctor.' Alroy bowed in silence.

'He bears his years well. You would hardly believe that he was my master.'

'I perceive that you inherit much of his erudition.'

'You are kind. If he have breathed one year, Rabbi Maimon will be a hundred and ten next Passover.'

'I doubt it not.'

'When he is gathered to his fathers, a great light will be extinguished in Israel. You wanted to know something about the Tombs of the Kings; I told you he was your man. How full he was! His mind, sir, is an egg.'

'A somewhat ancient one. I fear his guidance will hardly bring me the enviable fortune of King Pirgandicus.'

'Between ourselves, good David, talking of King Pirgandicus, I cannot help fancying that the learned Maimon made a slight mistake. I hold Pirgandicus was only a prince. It was after the Captivity, and I know no authority for any of our rulers since the destruction assuming a higher title. Clearly a prince, eh? But, though I would whisper it to no one but you, I think our worthy friend grows a little old. We should remember his years, sir. A hundred and ten next Passover. 'Tis a great burden.'

'Ay! with his learning added, a very fearful burden indeed!'

'You have been a week in Jerusalem, and have not yet visited our synagogue. It is not of cedar and ivory, but it is still a temple. This way. It is only a week that you have been here? Why, you look another man! I shall never forget our first meeting: you did not know me. That was good, eh? And when I told you I was the chief Rabbi Zimri, how you changed! You have quite regained your appetite. Ah! 'tis pleasant to mix once more with our own people. To the left. So! we must descend a little. We hold our meetings in an ancient cemetery. You have a finer temple, I warrant me, in Bagdad. Jerusalem is not Bagdad. But this has its conveniences. 'Tis safe, and we are not very rich, nor wish to seem so.'

A long passage brought them to a number of small, square, low chambers[41] leading into each other. They were lighted by brass lamps, placed at intervals in vacant niches, that once held corpses, and which were now soiled by the smoky flame. Between two and three hundred individuals were assembled in these chambers, at first scarcely distinguishable by those who descended from the broad daylight; but by degrees the eyesight became accustomed to the dim and vaporous atmosphere, and Al-roy recognised in the final and more illumined chamber a high cedar cabinet, the type of the ark, and which held the sacred vessels and the sanctified copy of the law.

Standing in lines, with their heads mystically covered,[42] the forlorn remnant of Israel, captives in their ancient city, avowed, in spite of all their sufferings, their fidelity to their God, and, notwithstanding all the bitterness of hope delayed, their faith in the fulfilment of his promises. Their simple service was completed, their prayers were read, their responses made, their law exhibited, and their charitable offerings announced by their high priest. After the service, the venerable Zimri, opening a volume of the Talmud, and fortified by the opinions of all those illustrious and learned doctors, the heroes of his erudite conversations with the aged Maimon, expounded the law to the congregation of the people.[43]

'It is written,' said the Rabbi, '"Thou shalt have none other God but me." Now know ye what our father Abraham said when Nimrod ordered him to worship fire? "Why not water," answered Abraham, "which can put out fire? why not clouds, which can pour forth water? why not the winds, which can produce clouds? why not God, which can create winds?"'

A murmur of approbation sounded throughout the congregation.

'Eliezer,' said Zimri, addressing himself to a young Rabbi, 'it is written, that he took a rib from Adam when he was asleep. Is God then a robber?'

The young Rabbi looked puzzled, and cast his eyes on the ground. The congregation was perplexed and a little alarmed.

'Is there no answer?' said Zimri.

'Rabbi,' said a stranger, a tall, swarthy African pilgrim, standing in a corner, and enveloped in a red mantle, over which a lamp threw a flickering light; 'Rabbi, some robbers broke into my house last night, and stole an earthen pipkin, but they left a golden vase in its stead.'

'It is well said; it is well said,' exclaimed the congregation. The applause was loud.

'Learned Zimri,' continued the African, 'it is written in the Gemara, that there was a youth in Jerusalem who fell in love with a beautiful damsel, and she scorned him. And the youth was so stricken with his passion that he could not speak; but when he beheld her, he looked at her imploringly, and she laughed. And one day the youth, not knowing what to do with himself, went out into the desert; and towards night he returned home, but the gates of the city were shut. And he went down into the valley of Jehoshaphat, and entered the tomb of Absalom and slept;[44] and he dreamed a dream; and next morning he came into the city smiling. And the maiden met him, and she said, "Is that thou; art thou a laugher?" and he answered, "Behold, yesterday being disconsolate, I went out of the city into the desert, and I returned home, and the gates of the city were shut, and I went down into the valley of Jehoshaphat, and I entered the tomb of Absalom, and I slept, and I dreamed a dream, and ever since then I have laughed." And the damsel said, "Tell me thy dream." And he answered and said, "I may not tell my dream only to my wife, for it regards her honour." And the maiden grew sad and curious, and said, "I am thy wife, tell me thy dream." And straightway they went and were married and ever after they both laughed. Now, learned Zimri, what means this tale, an idle jest for a master of the law, yet it is written by the greatest doctor of the Captivity?'

'It passeth my comprehension,' said the chief Rabbi.

Rabbi Eliezer was silent; the congregation groaned.

'Now hear the interpretation,' said the African. 'The youth is our people, and the damsel is our lost Sion, and the tomb of Absalom proves that salvation can only come from the house of David. Dost thou hear this, young man?' said the African, coming forward and laying his hand on Alroy. 'I speak to thee, because I have observed a deep attention in thy conduct.'

The Prince of the Captivity started, and shot a glance at the dark visage before him, but the glance read nothing. The upper part of the countenance of the African was half concealed by masses of dark matted hair, and the lower by his uncouth robes. A flashing eye was its only characteristic, which darted forth like lightning out of a black cloud.

'Is my attention the only reason that induces you to address me?' inquired Alroy.

'Whoever gave all his reasons?' replied the African, with a laughing sneer.

'I seek not to learn them. Suffice it, stranger, that how much soever you may mean, as much I can understand.'

"Tis well. Learned Zimri, is this thy pupil? I congratulate thee. I will match him against the hopeful Eliezer.' So saying, the lofty African stalked out of the chamber. The assembly also broke up. Alroy would willingly have immediately followed the African, and held some further and more private conversation with him; but some minutes elapsed, owing to the officious attentions of Zimri, before he could escape; and, when he did, his search after the stranger was vain. He inquired among the congregation, but none knew the African. He was no man's guest and no man's debtor, and apparently had never before been seen.

The trumpet was sounding to close the gates, as Alroy passed the Zion entrance. The temptation was irresistible. He rushed out, and ran for more than one hundred yards without looking back, and when he did, he had the satisfaction of ascertaining that he was fairly shut out for the night. The sun had set, still the Mount of Olives was flushed with the reflection of his dying beams, but Jehoshaphat at its feet was in deep shadow.

He wandered among the mountains for some time, beholding Jerusalem from a hundred different points of view, and watching the single planets and clustering constellations that gradually burst into beauty, or gathered into light. At length, somewhat exhausted, he descended into the vale. The scanty rill of Siloah[45] looked like a thread of silver winding in the moonlight. Some houseless wretches were slumbering under the arch of its fountain. Several isolated tombs of considerable size[46] rose at the base of Olivet, and the largest of these Alroy entered. Proceeding through a narrow passage, he entered a small square chamber. On each side was an empty sarcophagus of granite, one with its lid broken. Between these the Prince of the Captivity laid his robe, and, wearied by his ramble, soon soundly slept.

After some hours he woke. He fancied that he had been wakened by the sound of voices. The chamber was not quite dark. A straggling moonbeam fought its way through an open fretwork pattern in the top of the tomb, and just revealed the dim interior. Suddenly a voice spoke, a strange and singular voice.

'Brother, brother, the sounds of the night begin.'

Another voice answered,

'Brother, brother, I hear them, too.'

'The woman in labour!'

'The thief at his craft!'

'The sentinel's challenge!'

'The murderer's step!'

'Oh! the merry sounds of the night!'

'Brother, brother, let us come forth and wander about the world.'

'We have seen all things. I'll lie here and listen to the baying hound. 'Tis music for a tomb.'

'Choice and rare. You are idle. I like to sport in the starry air. Our hours are few, they should be fair.'

'What shall we see, Heaven or Earth?' 'Hell for me, 'tis more amusing.' 'As for me, I am sick of Hades.' 'Let us visit Solomon!' 'In his unknown metropolis?'

'That will be rare.'

'But where, oh! where?'

'Even a spirit cannot tell. But they say, but they say, I dare not whisper what they say.'

'Who told you?'

'No one. I overheard an Afrite whispering to a female Ghoul he wanted to seduce.'

'Hah! hah! hah! hah! choice pair, choice pair! We are more ethereal.'

'She was a beauty in her way. Her eyes were luminous, though somewhat dank, and her cheek tinged with carnation caught from infant blood.'

'Oh! gay; oh! gay; what said they?'

'He was a deserter without leave from Solomon's body-guard. The trull wriggled the secret out.'

'Tell me, kind brother.'

'I'll show, not tell.'

'I pr'ythee tell me.'

'Well, then, well. In Genthesma's gloomy cave there is a river none has reached, and you must sail, and you must sail—— Brother!'

'Ay.'

'Methinks I smell something too earthly.'

'What's that?'

'The breath of man.'

'Scent more fatal than the morning air! Away, away!'

In the range of mountains that lead from Olivet to the river Jordan is the great cavern of Genthesma, a mighty excavation formed by the combined and immemorial work of Nature and of Art; for on the high basaltic columns are cut strange characters and unearthly forms,[47] and in many places the natural ornaments have been completed by the hands of the sculptor into symmetrical entablatures and fanciful capitals, the work, they say, of captive Dives and conquered Afrites for the great king.

It was midnight; the cold full moon showered it brilliancy upon this narrow valley, shut in on all sides by black and barren mountains. A single being stood at the entrance of the cave.

It was Alroy. Desperate and determined, after listening to the spirits in the tomb, he resolved to penetrate the mysteries of Genthesma. He took from his girdle a flint and steel, with which he lighted a torch and then he entered.

The cavern narrowed as he cautiously advanced, and soon he found himself at the head of an evidently artificial gallery. A crowd of bats rushed forward and extinguished his torch [48] He leant down to relight it and in so doing observed that he had trod upon an artificial pavement.

The gallery was of great extent, with a gradual declination [49] Being in a straight line with the mouth of the cavern, the moonlit scene was long visible, but Alroy, on looking round, now perceived that the exterior was shut out by the eminence that he had left behind him. The sides of the gallery were covered with strange and sculptured forms.

The Prince of the Captivity proceeded along this gallery for nearly two hours. A distant murmur of falling water, which might have been distinguished nearly from the first, increased in sound as he advanced, and now, from the loud roar and dash at hand, he felt that he was on the brink of some cataract. It as very dark. His heart trembled. He felt his footing ere he ventured to advance. The spray suddenly leaped forward and extinguished his torch.

His eminent danger filled him with terror, and he receded some paces, but in vain endeavoured to reillumine his torch, which was soaked with water.

His courage deserted him. Energy and exertion seemed hopeless. He was about to deliver himself up to despair, when and expanding lustre attracted his attention in the opposing gloom.

A small and bright red cloud seemed sailing towards him. It opened, discharged from its bosom as silvery star, and dissolved again into darkness. But the star remained, the silvery star, and threw a long line of tremulous light upon the vast and raging rapid, which now, fleet and foaming, revealed itself on all sides to the eye of Alroy.

The beautiful interposition in his favour re-animated the adventurous pilgrim. A dark shadow in the foreground, breaking the line of light shed by the star upon the waters, attracted his attention. He advanced, regained his former footing, and more nearly examined it. It was a boat, and in the boat, mute and immovable, sat one of those vast, singular, and hidden forms which eh had observed sculptured on the walls of the gallery.

David Alry, committing his fortunes to the God of Israel, leapt into the boat.

And at the same moment the Afrite, for it was one of those dread beings,[50] raised the oars, and the barque moved. The falling waters suddenly parted in the long line of the star's reflection, and the barque glided through their high and severed masses.

In this wise they proceeded for a few minutes, until they entered a beautiful and moonlit lake. In the distance was mountainous country. Alroy examined his companion with a feeling of curiosity not unmixed with terror. It was remarkable that Alroy could never succeed in any way in attracting his notice. The Afrite seemed totally unconscious of the presence of his passenger. At length the boat reached the opposite shore of the lake, and the Prince of the Captivity debarked.

He debarked at the head of an avenue of colossal lions of red granite,[51] extending far as the eye could reach, and ascending the side of the mountain, which was cut into a flight of magnificent steps. The easy ascent was in consequence soon accomplished, and Alroy, proceeding along the avenue of lions, soon gained the summit of the mountain.

To his infinite astonishment he beheld Jerusalem. That strongly-marked locality could not be mistaken: at his feet were Jehoshaphat, Kedron, Siloah; he stood upon Olivet; before him was Zion. But in all other respects, how different was the landscape from the one that he had gazed upon a few days back, for the first time! The surrounding hills sparkled with vineyards, and glowed with summer palaces, and voluptuous pavilions, and glorious gardens of pleasure. The city, extending all over Mount Sion, was encompassed with a wall of white marble, with battlements of gold; a gorgeous mass of gates and pillars, and gardened terraces; lofty piles of rarest materials, cedar, and ivory, and precious stones; and costly columns of the richest workmanship and the most fanciful orders, capitals of the lotus and the palm, and flowing friezes of the olive and the vine.

And in the front a mighty Temple rose, with inspiration in its very form; a Temple so vast, so sumptuous, that there needed no priest to tell us that no human hand planned that sublime magnificence!

'God of my fathers!' said Alroy, 'I am a poor, weak thing, and my life has been a life of dreams and visions, and I have sometimes thought my brain lacked a sufficient master; where am I? Do I sleep or live? Am I a slumberer or a ghost? This trial is too much.' He sank down, and hid his face in his hands: his over-exerted mind appeared to desert him: he wept.

Many minutes elapsed before Alroy grew composed. His wild bursts of weeping sank into sobs, and the sobs died off into sighs. And at length, calm from exhaustion, he again looked up, and lo! the glorious city was no more! Before him was a moon-lit plain, over which the avenue of lions still advanced, and appeared to terminate only in the mountainous distance.

This limit the Prince of the Captivity at length reached, and stood before a stupendous portal, cut out of the solid rock, four hundred feet in height, and supported by clusters of colossal Caryatides.[52] Upon the portal were engraven some Hebrew characters, which upon examination proved to be the same as those upon the talisman of Jabaster. And so, taking from his bosom that all-precious and long-cherished deposit, David Alroy, in obedience to his instructions, pressed the signet against the gigantic portal.

The portal opened with a crash of thunder louder than an earthquake. Pale, panting, and staggering, the Prince of the Captivity entered an illimitable hall, illumined by pendulous balls of glowing metal. On each side of the hall, sitting on golden thrones, was ranged a line of kings, and, as the pilgrim entered, the monarchs rose, and took off their diadems, and waved them thrice, and thrice repeated, in solemn chorus, 'All hail, Alroy! Hail to thee, brother king! Thy crown awaits thee!'

The Prince of the Captivity stood trembling, with his eyes fixed upon the ground, and leaning breathless against a column. And when at length he had a little recovered himself, and dared again to look up, he found that the monarchs were re-seated; and, from their still and vacant visages, apparently unconscious of his presence. And this emboldened him, and so, staring alternately at each side of the hall, but with a firm, perhaps desperate step, Alroy advanced.

And he came to two thrones which were set apart from the others in the middle of the hall. On one was seated a noble figure, far above the common stature, with arms folded and downcast eyes. His feet rested upon a broken sword and a shivered sceptre, which told that he was a monarch, in spite of his discrowned head.

And on the opposite throne was a venerable personage, with a long flowing beard, and dressed in white raiment. His countenance was beautiful, although ancient. Age had stolen on without its imperfections, and time had only invested it with a sweet dignity and solemn grace. The countenance of the king was upraised with a seraphic gaze, and, as he thus looked up on high, with eyes full of love, and thanksgiving, and praise, his consecrated fingers seemed to touch the trembling wires of a golden harp.

And further on, and far above the rest, upon a throne that stretched across the hall, a most imperial presence straightway flashed upon the startled vision of Alroy. Fifty steps of ivory, and each step guarded by golden lions,[53] led to a throne of jasper. A dazzling light blazed forth from the glittering diadem and radiant countenance of him who sat upon the throne, one beautiful as a woman, but with the majesty of a god. And in one hand he held a seal, and in the other a sceptre.

And when Alroy had reached the foot of the throne, he stopped, and his heart misgave him. And he prayed for some minutes in silent devotion, and, without daring to look up, he mounted the first step of the throne, and the second, and the third, and so on, with slow and faltering feet, until he reached the forty-ninth step.

The Prince of the Captivity raised his eyes. He stood before the monarch face to face. In vain Alroy attempted to attract his attention, or to fix his gaze. The large dark eyes, full of supernatural lustre, appeared capable of piercing all things, and illuminating all things, but they flashed on without shedding a ray upon Alroy.

Pale as a spectre, the pilgrim, whose pilgrimage seemed now on the point of completion, stood cold and trembling before the object of all his desires and all his labours. But he thought of his country, his people, and his God; and, while his noiseless lips breathed the name of Jehovah, solemnly he put forth his arm, and with a gentle firmness grasped the unresisting sceptre of his great ancestor.

And, as he seized it, the whole scene vanished from his sight!

Hours or years might have passed away, so far as the sufferer was concerned, when Alroy again returned to self-consciousness. His eyes slowly opened, he cast around a vacant stare, he was lying in the cavern of Genthesma. The moon had set, but the morn had not broken. A single star glittered over the brow of the black mountains. He faintly moved his limbs; he would have raised his hand to his bewildered brain, but found that it grasped a sceptre. The memory of the past returned to him. He tried to rise, and found that he was reposing in the arms of a human being. He turned his head; he met the anxious gaze of Jabaster!

CHAPTER VII.

Conquest of the Seljuks

'YOUR face is troubled, uncle.' 'So is my mind.' 'All may go well.' 'Miriam, we have seen the best. Prepare yourself for sorrow, gentle girl. I care not for myself, for I am old, and age makes heroes of us all. I have endured, and can endure more. As we approach our limit, it would appear that our minds grow callous. I have seen my wealth, raised with the labours of a thoughtful life, vanish in a morn: my people, a fragile remnant, nevertheless a people, dispersed, or what is worse. I have wept for them, although no tear of selfish grief has tinged this withered cheek. And, were I but alone, ay! there's the pang. The solace of my days is now my sorrow.'

'Weep not for me, dear uncle. Rather let us pray that our God will not forsake us.'

'We know not when we are well. Our hours stole tranquilly along, and then we murmured. Prospering, we murmured, and now we are rightly stricken. The legend of the past is Israel's bane. The past is a dream; and, in the waking present, we should discard the enervating shadow. Why should we be free? We murmured against captivity. This *is* captivity: this damp, dim cell, where we are brought to die.

'O! youth, rash youth, thy being is destruction. But yesterday a child, it seems but yesterday I nursed him in these arms, a thoughtless child, and now our house has fallen by his deeds. I will not think of it; 'twill make me mad.'

'Uncle, dearest uncle, we have lived together, and we will die together, and both in love; but, I pray you, speak no harsh word of David.'

'Shall I praise him?'

'Say nothing. What he has done, if done in grief, has been done all in honour. Would you that he had spared Alschiroch?'

'Never! I would have struck him myself. Brave boy, he did his duty; and I, I, Miriam, thy uncle, at whom they wink behind his back and call him niggard, was I wanting in that hour of trial? Was my treasure spared to save my people? Did I shrink from all the toil and trouble of that time? A trying time, my Miriam, but compared with this, the building of the Temple——'

'You were then what you have ever been, the best and wisest. And since our fathers' God did not forsake us, even in that wilderness of wildest woe, I offer gratitude in present faith, and pay him for past mercies by my prayers for more.'

'Well, well, life must end. The hour approaches when we must meet our rulers and mock trial; precious justice that begins in threats and ends in torture. You are silent, Miriam.'

'I am speaking to my God.'

'What is that noise? A figure moves behind the dusky grate. Our gaoler. No, no, it is Caleb! Faithful child, I fear you have perilled much.'

'I enter with authority, my lord, and bear good tidings.'

'He smiles! Is't possible? Speak on, speak on!'

'Alroy has captured the harem of our Governor, as they journeyed from Bagdad to this city, guarded by his choicest troops. And he has sent to offer that they shall be exchanged for you and for your household. And Hassan has answered that his women shall owe their freedom to nothing but his sword. But, in the meantime, it is agreed between him and the messenger of your nephew, that both companies of prisoners shall be treated with all becoming courtesy. You, therefore, are remanded to your palace, and the trumpet is now sounding before the great mosque to summon all the host against Alroy, whom Hassan has vowed to bring to Hamadan dead or alive.'

'The harem of the Governor, guarded too by his choicest troops! 'Tis a great deed. He did remember us. Faithful boy! The harem of the Governor! his choicest troops! 'Tis a very great deed. Me-thinks the Lord is with him. He has his great father's heart. Only think of David, a child! I nursed him, often. Caleb! Can this be David, our David, a child, a girl? Yet he struck Alschiroch! Miriam! where is she? Worthy Caleb, look to your mistress; she has fallen. Quite gone! Fetch water. 'Tis not very pure, but we shall be in our palace soon. The harem of the Governor! I can't believe it. Sprinkle, sprinkle. David take them prisoners! Why, when they pass, we are obliged to turn our heads, and dare not look. More water: I'll rub her hand. 'Tis warmer! Her eyes open! Miriam, choice news, my child! The harem of the Governor! I'll not believe it!

'Once more within our walls, Caleb. Life is a miracle. I feel young again. This is home; and yet I am a prisoner. You said the host were assembling; he can have no chance. Think you, Caleb, he has any chance? I hope he will die. I would not have him taken. I fear their tortures. We will die too; we will all die. Now I am out of that dungeon, me-thinks I could even fight. Is it true that he has joined with robbers?'

'I saw the messenger, and learnt that he first repaired to some bandits in the ruins in the desert. He had become acquainted with them in his pilgrimage. They say their leader is one of our people.'

'I am glad of that. He can eat with him. I would not have him eat unclean things with the Ishmaelites.'

'Lord, sir! our people gather to him from all quarters. 'Tis said that Jabaster, the great Cabalist, has joined him from the mountains with ten thousand men.'

'The great Jabaster! then there is some chance. I know Jabaster well. He is too wise to join a desperate cause. Art sure about Jabaster? 'Tis a great name, a very potent spirit. I have heard such things of that Jabaster, sir, would make you stare like Saul before the spirit! Only think of our David, Caleb, making all this noise! I am full of hope. I feel not like a prisoner. He beat the harem guard, and, now he has got Jabaster, he will beat them all.'

'The messenger told me he captured the harem, only to free his uncle and his sister.'

'He ever loved me; I have done my duty to him; I think I have. Jabaster! why, man, the name is a spell I There are men at Bagdad who will get up in the night to join Jabaster. I hope David will follow his counsels in all things. I would I had seen his servant, I could have sent him a message.'

'Lord, sir! the Prince Alroy has no great need of counsellors, I can tell you. 'Tis said he bears the sceptre of great Solomon, which he himself obtained in the unknown tombs of Palestine.'

'The sceptre of Solomon! could I but believe it! 'Tis an age of wonders! Where are we? Call for Miriam, I'll tell her this. Only think of David, a mere child, our David with the sceptre of Solomon! and Jabaster too! I have great faith. The Lord confound his enemies!'

'Gentle Rachel, I fear I trouble you; sweet Beruna, I thank you for your zeal. I am better now; the shock was great. These are strange tidings, maidens.'

'Yes, dear lady! who would have thought of your brother turning out a Captain?'

'I am sure I always thought he was the quietest person in the world,' said Beruna, 'though he did kill Alschiroch.'

'One could never get a word out of him,' said Rachel.

'He was always moping alone,' said Beruna.

'And when one spoke to him he always turned away,' said Leah.

'Or blushed,' added Imra.

'Well, for my part,' said the beautiful Bathsheba, 'I always thought Prince David was a genius. He had such beautiful eyes!'

'I hope he will conquer Hassan,' said Rachel.

'So do I,' said Beruna.

'I wonder what he has done with the harem,' said Leah.

'I don't think he will dare to speak to them,' said Imra.

'You are very much mistaken,' said Bathsheba.

'Hark!' said Miriam.

"Tis Hassan,' said Bathsheba; 'may he never return!'

The wild drum of the Seljuks sounded, then a flourish of their fierce trumpets, and soon the tramp of horse. Behind the blinds of their chamber, Miriam and her maidens beheld the magnificent troop of tur-baned horsemen, who, glittering with splendid armour and bright shawls, and proudly bounding on their fiery steeds, now went forth to crush and conquer the only hope of Israel. Upon an Arab, darker than night, rode the superb Hassan, and, as he passed the dwelling of his late prisoners, whether from the exulting anticipation of coming triumph, or from a soft suspicion that, behind that lattice, bright eyes and brilliant faces were gazing on his state, the haughty but handsome Seljuk flourished his scimitar over his head, as he threw his managed steed into attitudes that displayed the skill of its rider.

'He is handsomer than Alschiroch,' said Rachel.

'What a shawl!' said Beruna.

'His scimitar was like lightning,' said Leah.

'And his steed like thunder,' said Imra.

'The evil eye fall on him!' said Bathsheba.

'Lord,' exclaimed Miriam, 'remember David and all his afflictions!'

The deserted city of the wilderness presented a very different appearance from that which met the astonished gaze of Alroy, when he first beheld its noble turrets, and wandered in its silent streets of palaces.

Without the gates was pitched a numerous camp of those low black tents common among the Kourds and Turkmans; the principal street was full of busy groups engaged in all the preparations of warfare, and all the bustling expedients of an irregular and adventurous life; steeds were stalled in ruined chambers, and tall camels raised their still visages among the clustering columns, or crouched in kneeling tranquillity amid fallen statues and prostrate obelisks.

Two months had scarcely elapsed since Alroy and Jabaster had sought Scherirah in his haunt, and announced to him their sacred mission. The callous heart of him, whose 'mother was a Jewess,' had yielded to their inspired annunciations. He embraced their cause with all the fervour of conversion, and his motley band were not long sceptical of a creed which, while it assuredly offered danger and adventure, held out the prospects of wealth and even empire. From the city of the wilderness the new Messiah sent forth his messengers to the neighbouring cities, to announce his advent to his brethren in captivity. The Hebrews, a proud and stiff-necked race, ever prone to rebellion, received the announcement of their favourite prince with transport. The descendant of David, and the slayer of Alschiroch, had double claims upon their confidence and allegiance, and the flower of the Hebrew youth in the neighbouring cities of the Caliphate repaired in crowds to pay their homage to the recovered sceptre of Solomon.

The affair was at first treated by the government with contempt, and the sultan of the Seljuks contented himself with setting a price upon the head of the murderer of his brother; but, when several cities had been placed under contribution, and more than one Moslem caravan stopped, and plundered in the name of the God of Abraham, of Isaac, and of Jacob, orders were despatched from Bagdad to the new governor of Hamadan, Hassan Subah, to suppress the robbers, or the rebels, and to send David Alroy dead or alive to the capital.

The Hebrew malcontents were well apprised by their less adventurous but still sympathising brethren of everything that took place at the head-quarters of the enemy. Spies arrived on the same day at the city of the wilderness, who informed Alroy that his uncle was thrown into a dungeon at Hamadan, and that a body of chosen troops were about to escort a royal harem from Bagdad into Persia.

Alroy attacked the escort in person, utterly discomfited them, and captured their charge. It proved to be the harem of the Governor of Hamadan, and if for a moment the too sanguine fancy of the captor experienced a passing pang of disappointment, the prize at least obtained, as we have seen, the freedom and security of his dear though distant friends. This exploit precipitated the expedition which was preparing at Hamadan for his destruction. The enraged Hassan Subah started from his divan, seized his scimitar, and without waiting for the auxiliaries he had summoned from the neighbouring chieftains, called to horse, and at the head of two thousand of the splendid Seljuk cavalry, hurried to vindicate his love and satiate his revenge.

Within the amphitheatre which he first entered as a prisoner, Alroy sat in council. On his right was Jabaster, Scherirah on his left. A youth, little his senior, but tall as a palm-tree, and strong as a young lion, was the fourth captain. In the distance, some standing, some reclining, were about fifty men completely armed.

'Are the people numbered, Abner?' inquired Alroy of the youth.

'Even so; three hundred effective horsemen, and two thousand footmen; but the footmen lack arms.'

'The Lord will send them in good time,' said Jabaster; 'meanwhile let them continue to make javelins.'

'Trust in the Lord,' murmured Scherirah, bending his head, with his eyes fixed on the ground.

A loud shout was heard throughout the city. Alroy started from his carpet. The messenger had returned. Pale and haggard, covered with sweat and sand, the faithful envoy was borne into the amphitheatre almost upon the shoulders of the people. In vain the guard endeavoured to stem the passage of the multitude. They clambered up the tiers of arches, they filled the void and crumbling seats of the antique circus, they supported themselves upon each other's shoulders, they clung to the capitals of the lofty columns. The whole multitude had assembled to hear the intelligence; the scene recalled the ancient purpose of the building, and Alroy and his fellow-warriors seemed like the gladiators of some old spectacle.

'Speak,' said Alroy, 'speak the worst. No news can be bitter to those whom the Lord will avenge.'

'Ruler of Israel! thus saith Hassan Subah,' answered the messenger: 'My harem shall owe their freedom to nothing but my sword. I treat not with rebels, but I war not with age or woman; and between Bostenay and his household on one side, and the prisoners of thy master on the other, let there be peace. Go, tell Alroy, I will seal it in his best blood. And lo! thy uncle and thy sister are again in their palace.'

Alroy placed his hand for a moment to his eyes, and then instantly resuming his self-possession, he enquired as to the movements of the enemy.

'I have crossed the desert on a swift dromedary[54] lent to me by Shelomi of the Gate, whose heart is with our cause. I have not tarried, neither have I slept. Ere to-morrow's sunset the Philistines will be here, led by Hassan Subah himself. The Lord of Hosts be with us! Since we conquered Canaan, Israel hath not struggled with such a power!'

A murmur ran through the assembly. Men exchanged enquiring glances, and involuntarily pressed each other's arms.

'The trial has come,' said a middle-aged Hebrew, who had fought twenty years ago with Jabaster.

'Let me die for the Ark!' said a young enthusiast of the band of Abner.

'I thought we should get into a scrape,' whispered Kisloch the Kourd to Calidas the Indian. 'What could have ever induced us to give up robbing in a quiet manner?'

'And turn Jews!' said the Guebre, with a sneer.

'Look at Scherirah,' said the Negro, grinning. 'If he is not kissing the sceptre of Solomon!'

'I wish to heaven he had only hung Alroy the first time he met him,' said Calidas.

'Sons of the Covenant!' exclaimed Alroy, 'the Lord hath delivered them into our hands. To-morrow eve we march to Hamadan!'

A cheer followed this exclamation.

'It is written,' said Jabaster, opening a volume, '"Lo! I will defend this city, to save it, for mine own sake, and for my servant David's sake."

'"And it came to pass that night that the angel of the Lord went out, and smote in the camp of the Assyrians, an hundred four score and five thousand; and when they arose early in the morning, behold! they were all dead corpses."

'Now, as I was gazing upon the stars this morn, and reading the celestial alphabet known to the true Cabalist,[55] behold! the star of the house of David and seven other stars moved, and met together, and formed into a circle. And the word they formed was a mystery to me; but lo! I have opened the book, and each star is the initial letter of each line of the Targum that I have now read to you. Therefore the fate of Sennacherib is the fate of Hassan Subah!'

'"Trust in him at all times, ye people; pour out your heart before him." god is a refuge for us. Selah!'

At this moment a female form appeared on the very top of the amphitheatre, upon the slight remains of the upper most tier of which a solitary arch alone was left. The chorus instantly died away, every tongue was silent, every eye fixed. Hushed, mute, and immovable, even Kisloch and his companions were appalled as they gazed upon Esther the Prophetess.

Her eminent position, her imposing action, the flashing of her immense eyes, her beautiful but awful countenance, her black hair, that hung almost to her knees, and the white light of the moon, just rising over the opposite side of the amphitheatre, and which threw a silvery flash upon her form, and seemed to invest her with some miraculous emanation, while all beneath her was in deep gloom,-these circumstances combined to render her an object of universal interest and attention, while in a powerful but high voice she thus addressed them:

'They come, they come! But will they go? Lo! hear ye this, O house of Jacob, which are called by the name of Israel, and are come forth out of the waters of Judah! I hear their drum in the desert, and the voice of their trumpets is like the wind of eve, but a decree hath gone forth, and it says, that a mortal shall be more precious than fine gold, yea, a man than the rich ore of Ophir.

'They come, they come! But will they go? I see the flash of their scimitars, I mark the prancing of their cruel steeds; but a decree hath gone forth, and it says, a gleaning shall be left among them, as in the shaking of the olive-tree; two or three berries on the top of the uppermost bough; four or five on the straggling branches.

'They come, they come! But will they go? Lo! a decree hath gone forth, and it says, Hamadan shall be to thee for a spoil, and desolation shall fall upon Babylon. And there shall the wild beasts of the desert lodge, and howling monsters shall fill their houses, and there shall the daughters of the ostrich dwell, and there shall the screech-owl pitch her tent, and there shall the night-raven lay her eggs, and there shall the satyrs hold their revels. And wolves shall howl to one another in their palaces, and dragons in their voluptuous pavilions. Her time is near at hand; her days shall not be prolonged; the reed and the lotus shall wither in her rivers; and the meadows by her canals shall be as the sands of the desert. For, is it a light thing that the Lord should send his servant to raise up the tribes of Jacob, and to restore the preserved of Israel? Sing, O heavens, and be joyful, O earth, and break forth into singing, O mountains, for the Lord hath comforted his people, and will have mercy upon his afflicted!'

She ceased; she descended the precipitous side of the amphitheatre with rapid steps, vaulting from tier to tier, and bounding with wonderful agility from one mass of ruin to another. At length she reached the level; and then, foaming and panting, she rushed to Alroy, threw herself upon the ground, embraced his feet, and wiped off the dust from his sandals with her hair.

The assembly broke into long and loud acclamations of supernatural confidence and sanguine enthusiasm. They beheld their Messiah wave his miraculous sceptre. They thought of Hassan Subah and his Seljuks only as of victims, and of to-morrow only as of a day which was to commence a new era of triumph, freedom, and empire!

Hassan Subah after five days' forced marches pitched his sumptuous pavilion in that beautiful Oasis, which had afforded such delightful refreshment to Alroy when a solitary pilgrim. Around for nearly a mile, were the tents of his warriors, and of the numerous caravan that had accompanied him, laden with water and provisions for his troops. Here, while he reposed, he also sought information as to the position of his enemy.

A party of observation, which he had immediately despatched, returned almost instantly with a small caravan that had been recently plundered by the robbers. The merchant, a venerable and pious Moslem, was ushered into the presence of the Governor of Hamadan.

'From the robbers' haunt?' enquired Hassan.

'Unfortunately so,' answered the merchant.

'Is it far?'

'A day's journey.'

'And you quitted it?'

'Yesterday morn.'

'What is their force?'

The merchant hesitated.

'Do they not make prisoners?' enquired the Governor, casting a scrutinising glance at his companion.

'Holy Prophet! what a miserable wretch am I!' exclaimed the venerable merchant, bursting into tears. 'A faithful subject of the Caliph, I am obliged to serve rebels, a devout Moslem, I am forced to aid Jews! Order me to be hanged at once, my lord,' continued the unfortunate merchant, wringing his hands. 'Order me to be hanged at once. I have lived long enough.'

'What is all this?' enquired Hassan; 'speak, friend, without fear.'

'I am a faithful subject of the Caliph,' answered the merchant; 'I am a devout Moslem, but I have lost ten thousand dirhems.'

'I am sorry for you, sir; I also have lost something, but my losses are nothing to you, nor yours to me.'

'Accursed be the hour when these dogs tempted me! Tell me, is it sin to break faith with a Jew?'

'On the contrary, I could find you many reverend Mollahs, who will tell you that such a breach is the highest virtue. Come! come, I see how it is: you have received your freedom on condition of not betraying your merciful plunderers. Promises exacted by terror are the bugbears of fools. Speak, man, all you know. Where are they? What is their force? Are we supposed to be at hand?'

'I am a faithful subject of the Caliph, and I am bound to serve him,' replied the merchant; 'I am a devout Moslem, and 'tis my duty to destroy all Giaours, but I am also a man, and I must look after my own interest. Noble Governor, the long and the short is, these scoundrels have robbed me of ten thousand dirhems, as my slaves will tell you: at least, goods to that amount. No one can prove that they be worth less. It is true that I include in that calculation the fifty per cent. I was to make on my shawls at Hamadan, but still to me it is as good as ten thousand dirhems. Ask my slaves if such an assortment of shawls was ever yet beheld.'

'To the point, to the point. The robbers?' 'I am at the point. The shawls is the point. For when I talked of the shawls and the heaviness of my loss, you must know that the captain of the robbers—'

'Alroy?'

'A fierce young gentleman, I do not know how they call him: said the captain to me, "Merchant, you look gloomy." "Gloomy," I said, "you would look gloomy if you were a prisoner, and had lost ten thousand dirhems." "What, is this trash worth ten thousand dirhems?" said he. "With the fifty per cent. I was to make at Hamadan." "Fifty per cent.," said he; "you are an old knave." "Knave! I should like to hear any one call me knave at Bagdad." "Well, knave or not, you may get out of this scrape." "How?" "Why you are a respectable-looking man," said he, "and are a good Moslem into the bargain, I warrant." "That I am," said I, "although you be a Jew: but how the faith is to serve me here I am sure I don't know, unless the angel Gabriel, as in the fifty-fifth verse of the twenty-seventh chapter of the Koran——"'

'Tush, tush!' exclaimed Hassan; 'to the point.'

'I always am at the point, only you put me out. However, to make it as short as possible, the captain knows all about your coming, and is frightened out of his wits, although he did talk big; I could easily see that. And he let me go, you see, with some of my slaves, and gave me an order for five thousand dirhems on one Bostenay, of Hamadan (perhaps you know him; is he a good man?), on condition that I would fall in with you, and, Mohammed forgive me, tell you a lie!'

'A lie!'

'Yes, a lie; but these Jewish dogs do not understand what a truly religious man is, and when I began to tell the lie, I was soon put out. Now, noble Hassan, if a promise to a Jew be not binding on a true believer, and you will see me straight with the five thousand dirhems, I will betray everything at once.'

'Be easy about the five thousand dirhems, good man, and tell me all.'

'You will see me paid?'

'My honour upon it.'

''Tis well! Know then, the infamous dogs are very weak, and terrified at the news of your progress: one, whom I think they call Jabaster, has departed with the great majority of the people into the interior of the desert, about seven hundred strong. I heard so; but mind, I do not know it. The young man, whom you call Alroy, being wounded in a recent conflict, could not depart with them, but remains among the ruins with some female prisoners, some treasure, and about a hundred companions hidden in sepulchres. He gave me my freedom on condition that I should fall in with you, and assure you that the dogs, full five thousand strong, had given you the go-by in the night, and marched towards Hamadan. They wanted me to frighten you; it was a lie, and I could not tell it. And now you know the plain truth; and if it be a sin to break faith with an infidel, you are responsible for it, as well as for the five thousand dirhems, which, by-the-bye, ought to have been ten.'

'Where is your order?'

''Tis here,' said the merchant, drawing it from his vest, 'a very business-like document, drawn upon one Bostenay, whom they described as very rich, and who is here enjoined to pay me five thousand dirhems, if, in consequence of my information, Hassan Subah, that is yourself, return forthwith to Hamadan without attacking them.'

'Old Bostenay's head shall answer for this.'

'I am glad of it. But were I you, I would make him pay me first.'

'Merchant,' said Hassan, 'have you any objection to pay another visit to your friend Alroy?'

'Allah forbid!'

'In my company?'

'That makes a difference.'

'Be our guide. The dirhems shall be doubled.'

'That will make up for the fifty per cent. I hardly like it; but in your company that makes a difference. Lose no time. If you push on, Alroy must be captured. Now or never! The Jewish dogs, to rifle a true believer!'

'Oglu,' said Hassan to one of his officers. 'To horse! You need not strike the tents. Can we reach the city by sunset, merchant?'

'An hour before, if you be off at once.' 'Sound the drums. To horse! to horse!' The Seljuks halted before the walls of the deserted city. Their commander ordered a detachment to enter and reconnoitre. They returned and reported its apparent desolation. Hassan Subah, then directing that a guard should surround the walls to prevent any of the enemy from escaping, passed with his warriors through the vast portal into the silent street. The still magnificence of the strange and splendid scene influenced the temper even of this ferocious cavalry. They gazed around them with awe and admiration. The fierceness of their visages was softened, the ardour of their impulse stilled. A supernatural feeling of repose stole over their senses. No one brandished his scimitar, the fiery courser seemed as subdued as his lord, and no sound was heard but the melancholy, mechanical tramp of the disciplined march, unrelieved by martial music, inviolate by oath or jest, and unbroken even by the ostentatious caracoling of any showy steed.

It was sunset; the star of eve glittered over the white Ionian fane that rose serene and delicate in the flashing and purple sky.

'This way, my lord!' said the merchant guide, turning round to Hassan Subah, who, surrounded by his officers, led the van. The whole of the great way of the city was filled with the Seljukian warriors. Their ebon steeds, their snowy turbans, adorned with plumes of the black eagle and the red heron, their dazzling shawls, the blaze of their armour in the sunset, and the long undulating perspective of beautiful forms and brilliant colours, this regiment of heroes in a street of palaces. War had seldom afforded a more imposing or more picturesque spectacle.

'This way, my lord!' said the merchant, pointing to the narrow turning that, at the foot of the temple, led through ruined streets to the amphitheatre.

'Halt!' exclaimed a wild shrill voice. Each warrior suddenly arrested his horse.

'Who spoke?' exclaimed Hassan Subah.

'I!' answered a voice. A female form stood in the portico of the temple, with uplifted arms.

'And who art thou?' enquired Hassan Subah, not a little disconcerted.

'Thine evil genius, Seljuk!'

Hassan Subah, pale as his ivory battle-axe, did not answer; every man within hearing shuddered; still the dread woman remained immovable within the porch of the temple.

'Woman, witch, or goddess,' at length exclaimed Hassan Subah, 'what wouldst thou here?'

'Seljuk! behold this star. 'Tis a single drop of light, yet who even of thy wild band can look upon it without awe? And yet thou worse than Sisera, thou comest to combat against those for whom even "the stars in their courses fought."'

'A Jewish witch!' exclaimed the Seljuk.

'A Jewish witch! Be it so; behold, then, my spell falls upon thee, and that spell is Destruction.

'Awake, awake, Deborah: awake, awake, utter a song; arise, Barak, and lead thy captivity captive, thou son of Abinoam!'

Immediately the sky appeared to darken, a cloud of arrows and javelins broke from all sides upon the çlevoted Seljuks: immense masses of stone and marble were hurled from all directions, horses were stabbed by spears impelled by invisible hands, and riders fell to the ground without a struggle, and were trampled upon by their disordered and affrighted brethren.

'We are betrayed,' exclaimed Hassan Subah, hurling a javelin at the merchant, but the merchant was gone. The Seljuks raised their famous war cry.

'Oglu, regain the desert,' ordered the chieftain.

But no sooner had the guard without the walls heard the war cry of their companions, than, alarmed, for their safety, they rushed to their assistance. The retreating forces of Subah, each instant diminishing as they retreated, were baffled in their project by the very eagerness of their auxiliaries. The unwilling contention of the two parties increased the confusion; and when the Seljuks, recently arrived, having at length formed into some order, had regained the gate, they found to their dismay that the portal was barricadoed and garrisoned by the enemy. Uninspired by the presence of their commander, who was in the rear, the puzzled soldiers were seized with a panic, and spurring their horses, dispersed in all directions of the city. In vain Hassan Subah endeavoured to restore order. The moment was past. Dashing with about thirty men to an open ground, which his quick eye had observed in his progress down the street, and dealing destruction with every blow, the dreaded Governor of Hamadan, like a true soldier, awaited an inevitable fate, not wholly despairing that some chance might yet turn up to extricate him from his forlorn situation.

And now, as it were by enchantment, wild armed men seemed to arise from every part of the city. From every mass of ruin, from every crumbling temple and mouldering mansion, from every catacomb and cellar, from behind every column and every obelisk, upstarted some desperate warrior with a bloody weapon. The massacre of the Seljuks was universal. The horsemen dashed wildly about the ruined streets, pursued by crowds of footmen; sometimes, formed in small companies, the Seljuks charged and fought desperately; but, however stout might be their resistance to the open foe, it was impossible to withstand their secret enemies. They had no place of refuge, no power of gaining even a moment's breathing time. If they retreated to a wall it instantly bristled with spears; if they endeavoured to form, in a court, they sank under the falling masses which were showered upon them. Strange shouts of denunciation blended with the harsh braying of horns, and the clang and clash of cymbals and tambours sounded in every quarter of the city.

'If we could only mount the walls, Ibrahim, and leap into the desert!' exclaimed Hassan Subah to one of his few remaining comrades; "tis our only chance. We die here like dogs! Could I but meet Alroy!'

Three of the Seljuks dashed swiftly across the open ground in front, followed by several Hebrew horsemen.

'Smite all, Abner. Spare none, remember Amalek,' exclaimed their youthful leader, waving his bloody scimitar.

'They are down; one, two, there goes the third. My javelin has done for him.'

'Your horse bleeds freely. Where's Jabaster?'

'At the gates; my arm aches with slaughter. The Lord hath delivered them into our hands. Could I but meet their chieftain!'

'Turn, bloodhound, he is here,' exclaimed Hassan Subah.

'Away, Abner, this affair is mine.'

'Prince, you have already slain your thousands.'

'And Abner his tens of thousands. Is it so? This business is for me only. Come on, Turk.'

'Art thou Alroy?'

'The same.'

'The slayer of Alschiroch?'

'Even so.'

'A rebel and a murderer.'

'What you please. Look to yourself.'

The Hebrew Prince flung a javelin at the Seljuk. It glanced from the breastplate; but Hassan Subah staggered in his seat. Recovering, he charged Alroy with great force. Their scimitars crossed, and the blade of Hassan shivered.

'He who sold me that blade told me it was charmed, and could be broken only by a caliph,' said Hassan Subah. 'He was a liar.'

'As it may be,' said Alroy, and he cut the Seljuk to the ground. Abner had dispersed his comrades. Alroy leaped from his fainting steed, and, mounting the ebon courser of his late enemy, dashed again into the thickest of the fight.

The shades of night descended, the clamour gradually decreased, the struggle died away. A few unhappy Moslemin who had quitted their saddles and sought concealment among the ruins, were occasionally hunted out, and brought forward and massacred. Long ere midnight the last of the Seljuks had expired.[56]

The moon shed a broad light upon the street of palaces crowded with the accumulated slain and the living victors. Fires were lit, torches illumined, the conquerors prepared the eager meal as they sang hymns of praise and thanksgiving.

A procession approached. Esther the prophetess, clashing her cymbals, danced before the Messiah of Israel, who leant upon his victorious scimitar, surrounded by Jabaster, Abner, Scherirah, and his chosen chieftains. Who could now doubt the validity of his mission? The wide and silent desert rang with the acclamations of his enthusiastic votaries.

Heavily the anxious hours crept on in the Jewish quarter of Hamadan. Again and again the venerable Bostenay discussed the chances of success with the sympathising but desponding elders. Miriam was buried in constant prayer. Their most sanguine hopes did not extend beyond the escape of their Prince.

A fortnight had elapsed, and no news had been received of the progress of the expedition, when suddenly, towards sunset, a sentinel on a watch-tower announced the appearance of an armed force in the distance. The walls were instantly lined with the anxious inhabitants, the streets and squares filled with curious crowds. Exultation sat on the triumphant brow of the Moslemin; a cold tremor stole over the fluttering heart of the Hebrew.

'There is but one God,' said the captain of the gate.

'And Mahomed is His prophet,' responded a sentinel.

'To-morrow we will cut off the noses of all these Jewish dogs.'

'The sceptre has departed,' exclaimed the despairing Bostenay.

'Lord, remember David!' whispered Miriam, as she threw herself upon the court of the palace, and buried her face in ashes.

The Mollahs in solemn procession advanced to the ramparts, to shed their benediction on the victorious Hassan Subah. The Muezzin ascended the minarets to watch the setting sun, and proclaim the power of Allah with renewed enthusiasm.

'I wonder if Alroy be dead or alive,' said the captain of the gate.

'If he be alive, he will be impaled,' responded a sentinel.

'If dead, the carcass will be given to the dogs,' rejoined the captain; 'that is the practice.'

'Bostenay will be hung,' said the sentinel.

'And his niece, too,' answered the captain.

'Hem!' said the sentinel. 'Hassan Subah loves a black eye.'

'I hope a true Moslem will not touch a Jewess,' exclaimed an indignant black eunuch.

'They approach. What a dust!' said the captain of the gate.

'I see Hassan Subah!' said the sentinel.

'So do I,' said the eunuch, 'I know his black horse.'

'I wonder how many dirhems old Bostenay is worth,' said the captain.

'Immense!' said the sentinel.

'No plunder, I suppose?' said the eunuch.

'We shall see,' said the captain; 'at any rate, I owe a thousand to old Shelomi. We need not pay now, you know.'

'Certainly not,' said the black eunuch. 'The rebels.'

A body of horsemen dashed forward. Their leader in advance reined in his fiery charger beneath the walls.

'In the name of the Prophet, who is that?' exclaimed the captain of the gate, a little confused.

'I never saw him before,' said the sentinel, 'although he is in the Seljuk dress. 'Tis some one from Bagdad, I guess.'

A trumpet sounded.

'Who keeps the gate?' called out the warrior.

'I am the captain of the gate,' answered our friend.

'Open it, then, to the King of Israel.'

'To whom?' enquired the astonished captain.

'To King David. The Lord hath delivered Hassan Subah and his host into our hands, and of all the proud Seljuks none remaineth. Open thy gates, I say, and lose no time. I am Jabaster, a lieutenant of the Lord; this scimitar is my commission. Open thy gates, and thou and thy people shall have that mercy which they have never shown; but if thou delayest one instant, thus saith the King our master, "I will burst open your portal, and smite, and utterly destroy all that you have, and spare them not; but slay both man and woman, infant and suckling, ox and sheep, camel and ass."'

'Call forth the venerable Lord Bostenay,' said the captain of the gate, with chattering teeth. 'He will intercede for us.'

'And the gentle Lady Miriam,' said the sentinel. 'She is ever charitable.'

'I will head the procession,' said the black eunuch; 'I am accustomed to women.'

The procession of Mollahs shuffled back to their college with profane precipitation; the sun set, and the astounded Muezzin stood with their mouths open, and quite forgot to announce the power of their Deity, and the validity of their Prophet. The people all called out for the venerable Lord Bostenay and the gentle Lady Miriam, and ran in crowds to see who could first kiss the hem of their garments.

The principal gate of Hamadan opened into the square of the great mosque. Here the whole population of the city appeared assembled. The gates were thrown open; Jabaster and his companions mounted guard. The short twilight died away, the shades of night descended. The minarets were illumined,[57] the houses hung with garlands, the ramparts covered with tapestry and carpets.

A clang of drums, trumpets, and cymbals announced the arrival of the Hebrew army. The people shouted, the troops without responded with a long cheer of triumph. Amid the blaze of torches, a youth waving his scimitar, upon a coal-black steed, bounded into the city, at the head of his guards, the people fell upon their knees, and shouted 'Long live Alroy!'

A venerable man, leading a beauteous maiden with downcast eyes, advanced. They headed a deputation of the chief inhabitants of the city. They came to solicit mercy and protection. At the sight of them, the youthful warrior leaped from his horse, flung away his scimitar, and clasping the maiden in his arms, exclaimed, 'Miriam, my sister, this, this indeed is triumph!'

'Drink,' said Kisloch the Kourd to Calidas the Indian; 'you forget, comrade, we are no longer Moslemin.'

'Wine, methinks, has a peculiarly pleasant flavour in a golden cup,' said the Guebre. 'I got this little trifle to-day in the Bazaar,' he added, holding up a magnificent vase studded with gems.

'I thought plunder was forbidden,' grinned the Negro.

'So it is,' replied the Guebre; 'but we may purchase what we please, upon credit.'

'Well, for my part, I am a moderate man,' exclaimed Calidas the Indian, 'and would not injure even these accursed dogs of Turks. I have not cut my host's throat, but only turned him into my porter, and content myself with his harem, his baths, his fine horses, and other little trifles.'

'What quarters we are in! There is nothing like a true Messiah!' exclaimed Kisloch, devoutly.

'Nothing,' said Calidas; 'though to speak truth, I did not much believe in the efficacy of Solomon's sceptre, till his Majesty clove the head of the valiant Seljuk with it.'

'But now there's no doubt of it,' said the Guebre.

'We should indeed be infidels if we doubted now,' replied the Indian.

'How lucky,' grinned the Negro, 'as I had no religion before, that I have now fixed upon the right one!'

'Most fortunate!' said the Guebre. 'What shall we do to amuse ourselves to-night?'

'Let us go to the coffee-houses and make the Turks drink wine,' said Calidas the Indian.

'What say you to burning down a mosque?' said Kisloch the Kourd.

'I had great fun with some Dervishes this morning,' said the Guebre. 'I met one asking alms with a wire run through his cheek,[58] so I caught another, bored his nose, and tied them both together!'

'Hah! hah! hah!' burst the Negro.

Asia resounded with the insurrection of the Jews, and the massacre of the Seljuks. Crowds of Hebrews, from the rich cities of Persia and the populous settlements on the Tigris and the Euphrates, hourly poured into Hamadan.

The irritated Moslemin persecuted the brethren of the successful rebel, and this impolicy precipitated their flight. The wealth of Bagdad flowed into the Hebrew capital. Seated on the divan of Hassan Subah, and wielding the sceptre of Solomon, the King of Israel received the homage of his devoted subjects, and despatched his envoys to Syria and to Egypt. The well-stored magazines and arsenals of Hamadan soon converted the pilgrims into warriors. The city was unable to accommodate the increased and increasing population. An extensive camp, under the command of Abner, was formed without the walls, where the troops were daily disciplined, and where they were prepared for greater exploits than a skirmish in a desert.

Within a month after the surrender of Hamadan, the congregation of the people assembled in the square of the great mosque, now converted into a synagogue. The multitude was disposed in ordered ranks, and the terrace of every house was crowded. In the centre of the square was an altar of cedar and brass, and on each side stood a company of priests guarding the victims, one young bullock, and two rams without blemish.

Amid the flourish of trumpets, the gates of the synagogue opened, and displayed to the wondering eyes of the Hebrews a vast and variegated pavilion planted in the court. The holy remnant, no longer forlorn, beheld that tabernacle of which they had so long dreamed, once more shining in the sun, with its purple and scarlet hangings, its curtains of rare skins, and its furniture of silver and gold.

A procession of priests advanced, bearing, with staves of cedar, run through rings of gold, a gorgeous ark, the work of the most cunning artificers of Persia.

Night and day had they laboured, under the direction of Jabaster, to produce this wondrous spectacle. Once more the children of Israel beheld the cherubim. They burst into a triumphant hymn of thanksgiving, and many drew their swords, and cried aloud to be led against the Canaanites.

From the mysterious curtains of the tabernacle, Alroy came forward, leading Jabaster. They approached the altar. And Alroy took robes from the surrounding priests, and put them upon Jabaster, and a girdle, and a breastplate of jewels. And Alroy took a mitre, and placed it upon the head of Jabaster, and upon the mitre he placed a crown; and pouring oil upon his head, the pupil anointed the master High Priest of Israel.

The victims were slain, the sin-offering burnt. Amid clouds of incense, bursts of music, and the shouts of a devoted people; amid odour, and melody, and enthusiasm, Alroy mounted his charger, and at the head of twenty thousand men, departed to conquer Media.

The extensive and important province of Aderbijan, of which Hamadan was the capital, was formed of the ancient Media. Its fate was decided by one battle. On the plain of Nehauend, Alroy met the hastily-raised levies of the Atabek of Kermanshah, and entirely routed them. In the course of a month, every city of the province had acknowledged the supremacy of the new Hebrew monarch, and, leaving Abner to complete the conquest of Louristan, Alroy entered Persia.

The incredible and irresistible progress of Alroy roused Togrul, the Turkish Sultan of Persia, from the luxurious indolence of the palaces of Nishapur. He summoned his emirs to meet him at the imperial city of Rhey, and crush, by one overwhelming effort, the insolent rebel.

Religion, valour, and genius, alike inspired the arms of Alroy, but he was, doubtless, not a little assisted by the strong national sympathy of his singular and scattered people, which ever ensured him prompt information of all the movements of his enemy. Without any preparation, he found agents in every court, and camp, and cabinet; and, by their assistance, he anticipated the designs of his adversaries, and turned even their ingenuity to their confusion. The imperial city of Rhey was surprised in the night, sacked, and burnt to the ground. The scared and baffled emirs who escaped, flew to the Sultan Togrul, tearing their beards, and prophesying the approaching termination of the world. The palaces of Nishapur resounded with the imprecations of their master, who, cursing the Jewish dogs, and vowing a pilgrimage to Mecca, placed himself at the head of a motley multitude of warriors, and rushed upon the plains of Irak, to exterminate Alroy.

The Persian force exceeded the Hebrew at least five times in number. Besides a large division of Seljuks, the Caucasus had poured forth its strange inhabitants to swell the ranks of the Faithful. The wild tribes of the Bactiari were even enlisted, with their fatal bows, and the savage Turkmans, tempted by the sultan's gold, for a moment yielded their liberty, and shook their tall lances in his ranks.

But what is a wild Bactiari, and what is a savage Turkman, and what even a disciplined and imperious Seljuk, to the warriors of the God of Abraham, of

Isaac, and of Jacob? At the first onset, Alroy succeeded in dividing the extended centre of Togrul, and separating the greater part of the Turks from their less disciplined comrades. At the head of his Median cavalry, the Messiah charged and utterly routed the warriors of the Caucasus. The wild tribes of the Bactiari discharged their arrows and fled, and the savage Turkmans plundered the baggage of their own commander.

The Turks themselves fought desperately; but, deserted by their allies, and surrounded by an inspired foe, their efforts were unavailing, and their slaughter terrible. Togrul was slain while heading a desperate and fruitless charge, and, after his fall, the battle resembled a massacre rather than a combat. The plain was glotted with Seljuk gore. No quarter was given or asked. Twenty thousand chosen troops fell on the side of the Turks; the rest dispersed and gained the mountains. Leaving Scherirah to restore order, Alroy the next morning pushed on to Nishapur at the head of three thousand horsemen, and summoned the city ere the inhabitants were apprised of the defeat and death of their sultan. The capital of Persia escaped the fate of Rhey by an inglorious treaty and a lavish tribute. The treasures of the Chosroes and the Gasnevides were despatched to Hamadan, on which city day dawned, only to bring intelligence of a victory or a conquest.

While Alroy dictated peace on his own terms in the palaces of Nishapur, Abner, having reduced Louristan, crossed the mountains, and entered Persia with the reinforcements he had received from Jabaster. Leaving the government and garrisoning of his new conquests to this valiant captain, Alroy, at the head of the conquerors of Persia, in consequence of intelligence received from Hamadan, returned by forced marches to that city.

Leaving the army within a day's march of the capital, Alroy, accompanied only by his staff, entered Hamadan in the evening, and, immediately repairing to the citadel, summoned Jabaster to council. The night was passed by the king and the high priest in deep consultation. The next morning, a decree apprised the inhabitants of the return of their monarch, of the creation of the new 'Kingdom of the Medes and Persians,' of which Hamadan was declared the capital, and Abner the viceroy, and of the intended and immediate invasion of Syria, and re-conquest of the Land of Promise.

The plan of this expedition had been long matured, and the preparations to effect it were considerably advanced. Jabaster had not been idle during the absence of his pupil. One hundred thousand warriors were now assembled[59] at the capital of the kingdom of the Medes and Persians; of these the greater part were Hebrews, but many Arabs, wearied of the Turkish yoke, and many gallant adventurers from the Caspian, easily converted from a vague idolatry to a religion of conquest, swelled the ranks of the army of the Lord of Hosts.

The plain of Hamadan was covered with tents, the streets were filled with passing troops, the bazaars loaded with military stores; long caravans of camels laden with supplies every day arrived from the neighbouring towns; each instant some high-capped Tatar with despatches[60] rushed into the city and galloped his steed up the steep of the citadel. The clang of arms, the prance of horses, the flourish of warlike music, resounded from all quarters. The business and the treasure of the world seemed, as it were in an instant, to have become concentrated in Hamadan. Every man had some great object; gold glittered in every hand. All great impulses were stirring; all the causes of human energy were in lively action. Every eye sparkled, every foot trod firm and fast. Each man acted as if the universal fate depended upon his exertions; as if the universal will sympathised with his particular desire. A vast population influenced by a high degree of excitement is the most sublime of spectacles.

The commander of the Faithful raised the standard of the Prophet on the banks of the Tigris. It was the secret intelligence of this intended event that had recalled Alroy so suddenly from Persia. The latent enthusiasm of the Moslemin was excited by the rare and mystic ceremony, and its effects were anticipated by previous and judicious preparations. The Seljuks of Bagdad alone amounted to fifty thousand men; the Sultan of Syria contributed the warriors who had conquered the Arabian princes of Damascus and Aleppo; while the ancient provinces of Asia Minor, which formed the rich and powerful kingdom of Seljukian Roum, poured forth a myriad of that matchless cavalry, which had so often baffled the armies of the Cæsars. Never had so imposing a force been collected on the banks of the Tigris since the reign of Haroun Alraschid. Each day some warlike Atabek, at the head of his armed train, poured into the capital of the caliphs,[61] or pitched his pavilion on the banks of the river; each day the proud emir of some remote principality astonished or affrighted the luxurious Babylonians by the strange or uncouth warriors that had gathered round his standard in the deserts of Arabia, or on the shores of the Euxine. For the space of twenty miles, the banks of the river were, on either side, far as the eye could reach, covered with the variegated pavilions, the glittering standards, the flowing streamers and twinkling pennons of the mighty host, of which Malek, the Grand Sultan of the Seljuks, and Governor of the Caliph's palace, was chief commander.

Such was the power assembled on the plains of Asia to arrest the progress of the Hebrew Prince, and to prevent the conquest of the memorable land promised to the faith of his fathers, and forfeited by their infidelity. Before the walls of Hamadan, Alroy reviewed the army of Israel, sixty thousand heavy-armed footmen, thirty thousand archers and light troops, and twenty thousand cavalry. Besides these, there had been formed a body of ten thousand picked horsemen, styled the 'Sacred Guard,' all of whom had served in the Persian campaign. In their centre, shrouded in a case of wrought gold, studded with carbuncles, and carried on a lusty lance of cedar, a giant—for the height of Elnebar exceeded that of common men by three feet—bore the sceptre of Solomon. The Sacred Guard was commanded by Asriel, the brother of Abner.

The army was formed into three divisions. All marched in solemn order before the throne of Alroy, raised upon the ramparts, and drooped their standards and lances as they passed their heroic leader. Bostenay, and Miriam, and the whole population of the city witnessed the inspiring spectacle from the walls. That same eve, Scherirah, at the head of forty thousand men, pushed on towards Bagdad, by Kermanshah; and Jabaster, who commanded in his holy robes, and who had vowed not to lay aside his sword until the rebuilding of the temple, conducted his division over the victorious plain of Nehauend. They were to concentrate at the pass of Kerrund, which conducted into the province of Bagdad, and await the arrival of the king.

At the dawn of day, the royal division and the Sacred Guard, the whole under the command of Asriel, quitted the capital. Alroy still lingered, and for some hours the warriors of his staff might have been observed lounging about the citadel, or practising their skill in throwing the jerreed as they exercised their impatient chargers before the gates.

The king was with the Lady Miriam, walking in the garden of their uncle. One arm was wound round her delicate waist, and with the other he clasped her soft and graceful hand. The heavy tears burst from her downcast eyes, and stole along her pale and pensive cheek. They walked in silence, the brother and the sister, before the purity of whose surpassing love even ambition vanished. He opened the lattice gate. They entered into the valley small and green; before them was the marble fountain with its columns and cupola, and in the distance the charger of Alroy and his single attendant.

They stopped, and Alroy gathered flowers, and placed them in the hair of Miriam. He would have softened the bitterness of parting with a smile. Gently he relaxed his embracing arm, almost insensibly he dropped her quivering hand.

'Sister of my soul,' he whispered, 'when we last parted here, I was a fugitive, and now I quit you a conqueror.'

She turned, she threw herself upon his neck, and buried her face in his breast.

'My Miriam, we shall meet at Bagdad.'

He beckoned to her distant maidens; they advanced, he delivered Miriam into their arms. He pressed her hand to his lips, and, rushing to his horse, mounted and disappeared.

A body of irregular cavalry feebly defended the pass of Kerrund. It was carried, with slight loss, by the vanguard of Scherirah, and the fugitives prepared the host of the caliph for the approach of the Hebrew army.

Upon the plain of the Tigris the enemy formed into battle array. The centre was commanded by Malek, the Grand Sultan of the Seljuks himself; the right wing, headed by the Sultan of Syria, was protected by the river; and the left, under the Sultan of Roum, was posted upon the advantageous position of some irregular and rising ground. Thus proud in the number, valour, discipline, and disposition of his forces, Malek awaited the conqueror of Persia.

The glittering columns of the Hebrews might even now be perceived defiling from the mountains, and forming at the extremity of the plain. Before nightfall the camp of the invaders was pitched within hearing of that of Malek. The moving lights in the respective tents might plainly be distinguished; and ever and anon the flourish of hostile music fell with an ominous sound upon the ears of the opposed foe-men. A few miles only separated those mighty hosts.

Upon to-morrow depended, perhaps, the fortunes of ages. How awful is the eve of battle!

Alroy, attended by a few chieftains, personally visited the tents of the soldiery, promising them on the morrow a triumph, before which the victories of Nehauend and Nishapur would sink into insignificance. Their fiery and excited visages proved at once their courage and their faith. The sceptre of Solomon was paraded throughout the camp in solemn procession. On the summit of a huge tumulus, perhaps the sepulchre of some classic hero, Esther, the prophetess, surrounded by the chief zealots of the host, poured forth her exciting inspirations. It was a grand picture, that beautiful wild girl, the groups of stern, devoted warriors, the red flame of the watch-fires mixing with the silver shadows of the moon as they illumined the variegated turbans and gleaming armour of her votaries!

In the pavilion of Alroy, Jabaster consulted with his pupil on the conduct of the morrow.

'This is a different scene from the cavern of the Caucasus,' said Alroy, as the high priest rose to retire.

'It has one great resemblance, sire; the God of our fathers is with us.'

'Ay! the Lord of Hosts. Moses was a great man. There is no career except conquest.'

'You muse.'

'Of the past. The present is prepared. Too much thought will mar it.'

'The past is for wisdom, the present for action, but for joy the future. The feeling that the building of the temple is at hand, that the Lord's anointed will once again live in the house of David, absorbs my spirit; and, when I muse over our coming glory, in my fond ecstasy I almost lose the gravity that doth beseem my sacred office.'

'Jerusalem; I have seen it. How many hours to dawn?'

'Some three.'

"Tis strange I could sleep. I remember, on the eve of battle I was ever anxious. How is this, Jabaster?'

'Your faith, sire, is profound.'

'Yes, I have no fear. My destiny is not complete. Good night, Jabaster. See, Asriel, valiant priest. Pharez!'

'My lord!'

'Rouse me at the second watch. Good night, boy.'

'Good night, my lord.'

'Pharez! Be sure you rouse me at the second watch. Think you it wants three hours to dawn?'

'About three hours, my lord.'

'Well! at the second watch, remember; good night.'

'It is the second watch, my lord.'

'So soon! Have I slept? I feel fresh as an eagle. Call Scherirah, boy.'

"Tis strange I never dream now. Before my flight my sleep was ever troubled. Say what they like, man is made for action. My life is now harmonious, and sleep has now become what nature willed it, a solace, not a contest. Before, it was a struggle of dark passions and bright dreams, in whose creative fancy and fair vision my soul sought refuge from the dreary bale of daily reality.

'I will withdraw the curtains of my tent. O most majestic vision! And have I raised this host? Over the wide plain, far as my eye can range, their snowy tents studding the purple landscape, embattled legions gather round their flags to struggle for my fate. It is the agony of Asia.

'A year ago, upon this very spot, I laid me down to die, an unknown thing, or known and recognised only to be despised, and now the sultans of the world come forth to meet me. I have no fear. My destiny is not complete. And whither tends it? Let that power decide which hitherto has fashioned all my course.

'Jerusalem, Jerusalem! ever harping on Jerusalem. With all his lore, he is a narrow-minded zealot whose dreaming memory would fondly make a future like the past. O Bagdad, Bagdad, within thy glittering halls, there is a charm worth all his Cabala!

'Hah! Scherirah! The dawn is near at hand, the stars are still shining. The air is very pleasant. Tomorrow will be a great day, Scherirah, for Israel and for you. You lead the attack. A moment in my tent, my brave Scherirah!'

The dawn broke; a strong column of the Hebrews, commanded by Scherirah, poured down upon the centre of the army of the caliph. Another column, commanded by Jabaster, attacked the left wing, headed by the Sultan of Roum. No sooner had Alroy perceived that the onset of Scherirah had succeeded in penetrating the centre of the Turks, than he placed himself at the head of the Sacred Guard, and by an irresistible charge completed their disorder and confusion. The division of the Sultan of Syria, and a great part of the centre, were entirely routed and driven into the river, and the remainder of the division of Malek was effectually separated from his left wing.

But while to Alroy the victory seemed already decided, a far different fate awaited the division of Jabaster. The Sultan of Roum, posted in an extremely advantageous position, and commanding troops accustomed to the discipline of the Romans of Constantinople, received the onset of Jabaster without yielding, and not only repelled his attack, but finally made a charge which completely disordered and dispersed the column of the Hebrews. In vain Jabaster endeavoured to rally his troops, in vain he performed prodigies of valour, in vain he himself struck down the standard-bearer of the sultan, and once even penetrated to the pavilion of the monarch. His division was fairly routed. The eagerness of the Sultan of Roum to effect the annihilation of his antagonists prevented him from observing the forlorn condition of the Turkish centre. Had he, after routing the division of Jabaster, only attacked Alroy in the rear, the fortune of the day might have been widely different. As it was, the eagle eye of Alroy soon detected his inadvertence, and profited by his indiscretion. Leaving Ithamar to keep the centre in check, he charged the Sultan of Roum with the Sacred Guard, and afforded Jabaster an opportunity of rallying some part of his forces. The Sultan of Roum, perceiving that the day was lost by the ill-conduct of his colleagues, withdrew his troops, retreated in haste, but in good order to

Bagdad, carried off the caliph, his harem, and some of his treasure, and effected his escape into Syria. In the meantime the discomfiture of the remaining Turkish army was complete. The Tigris was dyed with their blood, and the towns through which the river flowed were apprised of the triumph of Alroy by the floating corpses of his enemies. Thirty thousand Turks were slain in battle: among them the Sultans of Bagdad and Syria, and a vast number of atabeks, emirs, and chieftains. A whole division, finding themselves surrounded, surrendered on terms, and delivered up their arms. The camps and treasures of the three sultans were alike captured, and the troops that escaped so completely dispersed, that they did not attempt to rally, but, disbanded and desperate, prowled over and plundered the adjoining provinces. The loss of the division of Jabaster was also severe, but the rest of the army suffered little. Alroy himself was slightly wounded. The battle lasted barely three hours. Its results were immense. David Alroy was now master of the East.

The plain was covered with the corpses of men and horses, arms and standards, and prostrate tents. Returning from the pursuit of the Sultan of Roum, Alroy ordered the trumpets to sound to arms, and, covered with gore and dust, dismounted from his charger, and stood before the pavilion of Malek, leaning on his bloody scimitar, and surrounded by his victorious generals.

'Ah, Jabaster!' said the conqueror, giving his hand to the pontiff, "twas well your troops had such a leader. No one but you could have rallied them.

You must drill your lads a little before they again meet the Cappadocian cavalry. Brave Scherirah, we shall not forget our charge. Asriel, tell the guard, from me, that the victory of the Tigris was owing to their scimitars. Ithamar, what are our freshest troops?'

'The legion of Aderbijan, sire.'

'How strong can they muster?'

'It counts twelve thousand men: we might collect two-thirds.'

'Valiant Ithamar, take the Aderbijans and a division of the guards, push on towards Bagdad, and summon the city. If his Sultanship of Roum offer battle, take up a position, and he shall quickly have his desire. For the present, after these hasty marches and sharp fighting, the troops must rest. I think he will not tarry. Summon the city, and say that if any resistance be offered, I will make it as desolate as old Babylon. Treat with no armed force. Where is the soldier that saved me a cracked skull; his name Benaiah?'

'I wait your bidding, sire.'

'You're a captain. Join the division of Ithamar, and win fresh laurels ere we meet again. Gentle Asriel, let your brother know our fortune.'

'Sire, several Tartars have already been despatched to Hamadan.'

"Tis well. Send another with these tablets to the Lady Miriam. Despatch the pavilion of Malek as a trophy for the town. Elnebar, Goliath of the Hebrews, you bore our sacred standard like a hero! How fares the prophetess? I saw her charging in our ranks, waving a sabre with her snowy arm, her long, dark hair streaming like a storm, from which her eyes flashed lightning.'

'The king bleeds,' said Jabaster.

'Slightly. It will do me service. I am somewhat feverish. A kingdom for a draught of water! And now for our wounded friends. Asriel, do you marshal the camp. It is the Sabbath eve.[62] Time presses.'

The dead were plundered, and thrown into the river, the encampment of the Hebrews completed. Alroy, with his principal officers, visited the wounded, and praised the valiant. The bustle which always succeeds a victory was increased in the present instance by the anxiety of the army to observe with grateful strictness the impending Sabbath.

When the sun set, the Sabbath was to commence. The undulating horizon rendered it difficult to ascertain the precise moment of the setting. The crimson orb sunk behind the purple mountains, the sky was flushed with a rich and rosy glow. Then might be perceived the zealots, proud in their Talmudical lore, holding a skein of white silk in their hands, and announcing the approach of the Sabbath by their observation of its shifting tints. While the skein was yet golden, the forge of the armourer still sounded, the fire of the cook still blazed, still the cavalry led their steeds to the river, and still the busy footmen braced up their tents and hammered at their palisades. The skein of silk became rosy, the armourer worked with renewed energy, the cook puffed with increased zeal, the horsemen scampered from the river, the footmen cast an anxious glance at the fading twilight.

The skein of silk became blue; a dim, dull, sepulchral, leaden tinge fell over its purity. The hum of gnats arose, the bat flew in circling whirls over the tents, horns sounded from all quarters, the sun had set, the Sabbath had commenced. 'The forge was mute, the fire extinguished, the prance of horses and the bustle of men in a moment ceased. A deep, a sudden, an all-pervading stillness dropped over that mighty host. It was night; the sacred lamp of the Sabbath sparkled in every tent of the camp, which vied in silence and in brilliancy with the mute and glowing heavens.

Morn came; the warriors assembled around the altar and the sacrifice. The high priest and his attendant Levites proclaimed the unity and the omnipotence of the God of Israel, and the sympathetic responses of his conquering and chosen people reechoed over the plain. They retired again to their tents, to listen to the expounding of the law; even the distance of a Sabbath walk was not to exceed that space which lies between Jerusalem and the Mourft of Olives. This was the distance between the temple and the tabernacle; it had been nicely measured, and every Hebrew who ventured forth from the camp this day might be observed counting the steps of a Sabbath-day's journey. At length the sun again set, and on a sudden fires blazed, voices sounded, men stirred, in the same enchanted and instantaneous manner that had characterised the stillness of the preceding eve. Shouts of laughter, bursts of music, announced the festivity of the coming night; supplies poured in from all the neighbouring villages, and soon the pious conquerors commemorated their late triumph in a round of banqueting.

On the morrow, a Tatar arrived from Ithamar, informing Alroy that the Sultan of Roum had retreated into Syria, that Bagdad was undefended, but that he had acceded to the request of the inhabitants that a deputation should wait upon Alroy before the troops entered the city, and had granted a safe conduct for their passage.

On the morrow, messengers announced the approach of the deputation. All the troops were under arms. Alroy directed that the suppliants should be conducted through the whole camp before they arrived at the royal pavilion, on each side of which the Sacred Guard was mustered in array. The curtains of his tent withdrawn displayed the conqueror himself, seated on a sumptuous divan. On his right hand stood Jabaster in his priestly robes, on his left Scherirah. Behind him, the giant Elnebar supported the sacred sceptre. A crowd of chieftains was ranged on each side of the pavilion.

Cymbals sounded, muffled kettle-drums, and the faint flourish of trumpets; the commencement of the procession might be detected in the long perspective of the tented avenue. First came a company of beauteous youths, walking two by two, and strewing flowers; then a band of musicians in flowing robes of cloth of gold, plaintively sounding their silver trumpets. After these followed slaves of all climes, bearing a tribute of the most rare and costly productions of their countries: Negroes with tusks and teeth of the elephant, plumes of ostrich feathers, and caskets of gold dust; Syrians with rich armour; Persians with vases of atar-gul, and Indians with panniers of pearls of Ormuz, and soft shawls of Cachemire. Encircled by his children, each of whom held alternately a white or fawn-coloured gazelle, an Arab clothed in his blue bornouz, led by a thick cord of crimson silk a tall and tawny giraffe. Fifty stout men succeeded two by two, carrying in company a silver shield laden with gold coin, or chased goblets studded with gems.

The clash of cymbals announced the presence of the robes of honour,[63] culled from the wardrobe of the commander of the Faithful; the silk of Aleppo and the brocade of Damascus, lined with the furs of the sable and the ermine, down from the breast of the swan, and the skins of white foxes.

After these followed two grey dromedaries, with furniture of silver, and many caparisoned horses, each led by a groom in rich attire. The last of these was a snow-white steed, upon whose front was the likeness of a ruby star, a courser of the sacred stud of Solomon, and crossed only by the descendants of the Prophet.

The muffled kettle-drums heralded the company of black eunuchs, with their scarlet vests and ivory battle-axes. They surrounded and shrouded from the vulgar gaze fourteen beautiful Circassian girls, whose brilliant visages and perfect forms were otherwise concealed by their long veils and ample drapery.

The gorgeous procession, as they approached the conqueror, bowed humbly to Alroy, and formed in order on each side of the broad avenue. The deputation appeared; twelve of the principal citizens of Bagdad, with folded arms, and downcast eyes, and disordered raiment. Meekly and mutely each touched the earth with his hand, and kissed it in token of submission, and then, moving aside, made way for the chief envoy and orator of the company, Honain!

Humbly, but gracefully, the physician of the caliph bowed before the conqueror of the East. His appearance and demeanour afforded a contrast to the aspect of his brother envoys; not less calm or contented his countenance, not less sumptuous or studied his attire, than when he first rescued Alroy in the bazaar of Bagdad from the grip of the false Abdallah.

He spoke, and every sound was hushed before the music of his voice.

'Conqueror of the world, that destiny with which it is in vain to struggle has placed our lives and fortunes in your power. Your slaves offer for your approbation specimens of their riches; not as tribute, for all is yours; but to show you the products of security and peace, and to induce you to believe that mercy may be a policy as profitable to the conqueror as to the conquered; that it may be better to preserve than to destroy; and wiser to enjoy than to extirpate.

'Fate ordained that we should be born the slaves of the caliph; that same fate has delivered his sceptre into your hands. We offer you the same devotion that we yielded to him, and we entreat the same protection which he granted to us.

'Whatever may be your decision, we must bow to your decree with the humility that recognises superior force. Yet we are not without hope. We cannot forget that it is our good fortune not to be addressing a barbarous chieftain, unable to sympathise with the claims of civilisation, the creations of art, and the finer impulses of humanity. We acknowledge your irresistible power, but we dare to hope everything from a prince whose genius all acknowledge and admire, who has spared some portion of his youth from the cares of government and the pursuits of arms to the ennobling claims of learning, whose morality has been moulded by a pure and sublime faith, and who draws his lineage from a sacred and celebrated race, the unrivalled antiquity of which even the Prophet acknowledges.'

He ceased: a buzz of approbation sounded throughout the pavilion, which was hushed instantly as the lips of the conqueror moved.

'Noble emir,' replied Alroy, 'return to Bagdad, and tell your fellow-subjects that the King of Israel grants protection to their persons, and security to their property.'

'And for their faith?' enquired the envoy, in a lower voice.

'Toleration,' replied Alroy, turning to Jabaster.

'Until further regulations,' added the high priest.

'Emir,' said Alroy, 'the person of the caliph will be respected.'

'May it please your highness,' replied Honain, 'the Sultan of Roum has retired with our late ruler.'

'And his harem?'

'And his harem.'

'It was needless. We war not with women.'

'Men, as well as women, must acknowledge the gracious mercy of your highness.'

'Benomi,' said Alroy, addressing himself to a young officer of the guard, 'command the guard of honour that will attend this noble emir on his return. We soldiers deal only in iron, sir, and cannot vie with the magnificence of Bagdad, yet wear this dagger for the donor's sake:' and Alroy held out to Honain a poniard flaming with gems.

The Envoy of Bagdad advanced, took the dagger, pressed it to his lips, and placed it in his vest.[64]

'Scherirah,' continued Alroy, 'this noble emir is your charge. See that a choice pavilion of the host be for his use, and that his train complain not of the rough customs of our camp.'

'May it please your highness,' replied Honain, 'I have fulfilled my office, and, with your gracious permission, would at once return. I have business only less urgent than the present, because it concerns myself.'

'As you will, noble emir. Benomi, to your post. Farewell, sir.'

The deputation advanced, bowed, and retired. Alroy turned to Jabaster.

'No common person that, Jabaster?'

'A very gracious Turk, sire.'

'Think you he is a Turk?'

'By his dress.'

'It may be so. Asriel, break up the camp. We'll march at once to Bagdad.'

The chiefs dispersed to make the necessary arrangements for the march. The news that the army was immediately to advance to Bagdad soon circulated throughout the camp, and excited the most lively enthusiasm. Every hand was at work, striking the tents, preparing the arms and horses. Alroy retired to his pavilion. The curtains were drawn. He was alone, and plunged in profound meditation.

'Alroy!' a voice sounded.

He started, and looked up. Before him stood Esther the prophetess.

'Esther! is it thou?'

'Alroy! enter not into Babylon.'

'Indeed.'

'As I live, the Lord hath spoken it. Enter not into Babylon.'

'Not enjoy my fairest conquest, maiden?'

'Enter not into Babylon.'

'What affrights thee?'

'Enter not into Babylon.'

'I shall surely change the fortunes of my life without a cause.'

'The Lord hath spoken. Is not that a cause?'

'I am the Lord's anointed. His warning has not reached me.'

'Now it reaches thee. Doth the king despise the prophetess of the Lord? It is the sin of Ahab.'

'Despise thee! Despise the mouth that is the herald of my victories! 'Twere rank blasphemy. Prophesy triumph, Esther, and Alroy will never doubt thy inspiration.'

'He doubts it now. I see he doubts it now. O my king, I say again, enter not into Babylon.'

'Beauteous maiden, those eyes flash lightning. Who can behold their wild and liquid glance, and doubt that Esther is inspired! Be calm, sweet girl, some dream disturbs thy fancy.'

'Alroy, Alroy, enter not into Babylon!'

'I have no fear, I bear a charmed life.'

'Ah me! he will not listen.' All is lost!'

'All is gained, my beautiful.'

'I would we were upon the Holy Mount, and gazing on the stars of sacred Zion.'

'Esther,' said Alroy, advancing, and gently taking her hand, 'the capital of the East will soon unfold its marvels to thy sight. Prepare thyself for wonders. Girl, we are no longer in the desert. Forget thy fitful fancies. Come, choose a husband from my generals, child, and I will give a kingdom for thy dower. I would gladly see a crown upon that imperial brow. It well deserves one.'

The prophetess turned her dark eyes full upon Alroy. What passed in her mind was neither evident nor expressed. She gazed intently upon the calm and inscrutable countenance of the conqueror, then flung away his hand, and rushed out of the pavilion.

CHAPTER VIII.

Bagdad and the Princess

THE waving of banners, the flourish of trumpets, the neighing of steeds, and the glitter of spears! On the distant horizon they gleam like the morning, when the gloom of the night shivers bright into day. Hark! the tramp of the foemen, like the tide of the ocean, flows onward and onward, and conquers the shore. From the brow of the mountain, like the rush of a river, the column defiling melts into the plain.

Warriors of Judah! holy men that battle for the Lord! The land wherein your fathers wept, and touched their plaintive psalteries; the haughty city where your sires bewailed their cold and distant hearths; your steeds are prancing on its plain, and you shall fill its palaces. Warriors of Judah! holy men that battle for the Lord!

March, onward march, ye valiant tribes, the hour has come, the hour has come! All the promises of ages, all the signs of sacred sages, meet in this ravishing hour. Where is now the oppressor's chariot, where your tyrant's purple robe? The horse and the rider are both overthrown, the horse and the rider are both overthrown!

Rise, Rachel, from thy wilderness, arise, and weep no more. No more thy lonely palm-tree's shade need shroud thy secret sorrowing. The Lord hath heard the widow's sigh, the Lord hath stilled the widow's tear. Be comforted, be comforted, thy children live again!

Yes! yes! upon the bounding plain fleet Asriel glances like a star, and stout Scherirah shakes his spear by stern Jabaster's scimitar. And He is there, the chosen one, hymned by prophetic harps, whose life is like the morning dew on Zion's holy hill: the chosen one, the chosen one, that leads his race to victory; warriors of Judah! holy men that battle for the Lord!

They come, they come, they come!

The ramparts of the city were crowded with the inhabitants, the river sparkled with ten thousand boats, the bazaars were shut, the streets lined with the populace, and the terrace of every house covered with spectators. In the morning, Ithamar had entered with his division and garrisoned the city. And now the vanguard of the Hebrew army, after having been long distinguished in the distance, approached the walls. A large body of cavalry dashed forward at full speed from the main force. Upon a milk-white charger, and followed by a glittering train of warriors, amid the shouts of the vast multitude, Alroy galloped up to the gates.

He was received by Ithamar and the members of the deputation, but Honain was not there. Accompanied by his staff and a strong detachment of the Sacred Guard, Alroy was conducted through the principal thoroughfares of the city, until he arrived at the chief entrance of the serail, or palace, of the caliph. The vast portal conducted him into a large quadrangular court, where he dismounted, and where he was welcomed by the captain of the eunuch guard. Accompanied by his principal generals and his immediate attendants, Alroy was then ushered through a suite of apartments which reminded him of his visit with Honain, until he arrived at the grand council-chamber of the caliphs.

The conqueror threw himself upon the gorgeous divan of the commander of the Faithful.

'An easy seat after a long march,' said Alroy, as he touched with his lips the coffee, which the chief of the eunuchs presented to him in a cup of transparent pink porcelain, studded with pearls.[65] 'Itha-mar, now for your report. What is the temper of the city? Where is his Sultanship of Roum?'

'The city, sire, is calm, and I believe content. The sultan and the caliph are still hovering on the borders of the province.'

'So I supposed. Scherirah will settle that. Let the troops be encamped without the walls, the garrison, ten thousand strong, must be changed monthly. Ithamar, you are governor of the city: Asriel commands the forces. Worthy Jabaster, draw up a report of the civil affairs of the capital. Your quarters are the College of the Dervishes. Brave Scherirah, I cannot afford you a long rest. In three days you must have crossed the river with your division. It will be quick work. I foresee that they will not fight. Meet me all here in council by tomorrow's noon. Farewell.'

The chieftains retired, the high priest lingered.

'Were it not an intrusion, sire, I would fain entreat a moment's audience.'

'My own Jabaster, you have but to speak.'

'Sire, I would speak of Abidan, as valiant a warrior as any in the host. It grieves me much, that by some fatality, his services seem ever overlooked.'

'Abidan! I know him well, a valiant man, but a dreamer, a dreamer.'

'A dreamer, sire! Believe me, a true son of Israel, and one whose faith is deep.'

'Good Jabaster, we are all true sons of Israel. Yet let me have men about me who see no visions in a mid-day sun. We must beware of dreamers.'

'Dreams are the oracles of God.'

'When God sends them. Very true, Jabaster. But this Abidan and the company with whom he consorts are filled with high-flown notions, caught from old traditions, which, if acted on, would render government impracticable; in a word, they are dangerous men.'

'The very flower of Israel! Some one has poisoned your sacred ear against them.'

'No one, worthy Jabaster. I have no counsellor except yourself. They may be the flower of Israel, but they are not the fruit. Good warriors, bad subjects: excellent means, by which we may accomplish greater ends. I'll have no dreamers in authority. I must have practical men about me, practical men. See how Abner, Asriel, Ithamar, Medad, see how these conform to what surrounds them, yet invincible captains, invincible captains. But then they are practical men, Jabaster; they have eyes and use them. They know the difference of times and seasons. But this Abidan, he has no other thought but the rebuilding of the temple: a narrow-souled bigot, who would sacrifice the essence to the form. The rising temple soon would fall again with such constructors. Why, sir, what think you, this same Abidan preached in the camp against my entry into what the quaint fanatic chooses to call "Babylon," because he had seen what he calls a vision.'

'There was a time your Majesty thought not so ill of visions.'

'Am I Abidan, sir? Are other men to mould their conduct or their thoughts by me? In this world I stand alone, a being of a different order from yourselves, incomprehensible even to you. Let this matter cease. I'll hear no more and have heard too much. To-morrow at council.'

The high priest withdrew in silence.

'He is gone; at length I am alone. I cannot bear the presence of these men, except in action. Their words, even their looks, disturb the still creation of my brooding thought. I am once more alone, and loneliness hath been the cradle of my empire. Now I do feel inspired. There needs no mummery now to work a marvel.

'The sceptre of Solomon! It may be so. What then? Here's now the sceptre of Alroy. What's that without his mind? The legend said that none should free our people but he who bore the sceptre of great Solomon. The legend knew that none could gain that sceptre, but with a mind to whose supreme volition the fortunes of the world would bow like fate. I gained it; I confronted the spectre monarchs in their sepulchre; and the same hand that grasped their shadowy rule hath seized the diadem of the mighty caliphs by the broad rushing of their imperial river.

'The world is mine: and shall I yield the prize, the universal and heroic prize, to realise the dull tradition of some dreaming priest, and consecrate a legend? He conquered Asia, and he built the temple. Are these my annals? Shall this quick blaze of empire sink to a glimmering and a twilight sway over some petty province, the decent patriarch of a pastoral horde? Is the Lord of Hosts so slight a God, that we must place a barrier to His sovereignty, and fix the boundaries of Omnipotence between the Jordan and the Lebanon? It is not thus written; and were it so, I'll pit my inspiration against the prescience of my ancestors. I also am a prophet, and Bagdad shall be my Zion. The daughter of the Voice! Well, I am clearly summoned. I am the Lord's servant, not Jabaster's. Let me make His worship universal as His power; and where's the priest shall dare impugn my faith, because His altars smoke on other hills than those of Judah?

'I must see Honain. That man has a great mind. He alone can comprehend my purpose. Universal empire must not be founded on sectarian prejudices and exclusive rights. Jabaster would massacre the Moslemin like Amalek; the Moslemin, the vast majority, and most valuable portion, of my subjects. He would depopulate my empire, that it might not be said that Ishmael shared the heritage of Israel. Fanatic! I'll send him to conquer Judah. We must conciliate. Something must be done to bind the conquered to our conquering fortunes. That bold Sultan of Roum: I wish Abner had opposed him. To run off with the harem! I have half a mind to place myself at the head of the pursuing force, and—— Passion and policy alike combine: and yet Honain is the man; I might send him on a mission. Could we make terms? I detest treaties. My fancy flies from all other topics. I must see him. Could I but tell him all I think! This door, whither leads it? Hah! methinks I do remember yon glittering gallery! No one in attendance. The discipline of our palace is somewhat lax. My warriors are no courtiers. What an admirable marshal of the palace Honain would make! Silence everywhere. So! 'tis well. These saloons I have clearly passed through before. Could I but reach the private portal by the river side, unseen or undetected! 'Tis not impossible. Here are many dresses. I will disguise myself. Trusty scimitar, thou hast done thy duty, rest awhile. 'Tis lucky I am beardless. I shall make a capital eunuch. So! a handsome robe. One dagger for a pinch, slippers powdered with pearls,[66] a caftan of cloth of gold, a Cachemire girdle, and a pelisse of sables. One glance at the mirror. Good! I begin to look like the conqueror of the world!'

It was twilight: a small and solitary boat, with a single rower, glided along the Tigris, and stopped at the archway of a house that descended into the river. It stopped, the boatman withdrew the curtains, and his single passenger disembarked, and ascended the stairs of the archway.

The stranger reached the landing-place, and unfastening a golden grate, proceeded along a gallery, and entered a beautiful saloon of white and green marble, opening into gardens. No one was in the apartment; the stranger threw himself upon a silver couch, placed at the side of a fountain that rose from the centre of the chamber and fell into a porphyry basin. A soft whisper roused the stranger from his reverie, a soft whisper that faintly uttered the word 'Honain.' The stranger looked up, a figure, enveloped in a veil, that touched the ground, advanced from the gardens.

'Honain!' said the advancing figure, throwing off the veil. 'Honain! Ah! the beautiful mute returned!'

A woman more lovely than the rosy morn, beheld an unexpected guest. They stood, the lady and the stranger, gazing on each other in silence. A man, with a light, entered the extremity of the hall. Carefully he closed the portal, slowly he advanced, with a subdued step; he approached the lady and the stranger.

'Alroy!' said the astonished Honain, the light fell from his hand.

'Alroy!' exclaimed the lady, with a bewildered air: she turned pale, and leant against a column.

'Daughter of the caliph!' said the leader of Israel; and he advanced, and fell upon his knee, and stole her passive hand. 'I am indeed that Alroy to whom destiny has delivered the empire of thy sire; but the Princess Schirene can have nothing to fear from one who values above all his victories this memorial of her goodwill;' and he took from his breast a rosary of pearls and emeralds, and, rising slowly, left it in her trembling hand.

The princess turned and hid her face in her arm, which reclined against the column.

'My kind Honain,' said Alroy, 'you thought me forgetful of the past; you thought me ungrateful. My presence here proves that I am not so. I come to enquire all your wishes. I come to gratify and to fulfil them, if that be in my power.'

'Sire,' replied Honain, who had recovered from the emotion in which he rarely indulged, and from the surprise which seldom entrapped him, 'Sire, my wishes are slight. You see before you the daughter of my master. An interview, for which I fear I shall not easily gain that lady's pardon, has made you somewhat acquainted with her situation and her sentiments. The Princess Schirene seized the opportunity of the late convulsions to escape from a mode of life long repugnant to all her feelings, and from a destiny at which she trembled. I was her only counsellor, and she may feel assured, a faithful, although perhaps an indiscreet one. The irresistible solicitation of the inhabitants that I should become their deputy to their conqueror prevented us from escaping as we had intended. Since then, from the movement of the troops, I have deemed it more prudent that we should remain at present here, although I have circulated the intelligence of my departure. In the kiosk of my garden, the princess is now a willing prisoner. At twilight she steals forth for the poor relaxation of my society, to listen to the intelligence which I acquire during the day in disguise. The history, sire, is short and simple. We are in your power: but instead of deprecating your interference, I now solicit your protection.'

'Dear Honain, 'tis needless. The Princess Schirene has only to express a wish that it may be fulfilled. I came to speak with you on weighty matters, Honain, but I retire, for I am an intruder now. Tomorrow, if it please you, at this hour, and in this disguise, I will again repair hither. In the meantime, this lady may perchance express to you her wishes, and you will bear them to me. If an escort to any country, if any palace or province for her rule and residence—— But I will not offer to one who should command. Lady! farewell. Pardon the past! Tomorrow, good Honain! prythee let us meet. Good even!'

'The royal brow was clouded,' said Ithamar to Asriel, as, departing from the council, they entered their magnificent barque.

'With thought; he has so much upon his mind, 'tis wondrous how he bears himself.'

'I have seen him gay on the eve of battle, and lively though calm, with weightier matters than now oppress him. His brow was clouded, but not, methinks, with *thought*; one might rather say with *temper*. Mark you, how he rated Jabaster?'

'Roundly! The stern priest writhed under it; and as he signed the ordinance, shivered his reed in rage. I never saw a man more pale.'

'Or more silent. He looked like an embodied storm. I tell you what, Asriel, that stern priest loves not us.'

'Have you just discovered that secret, Ithamar? We are not of his school. Nor, in good faith, is our ruler. I am glad to see the king is so staunch about Abidan. Were he in council he would support Jabaster.'

'Oh! his mere tool. What think you of Scherirah?'

'I would not trust him. As long as there is fighting, he will meddle with nothing else; but, mark my words, Ithamar: in quiet times he will support the priest.'

'Medad will have a place in council. He is with us.'

'Heart and soul. I would your brother were here, Asriel: he alone could balance Jabaster. Alroy loves your brother like himself. Is it true that he marries the Lady Miriam?'

'So the king wishes. 'Twill be a fine match for Abner.'

'The world is all before us. I wonder who will be viceroy of Syria.'

'When we conquer it. Not Scherirah. Mark my words, Ithamar: he never will have a government. You or I perchance. For my own part, I would rather remain as I am.'

'Yours is a good post; the best.'

'With the command of the city. It should go with the guard.'

'Well, then, help me in getting Syria, and you can ask for my command.'

'Agreed. Jabaster will have it that, in a Hebrew monarchy, the chief priest is in fact the grand vizir.'

'Alroy will be his own minister.'

'I am not so sure of that. He may choose to command the Syrian expedition in person; he must leave some head at Bagdad. Jabaster is no general.'

'Oh! none at all. Alroy will be glad to leave him at home. The Sultan of Roum may not be always so merciful.'

'Hah! hah! that was an escape!'

'By heavens! I thought it was all over. You made a fine charge.'

'I shall never forget it. I nearly ran over Jabaster.'

'Would that you had!'

It is the tender twilight hour when maidens in their lonely bower sigh softer than the eve! The languid rose her head upraises, and listens to the nightingale, while his wild and thrilling praises from his trembling bosom gush: the languid rose her head upraises, and listens with a blush.

In the clear and rosy air, sparkling with a single star, the sharp and spiry cypress-tree rises like a gloomy thought, amid the flow of revelry. A singing bird, a single star, a solemn tree, an odorous flower, are dangerous in the tender hour, when maidens in their twilight bower sigh softer than the eve!

The daughter of the caliph comes forth to breathe the air: her lute her only company. She sits her down by a fountain's side, and gazes on the waterfall. Her cheek reclines upon her arm, like fruit upon a graceful bough. Very pensive is the face of that bright and beauteous lady. She starts; a warm voluptuous lip presses her soft and idle hand. It is her own gazelle. With his large and lustrous eyes, more eloquent than many a tongue, the fond attendant mutely asks the cause of all her thoughtfulness.

'Ah! bright gazelle! Ah! bright gazelle!' the princess cried, the princess cried; 'thy lips are softer than the swan, thy lips are softer than the swan; but his breathed passion when they pressed, my bright gazelle! my bright gazelle!

'Ah! bright gazelle! Ah! bright gazelle!' the princess cried, the princess cried; 'thine eyes are like the stars of night, thine eyes are like the stars of night; but his glanced passion when they gazed, my bright gazelle! my bright gazelle!'

She seized her lute, she wildly threw her fingers o'er its thrilling strings, and, gazing on the rosy sky, to borrow all its poetry, thus, thus she sang—thus, thus she sang:

He rose in beauty like the morn
That brightens in bur Syrian skies;
Dark passion glittered in his eyes,
And Empire sparkled in his form!

My soul! thou art the dusky earth,
On which his sunlight fell;
The dusky earth, that dim no longer,
Now breathes with light, now beams with love!

He rose in beauty, like the morn
That brightens in our Syrian skies;
Dark passion glittered in his eyes,
And Empire sparkled in his form!

'Once more, once more! Ah! sing that strain once more!'

The princess started and looked round. Before her stood Alroy. She rose, she would have retired; but, advancing, the conqueror stole her hand.

'Fair princess,' said Alroy, 'let it not be said that my presence banished at once beauty and music.'

'Sire, I doubt not that Honain awaits you. Let me summon him.'

'Lady, it is not with Honain that I would speak.'

He seated himself by her side. His countenance was pale, his heart trembled.

'This garden,' at length he observed in a low voice, 'this garden, a brief, brief space has glided away since first I wandered within its beauteous limits, and yet those days seem like the distant memory of another life.'

'It is another life,' said the princess. 'Ourselves, the world, all forms and usages, all feelings and all habits, verily they have changed, as if we had breathed within another sphere.'

''Tis a great change.'

'Since first you visited my bright kiosk. Pretty bauble! I pray it may be spared.'

'It is sacred, like yourself.'

'You are a courteous conqueror.'

'I am no conqueror, fair Schirene, but a slave more lowly than when I first bowed humbly in your presence.'

'And bore away a token not forgotten. Your rosary is here.'

'Let me claim it. It has been my consolation in much peril, beauteous lady. On the eve of battle I wound it round my heart.'

She held forth the rosary, and turned away her head. Her hand remained in his; he pressed it to his lips. His right arm retained her hand; he wound the other round her waist, as he fell upon his knee.

'O beautiful! O more than beautiful! for thou to me art like a dream unbroken,' exclaimed the young leader of Israel, 'let me, let me breathe my adoration. I offer thee not empire: I offer thee not wealth; I offer thee not all the boundless gratification of magnificent fancy,—these may be thine, but all these thou hast proved; but, if the passionate affections of a spirit which never has yielded to the power of woman or the might of man, if the deep devotion of the soul of Alroy, be deemed an offering meet for the shrine of thy surpassing loveliness, I worship thee, Schirene. I worship thee, I worship thee!

'Since I first gazed upon thee, since thy beauty first rose upon my presence like a star bright with my destiny, in the still sanctuary of my secret love, thy idol has ever rested. Then, then, I was a thing whose very touch thy creed might count a contumely. I have avenged the insults of long centuries in the best blood of Asia; I have returned, in glory and in pride, to claim my ancient sceptre; but sweeter far than vengeance, sweeter far than the quick gathering of my sacred tribes, the rush of triumph and the blaze of empire, is this brief moment of adoring love, wherein I pour the passion of my life!

'O my soul, my life, my very being! thou art silent, but thy silence is sweeter than others' speech. Yield, yield thee, dear Schirene, yield to thy suppliant! Thy faith, thy father's faith, thy native customs, these, these shall be respected, beauteous lady! Pharaoh's daughter yielded her dusky beauty to my great ancestor. Thy face is like the bright inspiring day! Let it not be said that the daughter of the Nile shared Israel's crown, the daughter of the Tigris spurned our sceptre. I am not Solomon, but I am one that, were Schirene the partner of my throne, would make his glowing annals read like a wearisome and misty tale to our surpassing lustre!'

He ceased, the princess turned her hitherto hidden countenance, and bowed it on his heart. 'O Alroy!' she exclaimed, 'I have no creed, no country, no life, but thee!'

'The king is late to-day.'

'Is it true, Asriel, there is an express from Hamadan?'

'Of no moment, Ithamar. I have private letters from Abner. All is quiet.'

"Tis much past the hour. When do you depart, Scherirah?'

'The troops are ready. I wait orders. This morning's council will perchance decide.'

'This morning's council is devoted to the settlement of the civil affairs of the capital,' remarked Jabaster.

'Indeed!' said Asriel. 'Is your report prepared, Jabaster?'

"Tis here,' replied the high priest. 'The Hebrew legislator requires but little musing to shape his order. He has a model which time cannot destroy, nor thought improve.'

Ithamar and Asriel exchanged significant glances. Scherirah looked solemn. There was a pause, which was broken by Asriel.

"Tis a noble city, this Bagdad. I have not yet visited your quarters, Jabaster. You are well placed.'

'As it may be. I hope we shall not tarry here long. The great point is still not achieved.'

'How far is it to the holy city?' enquired Scherirah.

'A month's march,' replied Jabaster.

'And when you get there?' enquired Ithamar.

'You may fight with the Franks,' replied Asriel.

'Jabaster, how large is Jerusalem?' enquired Ithamar. 'Is it true, as I have sometimes heard, that it is not bigger than the serail here, gardens and all?'

'Its glory hath departed,' replied the high priest; 'the bricks have fallen, but we will rebuild with marble; and Zion, that is now without the Christian walls, shall yet sparkle, as in the olden time, with palaces and pavilions.'

A flourish of trumpets, the portals flew open, and Alroy entered, leaning on the arm of the Envoy of Bagdad.

'Valiant leaders,' said Alroy to the astonished chieftains, 'in this noble stranger, you see one like yourselves entrusted with my unbounded confidence. Jabaster, behold thy brother!'

'Honain! art *thou* Honain?' exclaimed the pontiff starting from his seat. 'I have a thousand messengers after thee.' With a countenance alternately pallid with surprise and burning with affection, Jabaster embraced his brother, and, overpowered with emotion, hid his face on his shoulder.

'Sire,' at length exclaimed the high priest, in a low and tremulous voice, 'I must pray your pardon that for an instant in this character I have indulged in any other thoughts than those that may concern your welfare. Tis past: and you, who know all, will forgive me.'

'All that respects Jabaster must concern my welfare. He is the pillar of my empire;' and holding forth his hand, Alroy placed the high priest on his right. 'Scherirah, you depart this eve.'

The rough captain bowed in silence.

'What is this?' continued Alroy, as Jabaster offered him a scroll. 'Ah! your report. "Order of the Tribes," "Service of the Lévites," "Princes of the People," "Elders of Israel!" The day may come when this may be effected. At present, Jabaster, we must be moderate, and content ourselves with arrangements which may ensure that order shall be maintained, property respected, and justice administered. Is it true that a gang has rifled a mosque?'

'Sire! of that I would speak. They are no plunderers, but men, perhaps too zealous, who have read and who have remembered that "Ye shall utterly destroy all the places wherein the nations which ye shall possess, served their gods upon the high mountains, and upon the hill, and under every green tree. And ye shall overthrow their altars, and——"'

'Jabaster, is this a synagogue? Come I to a council of valiant statesmen or dreaming Rabbis? For a thousand years we have been quoting the laws we dared not practise. Is it with such aid that we captured Nishapur and crossed the Tigris? Valiant, wise Jabaster, thou art worthy of better things, and capable of all. I entreat thee, urge such matters for the last time. Are these fellows in custody?'

'They were in custody. I have freed them.'

'Freed them! Hang them! Hang them in the most public grove. Is this the way to make the Moslem a duteous subject? Jabaster! Israel honours thee; and I, its chief, know that one more true, more valiant, or more learned, crowds not around our standard; but I see, the caverns of the Caucasus are not a school for empire.'

'Sire, I had humbly deemed the school for empire was the law of Moses.'

'Ay! adapted to these times.'

'Can aught divine be changed?'

'Am I as tall as Adam? If man, the crown, the rose of all this fair creation, the most divine of all divine inventions, if Time have altered even this choicest of all godlike works, why shall it spare a law made but to rule his conduct? Good Jabaster, we must establish the throne of Israel, that is my mission, and for the means, no matter how, or where. Asriel, what news of Medad?'

'All is quiet between the Tigris and Euphrates. It would be better to recall his division, which has been much harassed. I thought of relieving him by Abidan.'

'I think so, too. We may as well keep Abidan out of the city. If the truth were known, I'll wager some of his company plundered the mosque. We must issue a proclamation on that subject. My good Jabaster, we'll talk over these matters alone. At present I will leave you with your brother. Scherirah, sup with me to-night; before you quit Asriel, come with me to my cabinet.'

'I must see the king!'

'Holy priest, his highness has retired. It is impossible.'

'I must see the king. Worthy Pharez, I take all peril on myself.'

'Indeed his highness' orders are imperative. You cannot see him.'

'Knowest thou who I am?'

'One whom all pious Hebrews reverence.'

'I say I must see the king.'

'Indeed, indeed, holy Jabaster, it cannot be.'

'Shall Israel perish for a menial's place? Go to; I *will see him.*'

'*Nay! if you will*, I'll struggle for my duty.'

'Touch not the Lord's anointed. Dog, you shall suffer for this!'

So saying, Jabaster threw aside Pharez, and, with the attendant clinging to his robes, rushed into the royal chamber.

'What is all this?' exclaimed Alroy, starting from the divan. 'Jabaster! Pharez, withdraw! How now, is Bagdad in insurrection?'

'Worse, much worse, Israel soon will be.'

'Ay!'

'My fatal brother has told me all, nor would I sleep, until I lifted up my voice to save thee.'

'Am I in danger?'

'In the wilderness, when the broad desert quivered beneath thy trembling feet, and the dark heavens poured down their burning torrents, thou wert less so. In that hour of death, One guarded thee, who never forgets His fond and faithful offspring, and now, when He has brought thee out of the house of bondage; now, when thy fortunes, like a noble cedar, swell in the air and shadow all the land; thou, the very leader of His people, His chosen one, for whom He hath worked such marvels, thy heart is turned from thy fathers' God, and hankers after strange abominations.'

Through the broad arch that led into the gardens of the serail, the moonlight fell upon the tall figure and the upraised arm of the priest; Alroy stood with folded arms at some distance, watching Jabaster as he spoke, with a calm but searching glance. Suddenly he advanced with a quick step, and, placing his hand upon Jabaster's arm, said, in a low, enquiring tone, 'You are speaking of this marriage?'

'Of that which ruined Solomon.'

'Listen to me, Jabaster,' said Alroy, interrupting him, in a calm but peremptory tone, 'I cannot forget that I am speaking to my master, as well as to my friend. The Lord, who knoweth all things, hath deemed me worthy of His mission. My fitness for this high and holy office was not admitted without proof. A lineage, which none else could offer, mystic studies shared by few, a mind that dared encounter all things, and a frame that could endure most, these were my claims. But no more of this. I have passed the great ordeal; the Lord of Hosts hath found me not unworthy of His charge; I have established His ancient people; His altars blaze with sacrifices; His priests are honoured, bear witness thou, Jabaster, His omnipotent unity is declared. What wouldst thou more?'

'All!'

'Then Moses knew you well. It is a stiff-necked people.'

'Sire, bear with me. If I speak in heat, I speak in zeal. You ask me what I wish: my answer is, a national existence, which we have not. You ask me what I wish: my answer is, the Land of Promise. You ask me what I wish: my answer is, Jerusalem. You ask me what I wish: my answer is, the Temple, all we have forfeited, all we have yearned after, all for which we have fought, our beauteous country, our holy creed, our simple manners, and our ancient customs.'

'Manners change with time and circumstances; customs may be observed everywhere. The ephod on thy breast proves our faith; and, for a country, is the Tigris less than Siloah, or the Euphrates inferior to the Jordan?'

'Alas! alas! there was a glorious prime when Israel stood aloof from other nations, a fair and holy thing that God had hallowed. We were then a chosen family, a most peculiar people, set apart for God's entire enjoyment. All about us was solemn, deep, and holy. We shunned the stranger as an unclean thing that must defile our solitary sanctity, and, keeping to ourselves and to our God, our lives flowed on in one great solemn tide of deep religion, making the meanest of our multitude feel greater than the kings of other lands. It was a glorious time: I thought it had returned; but I awake from this, as other dreams.'

'We must leave off dreaming, good Jabaster, we must act. Were I, by any chance, to fall into one of those reveries, with which I have often lost the golden hours at Hamadan, or in our old cave, I should hear, some fine morning, his Sultanship of Roum rattling at my gates.' Alroy smiled as he spoke; he would willingly have introduced a lighter tone into the dialogue, but the solemn countenance of the priest was not sympathetic with his levity.

'My heart is full, and yet I cannot speak: the memory of the past overpowers my thought. I had vainly deemed that my voice, inspired by the soul of truth, might yet preserve him; and now I stand here in his presence, silent and trembling, like a guilty thing. O, my prince! my pupil!' said the priest, advancing, falling on his knee, and seizing the robe of Alroy, 'by thy sacred lineage; by the sweet memory of thy ardent youth, and our united studies, by all thy zealous thoughts, and solemn musings, and glorious aspirations after fame; by all thy sufferings, and by all thy triumphs, and chiefly by the name of that great God, who hath elected thee his favoured child; by all the marvels of thy mighty mission, I do adjure thee! Arise, Alroy, arise and rouse thyself. The lure that snared thy fathers may trap thee, this Delilah may shear thy mystic locks. Spirits like thee act not by halves. Once fall out from the straight course before thee, and, though thou deemest 'tis but to saunter 'mid the summer trees, soon thou wilt find thyself in the dark depths of some infernal forest, where none may rescue thee!'

'What if I do inherit the eager blood of my great ancestor, at least I hold his sceptre. Shall aught of earthly power prevail against the supernatural sway of Heaven and Hades?'

'Sire, sire, the legend that came from Sinai is full of high instruction. But shape thy conduct by its oracles, and all were well. It says our people can be established only by him who rules them with the rod of Solomon. Sire, when the Lord offered his pleasure to that mighty king, thou knowest his deep discretion. Riches and length of days, empire and vengeance, these were not the choice of one to whom all accidents were proffered. The legend bears an inward spirit, as well as an outward meaning. The capture of the prize was a wise test of thy imperial fitness. Thou hast his sceptre, but, without his wisdom, 'tis but a staff of cedar.'

'Hah! Art thou there? I am glad to see Jabaster politic. Hear me, my friend. What my feelings be unto this royal lady, but little matters. Let them pass, and let us view this question by the light wherein you have placed it, the flame of policy and not of passion. I am no traitor to the God of Israel, in whose name I have conquered, and in whose name I shall rule; but thou art a learned doctor, thou canst inform us. I have heard no mandate to yield my glorious empire for my meanest province. I am Lord of Asia, so would I have my long posterity. Our people are but a remnant, a feeble fraction of the teeming millions that own my sway. What I hold I can defend; but my children may not inherit the spirit of their sire. The Moslemin will recognise their rule with readier hearts, when they remember that a daughter of their caliphs gave them life. You see I too am politic, my good Jabaster!'

'The policy of the son of Kareah[67], 'twas fatal. He preferred Egypt to Judah, and he suffered. Sire, the Lord hath blessed Judah: it is His land. He would have it filled by His peculiar people, so that His worship might ever flourish. For this He has, by many curious rites and customs, marked us out from all other nations, so that we cannot, at the same time, mingle with them and yet be true to Him. We must exist alone. To preserve that loneliness is the great end and essence of our law. What have we to do with Bagdad, or its people, where every instant we must witness some violation of our statutes? Can we pray with them? Can we eat with them? Alike in the highest duties, and the lowest occupations of existence, we cannot mingle. From the altar of our God to our domestic boards, we are alike separated from them. Sire, you may be King of Bagdad, but you cannot, at the same time, be a Jew.'

'I am what I am. I worship the Lord of Hosts. Perhaps, in His mercy, He will accept the days of Nishapur and the Tigris as a compensation for some slight relaxation in the ritual of the baker and the bath.'

'And mark my words: it was by the ritual of the baker and the bath that Alroy rose, and without it he will fall. The genius of the people, which he shared, raised him; and that genius has been formed by the law of Moses. Based on that law, he might indeed have handed down an empire to his long posterity; and now, though the tree of his fortunes seems springing up by the water-side, fed by a thousand springs, and its branches covered with dew, there is a gangrene in the sap, and to-morrow he may shrink like a shrivelled gourd. Alas! alas! for Israel! We have long fed on mallows; but to lose the vintage in the very day of fruition, 'tis very bitter. Ah! when I raised thy exhausted form in the cavern of Genthesma, and the star of David beamed brightly in the glowing heavens upon thy high fulfilment, who could have dreamed of a night like this? Farewell, sire.'

'Stop, Jabaster! earliest, dearest friend, prythee, prythee stop!'

The priest slowly turned, the prince hesitated.

'Part not in anger, good Jabaster.'

'In sorrow, sire, only in sorrow; but deep and terrible.'

'Israel is Lord of Asia, my Jabaster. Why should we fear?'

'Solomon built Tadmor in the wilderness, and his fleet brought gold from Ophir; and yet Alroy was born a slave.'

'But did not die one. The sultans of the world have fallen before me. I have no fear. Nay, do not go. At least you will give some credence to the stars, my learned Cabalist. See, my planet shines as brightly as my fortunes.' Alroy withdrew the curtain, and with Jabaster stepped out upon the terrace. A beautiful star glittered on high. As they gazed, its colour changed, and a blood-red meteor burst from its circle, and fell into space. The conqueror and the priest looked at each other at the same time. Their countenances were pale, enquiring, and agitated.

'Sire,' said Jabaster, 'march to Judah.'

'It portends war,' replied Alroy, endeavouring to recover himself. 'Perchance some troubles in Persia.'

'Troubles at home, no other. The danger is nigh. Look to thyself.'

A wild scream was heard in the gardens. It sounded thrice.

'What is this?' exclaimed Alroy, really agitated. 'Rouse the guard, Jabaster, search the gardens.'

''Tis useless and may do harm. It was a spirit that shrieked.'

'What said it?'

'*Mené, Mené, Tekel, Upharsin!*'

'The old story, the priest against the king,' said Honain to Alroy, when at his morrow's interview, he had listened to the events of the preceding night. 'My pious brother wishes to lead you back to the Theocracy, and is fearful that, if he prays at Bagdad instead of Zion, he may chance to become only the head of an inferior sect, instead of revelling in the universal tithes of a whole nation. As for the meteor, Scherirah must have crossed the river about the same time, and the Sultan of Roum may explain the bloody portent. For the shriek, as I really have no acquaintance with spirits, I must leave the miraculous communication to the favoured ears and initiated intelligences of your highness and my brother. It seems that it differed from "the Daughter of the Voice" in more respects than one, since it was not only extremely noisy, but, as it would appear, quite unintelligible except to the individual who had an interest in the interpretation, an ingenious one, I confess. When I enter upon my functions as your highness's chamberlain, I will at least guarantee that your slumbers shall not be disturbed either by spirits or more unwelcome visitors.'

'Enter upon them at once, good Honain. How fares my Persian rose to-day, my sweet Schirene?'

'Feeding on your image in your absence. She spares no word to me, I do assure your highness.'

'Nay, nay, we know you are a general favourite with the sex, Honain. I'faith I'm jealous.'

'I would your highness had cause,' said Honain, demurely.

The approaching marriage between the King of the Hebrews and the Princess of Bagdad was published throughout Asia. Preparations were made on the plain of the Tigris for the great rejoicing. Whole forests were felled to provide materials for the buildings and fuel for the banqueting. All the governors of provinces and cities, all the chief officers and nobility of both nations, were specially invited, and daily arrived in state at Bagdad. Among them the Viceroy of the Medes and Persians, and his recent bride, the Princess Miriam, were conspicuous, followed by a train of nearly ten thousand persons.

A throne, ascended by one hundred steps covered with crimson cloth, and crowned by a golden canopy, was raised in the middle of the plain; on each side was a throne less elevated, but equally gorgeous. In the front of these thrones an immense circus was described, formed by one hundred chartaks or amphitheatres, ample room for the admittance of the multitude being left between the buildings. These chartaks were covered with bright brocades and showy carpets; on each was hoisted a brilliant banner. In some of them were bands of choice musicians, in others companies of jugglers, buffoons, and storiers. Five chartaks on each side of the thrones were allotted for the convenience of the court; the rest were filled by the different trades of the city. In one the fruiterers had formed a beautiful garden, glowing with pomegranates and gourds and watermelons, oranges, almonds, and pistachio-nuts; in another the butchers exhibited their meats carved in fanciful shapes, and the skins of animals formed into ludicrous figures. Here assembled the furriers, all dressed in masquerade, like leopards, lions, tigers and foxes; and in another booth mustered the upholsterers, proud of a camel made of wood, and reeds, and cord, and painted linen, a camel which walked about as if alive, though ever and anon a curtain drawn aside discovered to the marvelling multitude the workman within, performing in his own piece. Further on might be perceived the cotton manufacturers, whose chartak was full of birds of all shapes and plumage, formed nevertheless of their curious plant; and, in the centre rose a lofty minaret, constructed of the same material, with the help of reeds, although every one imagined it to be built with bricks and mortar. It was covered with embroidered work, and on the top was placed a stork, so cunningly devised that the children pelted it with pistachio-nuts. The saddlers showed their skill in two litters, open at top, each carried on a dromedary, and in each a beautiful woman, who diverted the spectators with light balls of gilt leather, throwing them up both with their hands and feet. Nor were the mat-makers backward in the proof of their dexterity, since, instead of a common banner, they exhibited a large standard of reeds worked with two lines of writing in Kufic, proclaiming the happy names of Alroy and Schirene.

But indeed in every chartak might be seen some wondrous specimens of the wealth of Bagdad, and of the ingenuity of its unrivalled artisans.

Around this mighty circus, on every side for the space of many miles, the plain was studded with innumerable pavilions. At measured intervals were tables furnished with every species of provision, and attended by appointed servants; flagons of wine and jars of sherbets, mingled with infinite baskets of delicious fruits and trays of refreshing confectionery. Although open to all comers, so great and rapid was the supply, that these banqueting tables seemed ever laden; and that the joys of the people might be complete, they were allowed to pursue whatever pleasures they thought fit without any restraint, by proclamation, in these terms.

'*This is the time of feasting, pleasure, and rejoicing. Let no person reprimand or complain of another: let not the rich insult the poor, or the strong the weak: let no one ask another, "why have you done this?"*'

Millions of people were collected in this Paradise. They rejoiced, they feasted, they frolicked, they danced, they sang. They listened to the tales of the Arabian story-teller, at once enchanted and enchanting, or melted to the strain of the Persian poet as he painted the moon-lit forehead of his heroine and the wasting and shadowy form of his love-sick hero; they beheld with amazement the feats of the juggler of the Ganges, or giggled at the practised wit and the practical buffoonery of the Syrian mime. And the most delighted could still spare a fascinating glance to the inviting gestures and the voluptuous grace of the dancing girls of Egypt.[68] Everywhere reigned melody and merriment, rarity and beauty. For once mankind forgot their cares, and delivered themselves up to infinite enjoyment.

'I grow courteous,' said Kisloch the Kourd, assisting a party into one of the shows.

'And I humane,' said Calidas the Indian. 'Fellow, how dare you violate the proclamation, by thrashing that child?' He turned to one of the stewards of the table, who was belabouring the unfortunate driver of a camel which had stumbled and in its fall had shivered its burden, two panniers of porcelain.

'Mind your own business, fellow,' replied the steward, 'and be thankful that for once in your life you can dine.'

'Is this the way to speak to an officer?' said Calidas the Indian; 'I have half a mind to cut your tongue out.'

'Never mind, little fellow,' said the Guebre, 'here is a dirhem for you. Run away and be merry.'

'A miracle!' grinned the Negro; 'he giveth alms.'

'And you are witty,' rejoined the Guebre. ''Tis a wondrous day.'

'What shall we do?' said Kisloch.

'Let us dine,' proposed the Negro.

'Ay! under this plane-tree,' said Calidas. ''Tis pleasant to be alone. I hate everybody but ourselves.'

'Here stop, you rascal,' said the Guebre. 'What's your name?'

'I am a Hadgee,' said our old friend Abdallah, the servant of the charitable merchant Ali, and who was this day one of the officiating stewards.

'Are you a Jew, you scoundrel?' said the Guebre, 'that is the only thing worth being. Bring some wine, you accursed Giaour!'

'Instantly,' said Kisloch, 'and a pilau.' 'And a gazelle stuffed with almonds,' said Calidas. 'And some sugar-plums,' said the Negro. 'Quick, you infernal Gentile, or I'll send this javelin in your back,' hallooed the Guebre.

The servile Abdallah hastened away, and soon bustled back, bearing two flagons of wine, and followed by four servants, each with a tray covered with dainties.

'Where are you going, you accursed scoundrels?' grumbled Kisloch; 'wait upon the true believers.' 'We shall be more free alone,' whispered Calidas. 'Away, then, dogs,' growled Kisloch. Abdallah and his attendants hurried off, but were soon summoned back.

'Why did you not bring Schiraz wine?' asked Calidas, with an eye of fire.

'The pilau is overdone,' thundered Kisloch. 'You have brought a lamb stuffed with pistachio-nuts, instead of a gazelle with almonds,' said the Guebre.

'Not half sugar-plums enough,' said the Negro. 'Everything is wrong,' said Kisloch. 'Go, and get us a kabob.'

In time, however, even this unmanageable crew were satisfied; and, seated under their plane-tree, and stuffing themselves with all the dainties of the East, they became more amiable as their appetites decreased. 'A bumper, Calidas, and a song,' said Kisloch. ''Tis rare stuff,' said the Guebre; 'come, Cally, it should inspire you.'

'Here goes, then; mind the chorus.'

Drink, drink, deeply drink,
Never feel, and never think;
What's love? what's fame? a sigh, a smile.
Friendship? but a hollow wile.
If you've any thought or woe,
Drown them in the goblet's flow.
Yes! dash them in this brimming cup;
Dash them in, and drink them up.
Drink, drink, deeply drink,
Never feel, and never think.

'Hark, the trumpets! The King and Queen! 'The procession is coming. Let's away.'

'Again! they must be near. Hurry, hurry, for good places.'

'Break all the cups and dishes. Come along!'

The multitude from all quarters hurried to the great circus, amid the clash of ten thousand cymbals and the blast of innumerable trumpets. In the distance, issuing from the gates of Bagdad, might be discerned a brilliant crowd, the advance company of the bridal procession.

There came five hundred maidens crowned with flowers, and beauteous as the buds that girt their hair. Their flowing robes were whiter than the swan, and each within her hand a palm-branch held. Followed these a band of bright musicians, clothed in golden robes, and sounding silver trumpets.

Then five hundred youths, brilliant as stars, clad in jackets of white-fox skin, and alternately bearing baskets of fruit or flowers.

Followed these a band of bright musicians, clothed in silver robes, and sounding golden trumpets.

Six choice steeds, sumptuously caparisoned, each led by an Arab groom.[69]

The household of Medad, in robes of crimson, lined with sable.

The standard of Medad.

Medad, on a coal-black Arab, followed by three hundred officers of his division, all mounted on steeds of pure race.

Slaves, bearing the bridal present of Medad; six Damascus sabres of unrivalled temper.[70]

Twelve choice steeds, sumptuously caparisoned, each led by an Anatolian groom.

The household of Ithamar, in robes of violet, lined with ermine.

The standard of Ithamar.

Ithamar, on a snow-white Anatolian charger, followed by six hundred officers of his division, all mounted on steeds of pure race.

Slaves bearing the marriage present of Ithamar; a golden vase of rubies borne on a violet throne.

One hundred Negroes, their noses bored, and hung with rings of brilliants, playing upon wind instruments and kettle-drums.

The standard of the City of Bagdad.

The deputation from the citizens of Bagdad.

Two hundred mules, with caparisons of satin, embroidered with gold, and adorned with small golden bells. These bore the sumptuous wardrobe, presented by the city to their princess. Each mule was attended by a girl, dressed like a Péri, with starry wings, and a man, masked as a hideous Dive.

The standard of Egypt.

The deputation from the Hebrews of Egypt, mounted on dromedaries, with silver furniture.

Fifty slaves, bearing their present to the princess, with golden cords, a mighty bath of jasper, beautifully carved, the sarcophagus of some ancient temple, and purchased for an immense sum.

The standard of Syria.

The deputation from the Hebrews of the Holy Land, headed by Rabbi Zimri himself, each carrying in his hand his offering to the nuptial pair, a precious vase, containing earth from the Mount of Zion.

The standard of Hamadan.

The deputation from the citizens of Hamadan, headed by the venerable Bostenay himself, whose sumptuous charger was led by Caleb.

The present of the city of Hamadan to David Al-roy, offered at his own suggestion; the cup in which the Prince of the Captivity carried his tribute, now borne full of sand.

Fifty choice steeds, sumptuously caparisoned, each led by a Median or Persian groom.

The household of Abner and Miriam, in number twelve hundred, clad in chain armour of ivory and gold.

The standard of the Medes and Persians.

Two white elephants, with golden litters, bearing the Viceroy and his Princess.

The offering of Abner to Alroy; twelve elephants of state, with furniture embroidered with jewels, each tended by an Indian clad in chain armour of ivory and gold.

The offering of Miriam to Schirene; fifty plants of roses from Rocnabad;[71] a white shawl of Cachemire fifty feet in length, which folded into the handle of a fan; fifty screens, each made of a feather of the roc;[72] and fifty vases of crystal full of exquisite perfumes, and each sealed with a talisman of precious stones.

After these followed the eunuch guard.

Then came the band of the serail, consisting of three hundred dwarfs, hideous indeed to behold, but the most complete musicians in the world.

The steeds of Solomon, in number one hundred, each with a natural star upon its front, uncaparisoned, and led only by a bridle of diamonds.

The household of Alroy and Schirene. Foremost, the Lord Honain riding upon a chestnut charger, shod with silver; the dress of the rider, pink with silver stars. From his rosy turban depended a tremulous aigrette of brilliants,[73] blazing with a thousand shifting tints.

Two hundred pages followed him; and then servants of both sexes, gorgeously habited, amounting to nearly two thousand, carrying rich vases, magnificent caskets, and costly robes. The treasurer and two hundred of his underlings came next, showering golden dirhems on all sides.

The sceptre of Solomon borne by Asriel himself.

A magnificent and lofty car, formed of blue enamel with golden wheels, and axletrees of turquoises and brilliants, and drawn by twelve snow-white and sacred horses, four abreast; in the car Alroy and Schirene.

Five thousand of the Sacred Guard closed the procession.

Amid the exclamations of the people, this gorgeous procession crossed the plain, and moved around the mighty circus. The conqueror and his bride ascended their throne; its steps were covered by the youths and maidens. On the throne upon their right sat the venerable Bostenay; on the left, the gallant Viceroy and his Princess. The chartaks on each side were crowded with the court.

The deputations made their offerings, the chiefs and captains paid their homage, the trades of the city moved before the throne in order, and exhibited their various ingenuity. Thrice was the proclamation made, amid the sound of trumpets, and then began the games.

A thousand horsemen dashed into the arena and threw the jerreed. They galloped at full speed; they arrested their fiery charges in mid course, and flung their long javelins at the minute but sparkling target, the imitative form of a rare and brilliant bird. The conquerors received their prizes from the hand of the princess herself, bright shawls, and jewelled daggers, and rosaries of gems. Sometimes the trumpets announced a prize from the vice-queen, sometimes from the venerable Bostenay, sometimes from the victorious generals, or the loyal deputations, sometimes from the united trades, sometimes from the City of Bagdad, sometimes from the City of Hamadan. The hours flew away in gorgeous and ceaseless variety.

'I would we were alone, my own Schirene,' said Alroy to his bride.

'I would so too; and yet I love to see all Asia prostrate at the feet of Alroy.'

'Will the sun never set? Give me thy hand to play with.'

'Hush! See, Miriam smiles.'

'Lovest thou my sister, my own Schirene?'

'None dearer but thyself.'

'Talk not of my sister, but ourselves. Thinkest thou the sun is nearer setting, love?'

'I cannot see; thine eyes they dazzle me, they are so brilliant, sweet!'

'Oh, my soul! I could pour out my passion on thy breast.'

'Thou art very serious.'

'Love is ever so.'

'Nay, sweet! It makes me wild and fanciful. Now I could do such things, but what I know not. I would we had wings, and then we would fly away.'

'See, I must salute this victor in the games. Must I unloose thy hand! Dear hand, farewell! Think of me while I speak, my precious life. 'Tis done. Give back thy hand, or else methinks I shall die. What's this?'

A horseman, in no holiday dress, but covered with dust, rushed into the circus, bearing in his hand a tall lance, on which was fixed a scroll. The marshals of the games endeavoured to prevent his advance, but he would not be stayed. His message was to the king alone. A rumour of news from the army circulated throughout the crowd. And news from the army it was. Another victory! Scherirah had defeated the Sultan of Roum, who was now a suppliant for peace and alliance. Sooth to say, the intelligence had arrived at dawn of day, but the courtly Honain had contrived that it should be communicated at a later and more effective moment.

There scarcely needed this additional excitement to this glorious day. But the people cheered, the golden dirhems were scattered with renewed profusion, and the intelligence was received by all parties as a solemn ratification by Jehovah, or by Allah, of the morning ceremony.

The sun set, the court rose, and returned in the same pomp to the serail. The twilight died away, a beacon fired on a distant eminence announced the entrance of Alroy and Schirene into the nuptial chamber, and suddenly, as by magic, the mighty city, every mosque, and minaret, and tower, and terrace, and the universal plain, and the numberless pavilions, and the immense circus, and the vast and winding river, blazed with light. From every spot a lamp, a torch, a lantern, tinted with every hue, burst forth; enormous cressets of silver radiancy beamed on the top of each chartak, and huge bonfires of ruddy flame started up along the whole horizon.

For seven days and seven nights this unparalleled scene of rejoicing, though ever various, never ceased. Long, long was remembered the bridal feast of the Hebrew prince and the caliph's daughter; long, long did the peasantry on the plains of Tigris sit down by the side of that starry river, and tell the wondrous tale to their marvelling posterity.

Now what a glorious man was David Alroy, lord of the mightiest empire in the world, and wedded to the most beautiful princess, surrounded by a prosperous and obedient people, guarded by invincible armies, one on whom Earth showered all its fortune, and Heaven all its favour; and all by the power of his own genius!

CHAPTER IX.

The Death of Jabaster

'TWAS midnight, and the storm still raged; 'mid the roar of the thunder and the shrieks of the wind, the floods of forky lightning each instant revealed the broad and billowy breast of the troubled Tigris. Jabaster stood gazing upon the wild scene from the gallery of his palace. His countenance was solemn, but disquieted.

'I would that he were here!' exclaimed the high priest. 'Yet why should I desire his presence, who heralds only gloom? Yet in his absence am I gay? I am nothing. This Bagdad weighs upon me like a cloak of lead: my spirit is dull and broken.'

'They say Alroy gives a grand banquet in the serail to-night, and toasts his harlot 'mid the thunderbolts. Is there no hand to write upon the wall? He is found wanting, he is weighed, and is indeed found wanting. The parting of his kingdom soon will come, and then, I could weep, oh! I could weep, and down these stern and seldom yielding cheeks pour the wild anguish of my desperate woe. So young, so great, so favoured! But one more step a God, and now a foul Belshazzar!

'Was it for this his gentle youth was passed in musing solitude and mystic studies? Was it for this the holy messenger summoned his most religious spirit? Was it for this he crossed the fiery desert, and communed with his fathers in their tombs? Is this the end of all his victories and all his vast achievements? To banquet with a wanton!

'A year ago, this very night, it was the eve of battle, I stood within his tent to wait his final word. He mused awhile, and then he said, "Good night, Jabaster!" I believed myself the nearest to his heart, as he has ever been nearest to mine, but that's all over. He never says, "Good night, Jabaster," now. Why, what's all this? Methinks I am a child.

'The Lord's anointed is a prisoner now in the light grating of a bright kiosk, and never gazes on the world he conquered. Egypt and Syria, even farthest Ind, send forth their messengers to greet Alroy, the great, the proud, the invincible. And where is he? In a soft Paradise of girls and eunuchs, crowned with flowers, listening to melting lays, and the wild trilling of the amorous lute. He spares no hours to council; all is left to his prime favourites, of whom the leader is that juggling fiend I sometime called my brother.

'Why rest I here? Whither should I fly? Methinks my presence is still a link to decency. Should I tear off the ephod, I scarcely fancy 'twould blaze upon another's breast. He goes not to the sacrifice; they say he keeps no fast, observes no ritual, and that their festive fantasies will not be balked, even by the Sabbath. I have not seen him thrice since the marriage. Honain has told her I did oppose it, and she bears to me a hatred that only women feel. Our strong passions break into a thousand purposes: women have one. Their love is dangerous, but their hate is fatal.

'See! a boat bounding on the waters. On such a night, but one would dare to venture.'

Now visible, now in darkness, a single lantern at the prow, Jabaster watched with some anxiety the slight bark buffeting the waves. A flash of lightning illumined the whole river, and tipped with a spectral light even the distant piles of building. The boat and the toiling figure of the single rower were distinctly perceptible. Now all again was darkness; the wind suddenly subsided; in a few minutes the plash of the oars was audible, and the boat apparently stopped beneath the palace.

There was a knocking at the private portal.

'Who knocks?' enquired Jabaster.

'A friend to Israel.'

'Abidan, by his voice. Art thou alone?'

'The prophetess is with me; only she.'

'A moment. I'll open the gate. Draw the boat within the arch.'

Jabaster descended from the gallery, and in a few moments returned with two visitors: the youthful prophetess Esther, and her companion, a man short in stature, but with a powerful and well-knit frame. His countenance was melancholy, and, with harshness in the lower part, not without a degree of pensive beauty in the broad clear brow and sunken eyes, unusual in Oriental visages.

'A rough night,' said Jabaster.

'To those who fear it,' replied Abidan. 'The sun has brought so little joy to me, I care not for the storm.'

'What news?'

'Woe! woe! woe!'

'Thy usual note, my sister. Will the day never come when we may change it?'

'Woe! woe! woe! unutterable woe!'

'Abidan, how fares it?'

'Very well.'

'Indeed!'

'As it may turn out.'

'You are brief.'

'Bitter.'

'Have you been to court, that you have learnt to be so wary in your words, my friend?'

'I know not what may happen. In time we may all become courtiers, though I fear, Jabaster, we have done too much to be rewarded. I gave him my blood, and you something more, and now we are at Bagdad. 'Tis a fine city. I wish to Heaven the shower of Sodom would rain upon its terraces.'

'I know thou hast something terrible to tell. I know it by that gloomy brow of thine, that lowers like the tempest. Speak out, man, I can bear the worst, for which I am prepared.'

'Take it, then. Alroy has proclaimed himself Caliph. Abner is made Sultan of Persia; Asriel, Ithamar, Medad, and the chief captains, Vizirs, Honain their chief.

Four Moslem nobles are sworn into the council. The Princess goes to mosque in state next Friday; 'tis said thy pupil doth accompany her.'

'I'll not believe it! By the God of Sinai, I'll not believe it! Were my own eye the accursed witness of the deed, I'd not believe it. Go to mosque! They play with thee, my good Abidan, they play with thee.'

'As it may be. Tis a rumour, but rumours herald deeds. The rest of my intelligence is true. I had it from my kinsman, stout Zalmunna. He left the banquet.'

'Shall I go to him? Methinks one single word, To mosque! only a rumour and a false one. I'll never believe it; no, no, no, never, never! Is he not the Lord's anointed? The ineffable curse upon this daughter ot the Moabite! No marvel that it thunders! By heavens, I'll go and beard him in his orgies!'

'You know your power better than Abidan. You bearded him before his marriage, yet——'

'He married. Tis true. Honain, their chief. And I kept his ring! Honain is my brother. Have I ne'er a dagger to cut the bond of brotherhood?'

'We have all daggers, Jabaster, if we knew but how to use them.'

''Tis strange, we met after twenty years of severance. You were not in the chamber, Abidan. 'Twas at council. We met after twenty years of severance. He is my brother. 'Tis strange, I say: I felt that man shrink from my embrace.'

'Honain is a philosopher, and believes in sympathy. 'Twould appear there was none between you. His system, then, absolves you from all ties.'

'You are sure the rest of the intelligence is true? I'll not believe the mosque, the rest is bad enough.'

'Zalmunna left the banquet. Hassan Subah's brother sat above him.'

'Subah's brother! 'Tis all over, then. Is he of the council?'

'Ay, and others.'

'Where now is Israel?'

'She should be in her tents.'

'Woe! woe! unutterable woe!' exclaimed the prophetess, who, standing motionless at the back of the chamber, seemed inattentive to their conversation.

Jabaster paced the gallery with agitated steps. Suddenly he stopped, and, walking up to Abidan, seized his arm, and looked him sternly in the face. 'I know thy thoughts, Abidan,' exclaimed the priest; 'but it cannot be. I have dismissed, henceforth and for ever I have dismissed all feeling from my mind; now I have no brother, no friend, no pupil, and, I fear, no Saviour. Israel is all in all to me. I have no other life. 'Tis not compunction, then, that stays my arm. My heart's as hard as thine.'

'Why stays it then?'

'Because with him we fall. He is the last of all his sacred line. There is no other hand to grasp our sceptre.'

'*Our* sceptre! what sceptre?'

'The sceptre of our kings.'

'Kings!'

'Ay, why dost thou look so dark?'

'How looked the prophet when the stiff-necked populace forsooth must have a king! Did he smile? Did he shout, and clap his hands, and cry, God save his Majesty! O, Jabaster! honoured, rare Jabaster! thou second Samuel of our lightheaded people! there was a time when Israel had no king except their God. Were we viler then? Did kings conquer Canaan? Who was Moses, who was Aaron, who was mighty Joshua? Was the sword of Gideon a kingly sword? Did the locks of Samson shade royal temples? Would a king have kept his awful covenant like solemn Jephtha? Royal words are light as air, when, to maintain them, you injure any other than a subject.

'Kings! why, what's a king? Why should one man break the equal sanctity of our chosen race? Is their blood purer than our own? We are all the seed of Abraham. Who was Saul, and who was David? I never heard that they were a different breed from our fathers. Grant them devout, which they were not; and brave and wise, which other men were; have their posterity a patent for all virtues? No, Jabaster! thou ne'er didst err, but when thou placedst a crown upon this haughty stripling. What he did, a thousand might have done. 'Twas thy mind inspired the deed. And now he is a king; and now Jabaster, the very soul of Israel, who should be our Judge and leader, Jabaster trembles in disgrace, while our unhallowed Sanhedrim is filled with Ammonites!'

'Abidan, thou hast touched me to the quick; thou hast stirred up thoughts that ever and anon, like strong and fatal vapours, have risen from the dark abyss of thought, and I have quelled them.'

'Let them rise, I say; let them drown the beams of that all-scorching sun we suffer under, that drinks all vegetation up, and makes us languish with a dull exhaustion!'

'Joy! joy! unutterable joy!'

'Hark! the prophetess has changed her note; and yet she hears us not. The spirit of the Lord is truly with her. Come, Jabaster, I see thy heart is opening to thy people's sufferings; thy people, my Jabaster, for art not thou our Judge? At least, thou shalt be.'

'Can we call back the Theocracy? Is't possible?'

'But say the word, and it is done, Jabaster. Nay, stare not. Dost thou think there are no true hearts in Israel? Dost thou suppose thy children have beheld, without a thought, the foul insults poured on thee; thee, their priest, their adored high priest, one who recalls the best days of the past, the days of their great Judges? But one word, one single movement of that mitred head, and—— But I speak unto a mind that feels more than I can express. Be silent, tongue, thou art a babbling counsellor. Jabaster's patriot soul needs not the idle schooling of a child. If he be silent, 'tis that his wisdom deems that the hour is not ripe, but when her leader speaks, Israel will not be slack.'

'The Moslemin in council! We know what must come next. Our national existence is in its last agony. Methinks the time is very ripe, Abidan.'

'Why, so we think, great sir; and say the word, and twenty thousand spears will guard the Ark. I'll answer for my men. Stout Scherirah looks grimly on the Moabites. A word from thee, and the whole Syrian army will join our banner, the Lion of Judah, that shall be our flag. The tyrant and his satraps, let them die, and then the rest must join us. We'll proclaim the covenant, and, leaving Babylon to a bloody fate, march on to Zion!'

'Zion, his youthful dream, Zion!'

'You muse!'

'King or no king, he is the Lord's anointed. Shall this hand, that poured the oil on his hallowed head, wash out the balmy signet with his blood? Must I slay him? Shall this kid be seethed even in its mother's milk?'

'His voice is low, and yet his face is troubled. How now, sir?'

'What art thou? Ah! Abidan, trusty, stanch Abidan! You see, Abidan, I was thinking, my good Abidan, all this may be the frenzy of a revel. Tomorrow's dawn may summon cooler counsels. The tattle of the table, it is sacred. Let us forget it; let us pass it over. The Lord may turn his heart. Who knows, who knows, Abidan!'

'Noble sir, a moment since your mind was like your faith, firm and resolved, and now——'

'School me not, school me not, good Abidan. There is that within my mind you cannot fathom; some secret sorrows which are all my own. Leave me, good friend, leave me awhile. When Israel calls me I shall not be wanting. Be sure of that, Abidan, be sure of that. Nay, do not go; the night is very rough, and the fair prophetess should not again stem the swelling river. I'll to my closet, and will soon return.'

Jabaster quitted the gallery, and entered a small apartment. Several large volumes, unclasped and open, were lying on various parts of the divan. Before them stood his brazen cabalistic table. He closed the chamber with a cautious air. He advanced into the centre of the apartment. He lifted up his hands to heaven, and clasped them with an expression almost of agony.

'Is it come to this?' he muttered in a tone of deep oppression. 'Is it come to this? What is't I have heard? what done? Down, tempting devil, down! O life! O glory! O my country, my chosen people, and my sacred creed! why do we live, why act? Why have we feeling for aught that's famous, or for aught that's holy? Let me die! let, let me die! The torture of existence is too great.'

He flung himself upon the couch; he buried his awful countenance in his robes. His mighty heart was convulsed with passion. There did he lie, that great and solemn man, prostrate and woe-begone.

'The noisy banquet lingers in my ear; I love to be alone.'

'With me?'

'Thou art myself; I have no other life.'

'Sweet bird! It is now a caliph.'

'I am what thou wiliest, soul of my sweet existence! Pomp and dominion, fame and victory, seem now but flawed and dimly-shaded gems compared with thy bright smile!'

'My plaintive nightingale, shall we hunt to-day?'

'Alas! my rose, I would rather lie upon this lazy couch, and gaze upon thy beauty!'

'Or sail upon the cool and azure lake, in some bright barque, like to a sea-nymph's shell, and followed by the swans?'

'There is no lake so blue as thy deep eye; there is no swan so white as thy round arm!'

'Or shall we launch our falcons in the air, and bring the golden pheasant to our feet?'

'I am the golden pheasant at thy feet; why wouldst thou richer prey?'

'Rememberest thou thy earliest visit to this dear kiosk, my gentle mute? There thou stoodst with folded arms and looks demure as day, and ever and anon with those dark eyes stealing a glance which made my cheek quite pale. Methinks I see thee even yet, shy bird. Dost know, I was so foolish when it quitted me, dost know I cried?'

'Ah, no! thou didst not cry?'

'Indeed, I think I did.'

'Tell me again, my own Schirene, indeed didst cry?'

'Indeed I did, my soul!'

'I would those tears were in some crystal vase, I'd give a province for the costly urn.'

She threw her arms around his neck and covered his face with kisses.

Sunset sounded from the minarets. They arose and wandered together in the surrounding paradise. The sky was tinted with a pale violet flush, a single star floating by the side of the white moon, that beamed with a dim lustre, soft and shapely as a pearl.

'Beautiful!' exclaimed the pensive Schirene, as she gazed upon the star. 'O, my Alroy, why cannot we ever live alone, and ever in a paradise?'

'I am wearied of empire,' replied Alroy with a smile, 'let us fly!'

'Is there no island, with all that can make life charming, and yet impervious to man? How little do we require! Ah! if these gardens, instead of being surrounded by hateful Bagdad, were only encompassed by some beautiful ocean!'

'My heart, we live in a paradise, and are seldom disturbed, thanks to Honain!'

'But the very consciousness that there are any other persons existing besides ourselves is to me painful. Every one who even thinks of you seems to rob me of a part of your being. Besides, I am weary of pomp and palaces. I should like to live in a sparry grot, and sleep upon a couch of sweet leaves!'

This interesting discussion was disturbed by a dwarf, who, in addition to being very small and very ugly, was dumb. He bowed before the Princess; and then had recourse to a great deal of pantomimic action, by which she discovered that it was dinnertime. No other person could have ventured to disturb the royal pair, but this little being was a privileged favourite.

So Alroy and Schirene entered the serail. An immense cresset-lamp, fed with perfumed oil, threw a soft light round the sumptuous chamber. At the end stood a row of eunuchs in scarlet dresses, and each holding a tall silver staff. The Caliph and the Sultana threw themselves upon a couch covered with a hundred cushions; on one side stood a group consisting of the captain of the guard and other officers of the household, on the other, of beautiful female slaves magnificently attired.

The line of domestics at the end of the apartment opened, and a body of slaves advanced, carrying trays of ivory and gold, and ebony and silver, covered with the choicest dainties, curiously prepared. These were in turn offered to the Caliph and the Sultana by their surrounding attendants. The Princess accepted a spoon made of a single pearl, the long, thin golden handle of which was studded with rubies, and condescended to partake of some saffron soup, of which she was fond. Afterwards she regaled herself with the breast of a cygnet, stuffed with almonds, and stewed with violets and cream. Having now a little satisfied her appetite, and wishing to show a mark of her favour to a particular individual, she ordered the captain of the guard instantly to send him the whole of the next course[74] with her compliments. Her attention was then engaged with a dish of those delicate ortolans that feed upon the vine-leaves of Schiraz, and with which the Governor of Nishapur took especial care that she should be well provided. Tearing the delicate birds to pieces with her still more delicate fingers, she insisted upon feeding Alroy, who of course yielded to her solicitations. In the meantime, they refreshed themselves with their favourite sherbet of pomegranates, and the golden wine of Mount Lebanon.[75] The Caliph, who could eat no more ortolans, although fed by such delicate fingers, was at length obliged to call for 'rice,' which was synonymous to commanding the banquet to disappear. The attendants now brought to each basins of gold, and ewers of rock crystal filled with rose water, with towels of that rare Egyptian linen which can be made only of the cotton that grows upon the banks of the Nile. While they amused themselves with eating sugar-plums, and drinking coffee flavoured with cinnamon, the female slaves danced before them in the most graceful attitudes to the melody of invisible musicians.

'My enchanting Schirene,' said the Caliph, 'I have dined, thanks to your attention, very well. These slaves of yours dance admirably, and are exceedingly beautiful. Your music, too, is beyond all praise; but, for my own part, I would rather be quite alone, and listening to one of your songs.'

'I have written a new one to-day. You shall hear it.' So saying, she clapped her little white hands, and all the attendants immediately withdrew.

'The stars are stealing forth, and so will I. Sorry sight! to view Jabaster, with a stealthy step, skulk like a thing dishonoured! Oh! may the purpose consecrate the deed! the die is cast.'

So saying, the High Priest, muffled up in his robe, emerged from his palace into the busy streets. It is at night that the vitality of Oriental life is most impressive. The narrow winding streets, crowded with a population breathing the now sufferable air, the illuminated coffee-houses, the groups of gay yet sober revellers, the music, and the dancing, and the animated recitals of the poet and the story-teller, all combine to invest the starry hours with a beguiling and even fascinating character of enjoyment and adventure.

It was the night after the visit of Abidan and the prophetess. Jabaster had agreed to meet Abidan in the square of the great mosque two hours after sunset, and thither he now repaired.

'I am somewhat before my time,' he said, as he entered the great square, over which the rising moon threw a full flood of light. A few dark shadows of human beings alone moved in the distance. The world was in the streets and coffee-houses. 'I am somewhat before my time,' said Jabaster. 'Conspirators are watchful. I am anxious for the meeting, and yet I dread it. Since he broke this business, I have never slept. My mind is a chaos. I will not think. If 'tis to be done, let it be done at once. I am more tempted to sheathe this dagger in Jabaster's breast than in Alroy's. If life or empire were the paltry stake, I would end a life that now can bring no joy, and yield authority that hath no charm; but Israel, Israel, thou for whom I have endured so much, let me forget Jabaster had a mother!

'But for this thought that links me with my God, and leads my temper to a higher state, how vain and sad, how wearisome and void, were this said world they think of! But for this thought, I could sit down and die. Yea! my great heart could crack, worn out, worn out; my mighty passions, with their fierce but flickering flame, sink down and die; and the strong brain that ever hath urged my course, and pricked me onward with perpetual thought, desert the rudder it so long hath held, like some baffled pilot in blank discomfiture, in the far centre of an unknown sea.

'Study and toil, anxiety and sorrow, mighty action, perchance Time, and disappointment, which is worse than all, have done their work, and not in vain. I am no longer the same Jabaster that gazed upon the stars of Caucasus. Methinks even they look dimmer than of yore. The glory of my life is fading. My leaves are sear, tinged, but not tainted. I am still the same in one respect; I have not left my God, in deed or thought. Ah! who art thou?'

'A friend to Israel.'

'I am glad that Israel hath a friend. Noble Abi-dan, I have well considered all that hath passed between us. Sooth to say, you touched upon a string I've played before, but kept it for my loneliness; a jarring tune, indeed a jarring tune, but so it is, and being so, let me at once unto your friends, Abi-dan.'

'Noble Jabaster, thou art what I deemed thee.'

'Abidan, they say the consciousness of doing justly is the best basis of a happy mind.'

'Even so.'

'And thou believest it?'

'Without doubt.'

'We are doing very justly?'

"Tis a weak word for such a holy purpose.'

'I am most wretched!'

The High Priest and his companion entered the house of Abidan. Jabaster addressed the already assembled guests.

'Brave Scherirah, it joys me to find thee here. In Israel's cause when was Scherirah wanting? Stout Zalmunna, we have not seen enough of each other: the blame is mine. Gentle prophetess, thy blessing!

'Good friends, why we meet here is known to all. Little did we dream of such a meeting when we crossed the Tigris. But that is nothing. We come to act, and not to argue. Our great minds, they are resolved: our solemn purpose requires no demonstration. If there be one among us who would have Israel a slave to Ishmael, who would lose all we have prayed for, all we have fought for, all we have won, and all for which we are prepared to die, if there be one among us who would have the Ark polluted, and Jehovah's altar stained with a Gentile sacrifice, if there be one among us who does not sigh for Zion, who would not yield his breath to build the Temple and gain the heritage his fathers lost, why, let him go! There is none such among us: then stay, and free your country!'

'We are prepared, great Jabaster; we are prepared, all, all!'

'I know it; you are like myself. Necessity hath taught decision. Now for our plans. Speak, Zalmunna.'

'Noble Jabaster, I see much difficulty. Alroy no longer quits his palace. Our entrance unwatched is, you well know, impossible. What say you, Scherirah?'

'I doubt not of my men, but war against Alroy is, to say nought of danger, of doubtful issue.'

'I am prepared to die, but not to fail,' said Abidan. 'We must be certain. Open war I fear. The mass of the army will side with their leaders, and they are with the tyrant. Let us do the deed, and they must join us.'

'Is it impossible to gain his presence to some sacrifice in honour of some by-gone victory; what think ye?'

'I doubt much, Jabaster. At this moment he little wishes to sanction our national ceremonies with his royal person. The woman assuredly will stay him. And, even if he come, success is difficult, and therefore doubtful.'

'Noble warriors, list to a woman's voice,' exclaimed the prophetess, coming forward. "Tis weak, but with such instruments, even the aspirations of a child, the Lord will commune with his chosen people. There is a secret way by which I can gain the gardens of the palace. To-morrow night, just as the moon is in her midnight bower, behold the accursed pile shall blaze. Let Abidan's troops be all prepared, and at the moment when the flames first ascend, march to the Seraglio gate as if with aid. The affrighted guard will offer no opposition. While the troops secure the portals, you yourselves, Zalmunna, Abidan, and Jabaster, rush to the royal chamber and do the deed. In the meantime, let brave Scherirah, with his whole division, surround the palace, as if unconscious of the mighty work. Then come you forward, show, if it need, with tears, the fated body to the soldiery, and announce the Theocracy.'

'It is the Lord who speaks,' said Abidan, who was doubtless prepared for the proposition. 'He has delivered them into our hands.'

'A bold plan,' said Jabaster, musing, 'and yet I like it. 'Tis quick, and that is something. I think 'tis sure.'

'It cannot fail,' exclaimed Zalmunna, 'for if the flame ascend not, still we are but where we were.'

'I am for it,' said Scherirah.

'Well, then,' said Jabaster, 'so let it be. Tomorrow's eve will see us here again prepared. Good night.'

'Good night, holy Priest. How seem the stars, Jabaster?'

'Very troubled; so have they been some days. What they portend I know not.'

'Health to Israel.'

'Let us hope so. Good night, sweet friends.'

'Good night, holy Jabaster. Thou art our cornerstone.'

'Israel hath no other hope but in Jabaster.'

'My Lord,' said Abidan, 'remain, I pray, one moment.'

'What is't? I fain would go.'

'Alroy must die, my Lord, but dost thou think a single death will seal the covenant?'

'The woman?'

'Ay! the woman! I was not thinking of the woman. Asriel, Ithamar, Medad?'

'Valiant soldiers! doubt not we shall find them useful instruments. I do not fear such loose companions. They follow their leaders, like other things born to obey. Having no head themselves, they must follow us who have.'

'I think so too. There is no other man who might be dangerous?'

Zalmunna and Scherirah cast their eyes upon the ground. There was a dead silence, broken by the prophetess.

'A judgment hath gone forth against Honain!' 'Nay! he is Lord Jabaster's brother,' said Abidan.

'It is enough to save a more inveterate foe to Israel, if such there be.'

'I have no brother, Sir. The man you speak of I will not slay, since there are others who may do that deed. And so again, good night.'

It was the dead of night, a single lamp burned in the chamber, which opened into an arched gallery that descended by a flight of steps into the gardens of the Serail.

A female figure ascended the flight with slow and cautious steps. She paused on the gallery, she looked around, one foot was in the chamber.

She entered. She entered a chamber of small dimensions, but richly adorned. In the farthest corner was a couch of ivory, hung with a gauzy curtain of silver tissue, which, without impeding respiration, protected the slumberer from the fell insects of an Oriental night. Leaning against an ottoman was a large brazen shield of ancient fashion, and near it some helmets and curious weapons.

'An irresistible impulse hath carried me into this chamber!' exclaimed the prophetess. 'The light haunted me like a spectre; and wheresoever I moved, it seemed to summon me.

'A couch and a slumberer!'

She approached the object, she softly withdrew the curtain. Pale and panting, she rushed back, yet with a light step. She beheld Alroy!

For a moment she leant against the wall, overpowered by her emotions. Again she advanced, and gazed on her unconscious victim.

'Can the guilty sleep like the innocent? Who would deem this gentle slumberer had betrayed the highest trust that ever Heaven vouchsafed to favoured man? He looks not like a tyrant and a traitor: calm his brow, and mild his placid breath! His long dark hair, dark as the raven's wing, hath broken from its fillet, and courses, like a wild and stormy night, over his pale and moon-lit brow. His cheek is delicate, and yet repose hath brought a flush; and on his lip there seems some word of love, that will not quit it. It is the same Alroy that blessed our vision when, like the fresh and glittering star of morn, he rose up in the desert, and bringing joy to others, brought to me only——

'Oh! hush my heart, and let thy secret lie hid in the charnel-house of crushed affections. Hard is the lot of woman: to love and to conceal is our sharp doom! O bitter life! O most unnatural lot! Man made society, and made us slaves. And so we droop and die, or else take refuge in idle fantasies, to which we bring the fervour that is meant for nobler ends.

'Beauteous hero! whether I bear thee most hatred or most love I cannot tell. Die thou must; yet I feel I should die with thee. Oh! that to-night could lead at the same time unto our marriage bed and funeral pyre. Must that white bosom bleed? and must those delicate limbs be hacked and handled by these bloody butchers? Is that justice? They lie, the traitors, when they call thee false to our God. Thou art thyself a god, and I could worship thee! See those beauteous lips; they move. Hark to the music!'

'Schirene, Schirene!'

'There wanted but that word to summon back my senses. Fool! whither is thy fancy wandering? I will not wait for tardy justice. I will do the deed myself. Shall I not kill my Sisera?' She seized a dagger from the ottoman, a rare and highly-tempered blade. Up she raised it in the air, and dashed it to his heart with superhuman force. It struck against the talisman which Jabaster had given to Alroy, and which, from a lingering superstition, he still wore; it struck, and shivered into a thousand pieces. The Caliph sprang from his couch; his eyes met the prophetess, standing over him in black despair, with the hilt of the dagger in her hand.

'What is all this? Schirene! Who art thou? Esther!' He jumped from the couch, called to Pharez, and seized her by both hands. 'Speak!' he continued. 'Art thou Esther? What dost thou here?'

She broke into a wild laugh; she wrestled with his grasp, and pulled him towards the gallery. He beheld the chief tower of the Serail in flames. Joining her hands together, grasping them both in one of his, and dragging her towards the ottoman, he seized a helmet and flung it upon the mighty shield. It sounded like a gong. Pharez started from his slumbers, and rushed into the chamber.

'Pharez! Treason! treason! Send instant orders that the palace gates be opened on no pretence whatever. Go, fly! See the captain himself. Summon the household. Order all to arms. Speed, for our lives!'

The whole palace was now roused. Alroy delivered Esther, exhausted, and apparently senseless, to a guard of eunuchs. Slaves and attendants poured in from all directions. Soon arrived Schirene, with dishevelled hair and hurried robes, attended by a hundred maidens, each bearing a torch.

'My soul, what ails thee?'

'Nothing, sweetest; all will soon be well,' replied Alroy, picking up, and examining the fragments of the shivered dagger, which he had just discovered.

'My life has been attempted; the palace is in flames; I suspect the city is in insurrection. Look to your mistress, maidens!' Schirene fell into their arms. 'I will soon be back.' So saying, he hurried to the grand court.

Several thousand persons, for the population of the Serail and its liberties was very considerable, were assembled in the grand court; eunuchs, women, pages, slaves, and servants, and a few soldiers; all in confusion and alarm, fire raging within, and mysterious and terrible outcries without. A cry of 'The Caliph! the Caliph!' announced the arrival of Alroy, and produced a degree of comparative silence.

'Where is the captain of the guard?' he exclaimed. 'That's well. Open the gates to none. Who will leap the wall and bear a message to Asriel? You? That's well too. To-morrow you shall yourself command. Where's Mesrour? Take the eunuch guard and the company of gardeners,[76] and suppress the flames at all cost. Pull down the intervening buildings. Abidan's troop arrived with succour, eh! I doubt it not. I expected them. Open to none. They force an entrance, eh! I thought so. So that javelin has killed a traitor. Feed me with arms. I'll keep the gate. Send again to Asriel. Where's Pharez?'

'By your side, my lord.'

'Run to the Queen, my faithful Pharez, and tell her that all's well. I wish it were! Didst ever hear a din so awful? Methinks all the tambours and cymbals of the city are in full chorus. Foul play, I guess. Oh! for Asriel! Has Pharez returned?'

'I am by your side, my lord.'

'How's the Queen?'

'She would gladly join your side.'

'No, no! Keep the gates there. Who says they are making fires before them? Tis true. We must sally, if the worst come to the worst, and die at least like soldiers. O Asriel! Asriel!'

'May it please your Highness, the troops are pouring in from all quarters.'

''Tis Asriel.'

'No, your Highness, 'tis not the guard. Methinks they are Scherirah's men.'

'Hum! What it all is, I know not; but very foul play I do not doubt. Where's Honain?'

'With the Queen, Sire.'

''Tis well. What's that shout?'

'Here's the messenger from Asriel. Make way! way!'

'Well! how is't, Sir?'

'Please your Highness, I could not reach the guard.'

'Could not reach the guard! God of my fathers! who should let thee?'

'Sire, I was taken prisoner.'

'Prisoner! By the thunder of Sinai, are we at war? Who made thee prisoner?'

'Sire, they have proclaimed thy death.'

'Who?'

'The council of the Elders. So I heard. Abidan, Zalmunna——'

'Rebels and dogs! Who else?'

'The High Priest.'

'Hah! Is it there? Pharez, fetch me some drink. Is it true Scherirah has joined them?'

'His force surrounds the Serail. No aid can reach us without cutting through his ranks.'

'Oh! that I were there with my good guard! Are we to die here like rats, fairly murdered? Cowardly knaves! Hold out, hold out, my men! 'Tis sharp work, but some of us will smile at this hereafter. Who stands by Alroy to-night bravely and truly, shall have his heart's content to-morrow. Fear not: I was not born to die in a civic broil. I bear a charmed life. So to it.'

'Go to the Caliph, good Honain, I pray thee, go. I can support myself, he needs thy counsel. Bid him not expose his precious life. The wicked men! Asriel must soon be here. What sayest thou?'

'There is no fear. Their plans are ill-devised. I have long expected this stormy night, and feel even now more anxious than alarmed.'

''Tis at me they aim; it is I whom they hate. The High Priest, too! Ay, ay! Thy proud brother, good Honain, I have ever felt he would not rest until he drove me from this throne, my right; or washed my hated name from out our annals in my life's blood. Wicked, wicked Jabaster! He frowned upon me from the first, Honain. Is he indeed thy brother?'

'I care not to remember. He aims at something further than thy life; but Time will teach us more than all our thoughts.'

The fortifications of the Serail resisted all the efforts of the rebels. Scherirah remained in his quarters, with his troops under arms, and recalled the small force that he had originally sent out as much to watch the course of events as to assist Abidan. Asriel and Ithamar poured down their columns in the rear of that chieftain, and by dawn a division of the guard had crossed the river, the care of which had been entrusted to Scherirah, and had thrown themselves into the palace. Alroy sallied forth at the head of these fresh troops. His presence decided a result which was perhaps never doubtful. The division of Abidan fought with the desperation that became their fortunes. The carnage was dreadful, but their discomfiture complete. They no longer acted in masses, or with any general system. They thought only of self-preservation, or of selling their lives at the dearest cost. Some dispersed, some escaped. Others entrenched themselves in houses, others fortified the bazaar. All the horrors of war in the streets were now experienced. The houses were in flames, the thoroughfares flowed with blood.

At the head of a band of faithful followers, Abidan proved himself, by his courage and resources, worthy of success. At length, he was alone, or surrounded only by his enemies. With his back against a building in a narrow street, where the number of his opponents only embarrassed them, the three foremost of his foes fell before his irresistible scimitar. The barricaded door yielded to the pressure of the multitude. Abidan rushed up the narrow stairs, and, gaining a landing-place, turned suddenly round, and cleaved the skull of his nearest pursuer. He hurled the mighty body at his followers, and, retarding their advance, himself dashed onward, and gained the terrace of the mansion. Three soldiers of the guard followed him as he bounded from terrace to terrace. One, armed with a javelin, hurled it at the chieftain. The weapon slightly wounded Abidan, who, drawing it from his arm, sent it back to the heart of its owner. The two other soldiers, armed only with swords, gained upon him. He arrived at the last terrace in the cluster of buildings. He stood at bay on the brink of the precipice. He regained his breath. They approached him. He dodged them in their course. Suddenly, with admirable skill, he flung his scimitar edgewise at the legs of his farthest foe, who stopped short, roaring with pain. The chieftain sprang at the foremost, and hurled him down into the street below, where he was dashed to atoms. A trap-door offered itself to the despairing eye of the rebel. He descended and found himself in a room filled with women. They screamed, he rushed through them, and descending a Staircase, entered a chamber tenanted by a bed-ridden old man. The ancient invalid enquired the cause of the uproar, and died of fright before he could receive an answer, at the sight of the awful being before him, covered with streaming blood. Abidan secured the door, washed his blood-stained face, and disguising himself in the dusty robes of the deceased Armenian, sallied forth to watch the fray. The obscure street was silent. The chieftain proceeded unmolested. At the corner he found a soldier holding a charger for his captain. Abidan, unarmed, seized a poniard from the soldier's belt, stabbed him to the heart, and vaulting on the steed, galloped towards the river. No boat was to be found; he breasted the stream upon the stout courser. He reached the opposite bank. A company of camels were reposing by the side of a fountain. Alarm had dispersed their drivers. He mounted the fleetest in appearance; he dashed to the nearest gate of the city. The guard at the gate refused him a passage. He concealed his agitation. A marriage procession, returning from the country, arrived. He rushed into the centre of it, and overset the bride in her gilded wagon. In the midst of the confusion, the shrieks, the oaths, and the scuffle, he forced his way through the gate, scoured over the country, and never stopped until he had gained the desert.

The uproar died away. The shouts of warriors, the shrieks of women, the wild clang of warfare, all were silent. The flames were extinguished, the carnage ceased. The insurrection was suppressed, and order restored. The city, all the houses of which were closed, was patrolled by the conquering troops, and by sunset the conqueror himself, in his hall of state, received the reports and the congratulations of his chieftains. The escape of Abidan seemed counterbalanced by the capture of Jabaster. After performing prodigies of valour, the High Priest had been overpowered, and was now a prisoner in the Serail. The conduct of Scherirah was not too curiously criticised; a commission was appointed to enquire into the mysterious affair; and Alroy retired to the bath[77] to refresh himself after the fatigues of the victory which he could not consider a triumph.

As he reposed upon his couch, melancholy and exhausted, Schirene was announced. The Princess threw herself upon his neck and covered him with embraces. His heart yielded to her fondness, his spirit became lighter, his depression melted away.

'My ruby!' said Schirene, and she spoke in a low smothered voice, her face hidden and nestled in his breast. 'My ruby! dost thou love me?'

He smiled in fondness as he pressed her to his heart.

'My ruby, thy pearl is so frightened, it dare not look upon thee. Wicked men! 'tis I whom they hate, 'tis I whom they would destroy.'

'There is no danger, sweet. 'Tis over now. Speak not, nay, do not think of it.'

'Ah! wicked men! There is no joy on earth while such things live. Slay Alroy, their mighty master, who, from vile slaves, hath made them princes! Ungrateful churls! I am so alarmed, I ne'er shall sleep again. What! slay my innocent bird, my pretty bird, my very heart! I'll not believe it. It is I whom they hate. I am sure they will kill me. You shall never leave me, no, no, no, no! You shall not leave me, love, never, never! Didst hear a noise? Methinks they are even here, ready to plunge their daggers in our hearts, our soft, soft hearts! I think you love me, child; indeed, I think you do!'

'Take courage, heart! There is no fear, my soul; I cannot love thee more, or else I would.'

'All joy is gone! I ne'er shall sleep again. O my soul! art thou indeed alive? Do I indeed embrace my own Alroy, or is it all a wild and troubled dream, and are my arms clasped round a shadowy ghost, myself a spectre in a sepulchre? Wicked, wicked men! Can it indeed be true? What, slay Alroy! my joy, my only life! Ah! woe is me; our bright felicity hath fled for ever!'

'Not so, sweet child; we are but as we were. A few quick hours, and all will be as bright as if no storm had crossed our sunny days.'

'Hast seen Asriel? He says such fearful things!'

'How now?'

'Ah me! I am desolate. I have no friend.'

'Schirene!'

'They will have my blood. I know they will have my blood.'

'Indeed, an idle fancy.'

'Idle! Ask Asriel, question Ithamar. Idle! 'tis written in their tablets, their bloody scroll of rapine and of murder. Thy death led only to mine, and, had they hoped my bird would but have yielded his gentle mate, they would have spared him. Ay! ay! 'tis I whom they hate, 'tis I whom they would destroy. This form, I fear it has lost its lustre, but still 'tis thine, and once thou saidst thou lovedst it; this form was to have been hacked and mangled; this ivory bosom was to have been ripped up and tortured, and this warm blood, that flows alone for thee, that fell Jabaster was to pour its tide upon the altar of his ancient vengeance. He ever hated me!'

'Jabaster! Schirene! Where are we, and what are we? Life, life, they lie, that call thee Nature! Nature never sent these gusts of agony. Oh! my heart will break. I drove him from my thought, and now she calls him up, and now must I remember he is my-prisoner! God of heaven, God of my fathers, is it come to this? Why did he not escape? Why must Abidan, a common cut-throat, save his graceless life, and this great soul, this stern and mighty being—— Ah me! I have lived long enough. Would they had not failed, would——'

'Stop, stop, Alroy! I pray thee, love, be calm. I came to soothe thee, not to raise thy passions. I did not say Jabaster willed thy death, though Asriel says so; 'tis me he wars against; and if indeed Jabaster be a man so near thy heart, if he indeed be one so necessary to thy prosperity, and cannot live in decent order with thy slave that's here, I know my duty, Sir. I would not have thy fortunes farred to save my single heart, although I think 'twill break. I will go, I will die, and deem the hardest accident of life but sheer prosperity if it profit thee.'

'O Schirene! what wouldst thou? This, this is torture.'

'To see thee safe and happy; nothing more.'

'I am both, if thou art.'

'Care not for me, I am nothing.'

'Thou art all to me.'

'Calm thyself, my soul. It grieves me much that when I came to soothe I have only galled thee. All's well, all's well. Say that Jabaster lives. What then? He lives, and may he prove more duteous than before; that's all.'

'He lives, he is my prisoner, he awaits his doom. It must be given.'

'Yes, yes!'

'Shall we pardon?'

'My lord will do that which it pleases him.'

'Nay, nay, Schirene, I pray thee be more kind. I am most wretched. Speak, what wouldst thou?'

'If I must speak, I say at once, his life.'

'Ah me!'

'If our past loves have any charm, if the hope of future joy, not less supreme, be that which binds thee to this shadowy world, as it does me, and does alone, I say his life, his very carnal life. He stands between us and our loves, Alroy, and ever has done. There is no happiness if Jabaster breathe; nor can I be the same Schirene to thee as I have been, if this proud rebel live to spy my conduct.'

'Banish him, banish him!'

'To herd with rebels. Is this thy policy?'

'O Schirene! I love not this man, although me-thinks I should: yet didst thou know but all!'

'I know too much, Alroy. From the first he has been to me a hateful thought. Come, come, sweet bird, a boon, a boon unto thy own Schirene, who was so frightened by these wicked men! I fear it has done more mischief than thou deemest. Ay! robbed us of our hopes. It may be so. A boon, a boon! It is not much I ask: a traitor's head. Come, give me thy signet ring. It will not; nay, then, I'll take it. What, resist! I know thou oft hast told me a kiss could vanquish all denial. There it is. Is't sweet? Shalt have another, and another too. I've got the ring! Farewell, my lovely bird, I'll soon return to pillow in thy nest.'

'She has got the ring! What's this? what's this? Schirene! art gone? Nay, surely not. She jests. Jabaster! A traitor's head! What ho! there. Pharez, Pharez!'

'My lord.'

'Passed the Queen that way?'

'She did, my lord.'

'In tears?'

'Nay! very joyful!'

'Call Honain, quick as my thought. Honain! Honain! He waits without. I have seen the best of life, that's very sure. My heart is cracking. She surely jests! Hah! Honain. Pardon these distracted looks. Fly to the Armoury! fly, fly!'

'For what, my lord?'

'Ay! for what, for what! My brain it wanders. Thy brother, thy great brother, the Queen, the Queen has stolen my signet ring, that is, I gave it her. Fly, fly! or in a word, Jabaster is no more. He is gone. Pharez! your arm; I swoon!'

'His Highness is sorely indisposed to-day.'

'They say he swooned this morn.'

'Ay, in the bath.'

'No, not in the bath. 'Twas when he heard of Jabaster's death.'

'How died he, Sir?'

'Self-strangled. His mighty heart could not endure disgrace, and thus he ended all his glorious deeds.'

'A great man!'

'We shall not soon see his match. The Queen had gained his pardon, and herself flew to the Armoury to bear the news; alas! too late.'

'These are strange times. Jabaster dead!'

'A very great event.'

'Who will be High Priest?'

'I doubt if the appointment will be filled up.'

'Sup you with the Lord Ithamar to-night?'

'I do.'

'I also. We'll go together. The Queen had gained his pardon. Hum! 'tis strange.'

'Passing so. They say Abidan has escaped?'

'I hear it. Shall we meet Medad to-night?'

''Tis likely.'

CHAPTER X.

The Fall of Alroy

SHE comes not yet! her cheerful form, not yet it sparkles in our mournful sky. She comes not yet! the shadowy stars seem sad and lustreless without their Queen. She comes not yet!'

'WE ARE THE WATCHERS OF THE MOON,[78] AND LIVE IN LONELINESS TO HERALD LIGHT.'

'She comes not yet! her sacred form, not yet it summons to our holy feast. She comes not yet! our brethren far wait mute and motionless the saintly beam. She comes not yet!'

'WE ARE THE WATCHERS OF THE MOON, AND LIVE IN LONELINESS TO HERALD LIGHT.'

'She comes, she comes! her beauteous form sails with soft splendour in the glittering air. She comes, she comes! The beacons fire, and tell the nation that the month begins! She comes, she comes!'

'WE ARE THE WATCHERS OF THE MOON, TO TELL THE NATION THAT THE MONTH BEGINS.'

Instantly the holy watchers fired the beacons on the mountain top, and anon a thousand flames blazed round the land. From Caucasus to Lebanon, on every peak a crown of light.

'Sire! a Tatar has arrived from Hamadan, who will see none but thyself. I have told him your Highness was engaged, and sent him to the Lord Honain; but all denial is lost upon him. And as I thought perhaps the Lady Miriam——'

'From Hamadan? You did well, Pharez. Admit him.'

The Tatar entered.

'Well, Sir; good news, I hope!'

'Sire, pardon me, the worst. I come from the Lord Abner, with orders to see the Caliph, and none else.'

'Well, Sir, you see the Caliph. Your mission? What of the Viceroy?'

'Sire, he bade me tell thee, that, the moment the beacon that announced the Feast of the New Moon was fired on Caucasus, the dreaded monarch of Karasmé, the great Alp Arslan, entered thy kingdom, and now overruns all Persia.'

'Hah! and Abner?'

'Is in the field, and prays for aid.'

'He shall have it. This is indeed great news! When left you Hamadan?'

'Night and day I have journeyed upon the swiftest dromedary. The third morn sees me at Bagdad.'

'You have done your duty. See this faithful courier be well tended, Pharez. Summon the Lord Honain.'

'Alp Arslan! Hah! a very famous warrior. The moment the beacon was fired. No sudden impulse then, but long matured. I like it not.'

'Sire,' said Pharez, re-entering, 'a Tatar has arrived from the frontiers of the province, who will see none but thyself. I have told him your Highness was deeply busied, and as methinks he brings but the same news, I——'

"Tis very likely; yet never *think*, good Pharez. I'll see the man.' The Tatar entered.

'Well, Sir, how now! from whom?'

'From Mozul. The Governor bade me see the Caliph and none else, and tell your Highness that the moment the beacon that announced the Feast of the New Moon was fired on the mountains, the fell rebel Abidan raised the standard of Judah in the province, and proclaimed war against your Majesty.'

'In any force?'

'The royal power keeps within their walls.'

'Sufficient answer. Part of the same movement. We shall have some trouble. Hast summoned Honain?'

'I have, Sire.'

'Go, see this messenger be duly served, and, Pharez, come hither: let none converse with them. You understand?'

'Your Highness may assure yourself.'

'Abidan come to life. He shall not escape so well this time. I must see Scherirah. I much suspect——what's this? More news!'

A third Tatar entered.

'May it please your Highness, this Tatar has arrived from the Syrian frontier.'

'Mischief in the wind, I doubt not. Speak out, knave!'

'Sire! pardon me; I bear but sad intelligence.'

'Out with the worst!'

'I come from the Lord Medad.'

'Well! has he rebelled? It seems a catching fever.'

'Ah! no, dread Sire, Lord Medad has no thought but for thy glory. Alas! alas! he has now to guard it against fearful odds. Lord Medad bade me see the Caliph and none else, and tell your Highness, that the moment the beacon which announced the Feast of the New Moon was fired on Lebanon, the Sultan of Roum and the old Arabian Caliph unfurled the standard of their Prophet, in great array, and are now marching towards Bagdad.'

'A clear conspiracy! Has Honain arrived? Summon a council of the Vizirs instantly. The world is up against me. Well! I'm sick of peace. They shall not find me napping!'

'You see, my lords,' said Alroy, ere the council broke up, 'we must attack them singly. There can be no doubt of that. If they join, we must combat at great odds. 'Tis in detail that we must route them. I will myself to Persia. Ithamar must throw himself between the Sultan and Abidan, Medad fall back on Ithamar. Scherirah must guard the capital. Honain, you are Regent. And so farewell. I shall set off to-night. Courage, brave companions. 'Tis a storm, but many a cedar survives the thunderbolt.'

The council broke up.

'My own Scherirah!' said the Caliph, as they retired, 'stay awhile. I would speak with you alone. Honain,' continued Alroy, following the Grand Vizir out of the chamber, and leaving Scherirah alone, 'Honain, I have not yet interchanged a word with you in private. What think you of all this?'

'Sire, I am prepared for the worst, but hope the best.'

''Tis wise. If Abner could only keep that Karasmian in check! I am about to speak with Scherirah alone. I do suspect him much.'

'I'll answer for his treason.'

'Hah! I do suspect him. Therefore I give him no command. I would not have him too near his old companion, eh? We will garrison the city with his rebels.'

'Sire, these are not moments to be nice. Scherirah is a valiant captain, a very valiant captain, but lend me thy signet ring, I pray thee, Sire.'

Alroy turned pale.

'No, Sir, it has left me once, and never shall again. You have touched upon a string that makes me sad. There is a burden on my conscience, why, or what, I know not. I am innocent, you know I am innocent, Honain!'

'I'll answer for your Highness. He who has enough of the milk of human kindness to spare a thing like Scherirah, when he stands in his way, may well be credited for the nobler mercy that spared his better.'

'Ah me! there's madness in the thought. Why is he not here? Had I but followed; tush! tush! Go see the Queen, and tell her all that has happened. I'll to Scherirah.'

The Caliph returned.

'Thy pardon, brave Scherirah; in these moments my friends will pardon lapse of courtesy.'

'Your Highness is too considerate.'

'You see, Scherirah, how the wind blows, brave heart. There's much to do, no doubt. I am in sad want of some right trusty friend, on whose devoted bosom I can pillow all my necessities. I was thinking of sending you against this Arslan, but perhaps 'tis better that I should go myself. These are moments one should not seem to shrink, and yet we know not how affairs may run; no, we know not. The capital, the surrounding province: one disaster and these false Moslemin may rise against us. I should stay here, but if I leave Scherirah, I leave myself. I feel that deeply; 'tis a consolation. It may be that I must fall back upon the city. Be prepared, Scherirah. Let me fall back upon supporting friends. You have a great trust. Oh! use it wisely! Worthily I am sure you must do.'

'Your Highness may rest assured I have no other thought but for your weal and glory. Doubt not my devotion, Sire. I am not one of those mealy-mouthed youths, full of their own deeds and lip-worship, Sire, but I have a life devoted to your service, and ready at all times to peril all things.'

'I know that, Scherirah, I know it; I feel it deeply. What think you of these movements?'

'They are not ill combined, and yet I doubt not your Majesty will prove your fortunes most triumphant.'

'Think you the soldiery are in good cue?' 'I'll answer for my own. They are rough fellows, like myself, a little too blunt, perhaps, your Highness. We are not holiday guards, but we know our duty, and we will do it.'

'That's well, that's all I want. I shall review the troops before I go. Let a donative be distributed among them; and, 'by-the-bye, I have always forgotten it, your legion should be called the Legion of Syria. We owe our fairest province to their arms.'

'I shall convey to them your Highness' wish. Were it possible, 'twould add to their devotion.'

'I do not wish it. They are my very children. Sup at the Serail to-night, Scherirah. We shall be very private. Yet let us drink together ere we part. We are old friends, you know. Hast not forgotten our ruined city?'

Alroy entered the apartment of Schirene. 'My soul! thou knowest all?'

She sprang forward and threw her arms around his neck.

'Fear not, my life, we'll not disgrace our Queen. 'Twill be quick work. Two-thirds of them have been beaten before, and for the new champion, our laurels must not fade, and his blood shall nourish fresh ones.'

'Dearest, dearest Alroy, go not thyself, I pray thee. May not Asriel conquer?'

'I hope so, in my company. For a time we part, a short one. 'Tis our first parting: may it be our last!'

'Oh! no, no, no: oh! say not we must part.'

'The troops are under arms; to-morrow's dawn will hear my trumpet.'

'I will not quit thee, no! I will not quit thee. What business has Schirene without Alroy? Hast thou not often told me I am thy inspiration? In the hour of danger shall I be wanting? Never! I will not quit thee; no, I will not quit thee.'

'Thou art ever present in my thoughts, my soul. In the battle I shall think of her for whom alone I conquer.'

'Nay, nay, I'll go, indeed I must, Alroy. I'll be no hindrance, trust me, sweet boy, I will not. I'll have no train, no, not a single maid. Credit me, I know how a true soldier's wife should bear herself. I'll watch thee sleeping, and I'll tend thee wounded, and when thou goest forth to combat I'll gird thy sabre round thy martial side, and whisper triumph with victorious kisses.'

'My own Schirene, there's victory in thine eyes. We'll beat them, girl.'

'Abidan, doubly false Abidan! would he were doubly hanged! Ere she died, the fatal prophetess foretold this time, and gloated on his future treachery.'

'Think not of him.'

'And the Karasmian; think you he is very strong?' 'Enough, love, for our glory. He is a potent warrior: I trust that Abner will not rob us of our intended victory.'

'So you triumph, I care not by whose sword. Dost go indeed to-morrow?'

'At break of dawn. I pray thee stay, my sweet!' 'Never! I will not quit thee. I am quite prepared. At break of dawn? 'Tis near on midnight now. I'll lay me down upon this couch awhile, and travel in my litter. Art sure Alp Arslan is himself in the field?'

'Quite sure, my sweet.'

'Confusion on his crown! We'll conquer. Goes Asriel with us?' 'Ay!'

'That's well; at break of dawn. I'm somewhat drowsy. Methinks I'll sleep awhile.'

'Do, my best heart; I'll to my cabinet, and at break of dawn I'll wake thee with a kiss.'

The Caliph repaired to his cabinet, where his secretaries were occupied in writing. As he paced the chamber, he dictated to them the necessary instructions.

'Who is the officer on guard?'

'Benaiah, Sire.'

'I remember him. He saved me a broken skull upon the Tigris. This is for him. The Queen accompanies us. She is his charge. These papers for the Vizir. Let the troops be under arms by daybreak. This order of the day for the Lord Asriel. Send this instantly to Hamadan. Is the Tatar despatched to Medad? 'Tis well. You have done your duty. Now to rest. Pharez?'

'My lord.'

'I shall not sleep to-night. Give me my drink. Go rest, good boy. I have no wants. Good night.'

'Good night, my gracious lord!'

'Let me ponder! I am alone. I am calm, and yet my spirit is not quick. I am not what I was. Four-and-twenty hours ago who would have dreamed of this? All at stake again! Once more in the field, and struggling at once for empire and existence! I do lack the mighty spirit of my former days. I am not what I was. I have little faith. All about me seems changed, and dull, and grown mechanical. Where are those flashing eyes and conquering visages that clustered round me on the battle eve, round me, the Lord's anointed? I see none such. They are changed, as I am. Why! this Abidan was a host, and now he fights against me. She spoke of the prophetess; I remember that woman was the stirring trumpet of our ranks, and now where is she? The victim of my justice! And where is he, the mightier far, the friend, the counsellor, the constant guide, the master of my boyhood; the firm, the fond, the faithful guardian of all my bright career; whose days and nights were one unbroken study to make me glorious? Alas! I feel more like a doomed and desperate renegade than a young hero on the eve of battle, flushed with the memory of unbroken triumphs!

'Hah! what awful form art thou that risest from the dusky earth before me? Thou shouldst be one I dare not name, yet will: the likeness of Jabaster. Away! why frownest thou upon me? I did not slay thee. Do I live, or dream, or what? I see him, ay! I see thee. I fear thee not, I fear nothing. I am Alroy.

'Speak, oh speak! I do conjure thee, mighty spectre, speak. By all the memory of the past, although 'tis madness, I do conjure thee, let me hear again the accents of my boyhood.'

'*Alroy, Alroy, Alroy!*'

'I listen, as to the last trump.'

'*Meet me on the plain of Nehauend.*'

"Tis gone! As it spoke it vanished. It was Jabaster! God of my fathers, it was Jabaster! Life is growing too wild. My courage is broken! I could lie down and die. It was Jabaster! The voice sounds in my ear like distant thunder: "*Meet me on the plain of Nehauend.*" I'll not fail thee, noble ghost, although I meet my doom. Jabaster! Have I seen Jabaster! Indeed! indeed! Methinks I'm mad. Hah! What's that?'

An awful clap of thunder broke over the palace, followed by a strange clashing sound that seemed to come from one of the chambers. The walls of the Serail rocked.

'An earthquake!' exclaimed Alroy. 'Would that the earth would open and swallow all! Hah! Pharez, has it roused thee, too? Pharez, we live in strange times.'

'Your Highness is very pale.'

'And so art thou, lad! Wouldst have me merry? Pale! we may well be pale, didst thou know all. Hah! that awful sound again! I cannot bear it, Pharez, I cannot bear it. I have borne many things, but this I cannot.'

'My lord, 'tis in the Armoury.'

'Run, see. No, I'll not be alone. Where's Benaiah? Let him go. Stay with me, Pharez, stay with me. I pray thee stay, my child.'

Pharez led the Caliph to a couch, on which Alroy lay pale and trembling. In a few minutes he inquired whether Benaiah had returned.

'Even now he comes, Sire.'

'Well, how is it?'

'Sire! a most awful incident. As the thunder broke over the palace, the sacred standard fell from its resting-place, and has shivered into a thousand pieces. Strange to say, the sceptre of Solomon can neither be found nor traced.'

'Say nothing of the past, as ye love me, lads. Let none enter the Armoury. Leave me, Benaiah, leave me, Pharez.'

They retired. Alroy watched their departure with a glance of inexpressible anguish. The moment that they had disappeared, he flew to the couch, and throwing himself upon his knees, and, covering his face with his hands, burst into passionate tears, and exclaimed, 'O! my God, I have deserted thee, and now thou hast deserted me!'

Sleep crept over the senses of the exhausted and desperate Caliph. He threw himself upon the divan, and was soon buried in profound repose. He might have slept an hour; he awoke suddenly. From the cabinet in which he slept, you entered a vast hall, through a lofty and spacious arch, generally covered with drapery, which was now withdrawn. To the astonishment of Alroy, this presence-chamber appeared at this moment to blaze with light. He rose from his couch, he advanced; he perceived, with feelings of curiosity and fear, that the hall was filled with beings, terrible indeed to behold, but to his sight more terrible than strange. In the colossal and mysterious forms that lined the walls of the mighty chamber, and each of which held in its extended arm a streaming torch, he recognised the awful Afrites. At the end of the hall, upon a sumptuous throne, surrounded by priests and courtiers, there was seated a monarch, on whom Alroy had before gazed, Solomon the Great! Alroy beheld him in state and semblance the same Solomon, whose sceptre the Prince of the Captivity had seized in the royal tombs of Judah.

The strange assembly seemed perfectly unconscious of the presence of the child of Earth, who, with a desperate courage, leant against a column of the arch, and watched, with wonder, their mute and motionless society. Nothing was said, nothing done. No one moved, no one, even by gesture, seemed sensible of the presence of any other apparition save himself.

Suddenly there advanced from the bottom of the hall, near unto Alroy, a procession. Pages and dancing girls, with eyes of fire and voluptuous gestures, warriors with mighty arms, and venerable forms with ample robes and flowing beards. And, as they passed, even with all the activity of their gestures, they made no sound; neither did the musicians, whereof there was a great band playing upon harps and psalteries, and timbrels and cornets, break, in the slightest degree, the almighty silence.

This great crowd poured on in beautiful order, the procession never terminating, yet passing thrice round the hall, bowing to him that was upon the throne, and ranging themselves in ranks before the Afrites.

And there came in twelve forms, bearing a great seal: the stone green, and the engraven characters of living flame, and the characters were those on the talisman of Jabaster, which Alroy still wore next to his heart. And the twelve forms placed the great seal before Solomon, and humbled themselves, and the King bowed. At the same moment Alroy was sensible of a pang next to his heart. He instantly put his hand to the suffering spot, and lo! the talisman crumbled into dust.

The procession ceased; a single form advanced. Recent experience alone prevented Alroy from sinking before the spectre of Jabaster. Such was the single form. It advanced, bearing the sceptre. It advanced, it knelt before the throne, it offered the sceptre to the crowned and solemn vision. And the form of Solomon extended its arm, and took the sceptre, and instantly the mighty assembly vanished!

Alroy advanced immediately into the chamber, but all was dark and silent. A trumpet sounded. He recognised the note of his own soldiery. He groped his way to a curtain, and, pulling it aside, beheld the first streak of dawn.

Once more upon his charger, once more surrounded by his legions, once more his senses dazzled and inflamed by the waving banners and the inspiring trumpets, once more conscious of the power still at his command, and the mighty stake for which he was about to play, Alroy in a great degree recovered his usual spirit and self-possession. His energy returned with his excited pulse, and the vastness of the impending danger seemed only to stimulate the fertility of his genius.

He pushed on by forced marches towards Media, at the head of fifty thousand men. At the end of the second day's march, fresh couriers arrived from Abner, informing him that, unable to resist the valiant and almost innumerable host of the King of Karasmé, he had entirely evacuated Persia, and had concentrated his forces in Louristan. Alroy, in consequence of this information, despatched orders to Scherirah, to join him with his division instantly, and leave the capital to its fate.

They passed again the mountains of Kerrund, and joined Abner and the army of Media, thirty thousand strong, on the river Abzah. Here Alroy rested one night, to refresh his men, and on the ensuing morn pushed on to the Persian frontier, unexpectedly attacked the advanced posts of Alp Arslan, and beat them back with great loss into the province. But the force of the King of Karasmé was so considerable, that the Caliph did not venture on a general engagement, and therefore he fell back, and formed in battle array upon the neighbouring plain of Nehauend, the theatre of one of his earliest and most brilliant victories, where he awaited the hourly-expected arrival of Scherirah.

The King of Karasmé, who was desirous of bringing affairs to an issue, and felt confident in his superior force, instantly advanced. In two or three days at farthest, it was evident that a battle must be fought that would decide the fate of the East.

On the morn ensuing their arrival at Nehauend, while the Caliph was out hunting, attended only by a few officers, he was suddenly attacked by an ambushed band of Karasmians. Alroy and his companions defended themselves with such desperation that they at length succeeded in beating off their assailants, although triple their number. The leader of the Karasmians, as he retreated, hurled a dart at the Caliph, which must have been fatal, had not a young officer of the guard interposed his own breast, and received the deadly wound. The party, in confusion, returned with all speed to the camp, Alroy himself bearing the expiring victim of desperate loyalty and military enthusiasm.

The bleeding officer was borne to the royal pavilion, and placed upon the imperial couch. The most skilful leech was summoned; he examined the wound, but shook his head. The dying warrior was himself sensible of his desperate condition. His agony could only be alleviated by withdrawing the javelin, which would occasion his immediate decease. He desired to be left alone with his Sovereign.

'Sire!' said the officer, 'I must die; and I die without a pang. To die in your service, I have ever considered the most glorious end. Destiny has awarded it to me;, and if I have not met my fate upon the field of battle, it is some consolation that my death has preserved the most valuable of lives. Sire! I have a sister.'

'Waste not thy strength, dear friend, in naming her. Rest assured I shall ever deem thy relatives my own.'

'I doubt it not. Would I had a thousand lives for such a master! I have a burden on my conscience, Sire, nor can I die in peace unless I speak of it.'

'Speak, speak freely. If thou hast injured any one, and the power or wealth of Alroy can redeem thy oppressed spirit, he will not spare, he will not spare, be assured of that.'

'Noble, noble master, I must be brief; for, although, while this javelin rests within my body, I yet may live, the agony is great. Sire, the deed of which I speak doth concern thee.'

'Ay!'

'I was on guard the day Jabaster died.'

'Powers of heaven! I am all ear. Speak on, speak on!'

'He died self-strangled, so they say?'

'So they ever told me.'

'Thou art innocent, thou art innocent! I thank my God, my King is innocent!'

'Rest assured of that, as there is hope in Israel. Tell me all.'

'The Queen came with the signet ring. To such authority I yielded way. She entered, and after her, the Lord Honain. I heard high words! I heard Jabaster's voice. He struggled, yes! he struggled; but his mighty form, wounded and fettered, could not long resist. Foul play, foul play, Sire! What could I do against such adversaries? They left the chamber with a stealthy step. Her eyes met mine. I never could forget that fell and glittering visage.'

'Thou ne'er hast spoken of this awful end?'

'To none but thee. And why I speak it now I cannot tell, save that it seems some inspiration urges me; and methinks they who did this may do even feller works, if such there be.'

'Thou hast robbed me of all peace and hope of peace; and yet I thank thee. Now I know the worth of life. I have never loved to think of that sad day; and yet, though I have sometimes dreamed of villainous work, the worst were innocence to thy dread tale.'

''Tis told; and now I pray thee secure thy secret, by drawing from my agonised frame this javelin.'

'Trusty heart, 'tis a sad office.'

'I die with joy if thou performest it.'

''Tis done.'

'God save Alroy.'

While Alroy, plunged in thought, stood over the body of the officer, there arose a flourish of triumphant music, and a eunuch, entering the pavilion, announced the arrival of Schirene from Kerrund. Almost immediately afterwards, the Princess descending from her litter, entered the tent; Alroy tore off his robe, and threw it over the corpse.

'My own,' exclaimed the Princess, as she ran up to the Caliph. 'I have heard all. Be not alarmed for me. I dare look upon a corpse. You know I am a soldier's bride. I am used to blood.'

'Alas!'

'Why so pale? Thou dost not kiss me! Has this unhinged thee so? 'Tis a sad deed; and yet tomorrow's dawn may light up thousands to as grim a fate. Why? thou tremblest! Alas! kind soul! The single death of this fond, faithful heart hath quite upset my love. Yet art thou used to battle. Why! this is foolishness. Art not glad to see me? What, not one smile! And I have come to fight for thee! I will be kissed!'

She flung herself upon his neck. Alroy faintly returned her embrace, and bore her to a couch. He clapped his hands, and two soldiers entered and bore away the corpse.

'The pavilion, Schirene, is now fitter for thy presence. Rest thyself; I shall soon return.' Thus speaking, he quitted her.

He quitted her; but her humbled look of sorrowful mortification pierced to his heart. He thought of all her love and all her loveliness, he called to mind all the marvellous story of their united fortunes. He felt that for her and her alone he cared to live, that without her quick sympathy, even success seemed unendurable. His judgment fluctuated in an eddy of passion and reason. Passion conquered. He dismissed from his intelligence all cognizance of good and evil; he determined, under all circumstances, to cling ever to her; he tore from his mind all memory of the late disclosure. He returned to the pavilion with a countenance beaming with affection; he found her weeping, he folded her in his arms, he kissed her with a thousand kisses, and whispered between each kiss his ardent love.

'Twas midnight. Schirene reposed in the arms of Alroy. The Caliph, who was restless and anxious for the arrival of Scherirah, was scarcely slumbering when the sound of a voice thoroughly aroused him. He looked around; he beheld the spectre of Jabaster. His hair stood on end, his limbs seemed to loosen, a cold dew crept over his frame, as he gazed upon the awful form within a yard of his couch. Unconsciously he disembarrassed his arms of their fair burden, and, rising on the couch, leant forward.

'*Alroy, Alroy, Alroy!*'

'I am here.'

'*To-morrow Israel is avenged!*'

'Who is that?' exclaimed the Princess, wakening.

In a frenzy of fear, Alroy, quite forgetting the spectre, turned and pressed his hand over her eyes. When he again looked round the apparition was invisible.

'What wouldst thou, Alroy?'

'Nothing, sweet! A soldier's wife must bear strange sights, yet I would save you some. One of my men, forgetful you were here, burst into my tent in such a guise as scarce would suit a female eye. I must away, my child. I'll call thy slaves. One kiss! Farewell! but for a time.'

'"To-morrow Israel will be avenged." What! in Karasmian blood? I have no faith. No matter. All is now beyond my influence. A rushing destiny carries me onward. I cannot stem the course, nor guide the vessel. How now! Who is the officer on guard?'

'Benomi, Sire, thy servant.'

'Send to the Viceroy. Bid him meet me here. Who is this?'

'A courier from the Lord Scherirah, Sire, but just arrived. He passed last night the Kerrund mountains, Sire, and will be with you by the break of day.'

'Good news. Go fetch Abner. Haste! He'll find me here anon. I'll visit the camp awhile. Well, my brave fellows, you have hither come to conquer again with Alroy. You have fought before, I warrant, on the plain of Nehauend. 'Tis a rich soil, and shall be richer with Karasmian gore.'

'God save your Majesty! Our lives are thine.'

'Please you, my little ruler,' said a single soldier, addressing Alroy; 'pardon my bluntness, but I knew you before you were a Caliph.'

'Stout heart, I like thy freedom. Pr'ythee say on.'

'I was a-saying, I hope you will lead us in the charge to-morrow. Some say you will not.'

'They say falsely.'

'I thought so. I'll ever answer for my little ruler, but then the Queen?'

'Is a true soldier's wife, and lives in the camp.'

'That's brave! There, I told you so, comrades; you would not believe me, but I knew our little ruler before you did. I lived near the gate at Hamadan, please your Highness: old Shelomi's son.'

'Give me thy hand; a real friend. What is't ye eat here, boys? Let me taste your mess. I'faith I would my cook could dress me such a pilau! Tis admirable!'

The soldiers gathered round their chieftain with eyes beaming with adoration. 'Twas a fine picture, the hero in the centre, the various groups around, some conversing with him, some cooking, some making coffee, all offering him by word or deed some testimonial of their devotion, and blending with that devotion the most perfect frankness.

'We shall beat them, lads!'

'There is no fear with you, you always conquer.'

'I do my best, and so do you. A good general without good troops is little worth.'

'I'faith that's true. One must have good troops. What think you of Alp Arslan?'

'I think he may give us as much trouble as all our other enemies together, and that's not much.'

'Brave, brave! God save Alroy!'

Benomi approached, and announced that the Viceroy was in attendance.

'I must quit you, my children,' said Alroy. 'We'll sup once more together when we have conquered.'

'God save you, Sire; and we will confound your enemies.'

'Good night, my lads. Ere the dawn break we may have hot work.'

'We are ready, we are ready. God save Alroy.'

'They are in good cue, and yet 'twas a different spirit that inspired our early days. That I strongly feel. These are men true to a leader who has never failed them, and confident in a cause that leads to plunder. They are but splendid mercenaries.

No more. Oh! where are now the fighting men of Judah! Where are the men who, when they drew their scimitars, joined in a conquering psalm of holy triumph! Last eve of battle you would have thought the field a mighty synagogue. Priests and altars, flaming sacrifices, and smoking censers, groups of fiery zealots hanging with frenzy on prophetic lips, and sealing with their blood and holiest vows a solemn covenant to conquer Canaan. All is changed, as I am. How now, Abner? You are well muffled!'

'Is it true Scherirah is at hand?'

'I doubt not all is right. Would that the dawn would break!'

'The enemy is advancing. Some of their columns are in sight. My scouts have dodged them. They intend doubtless to form upon the plain.'

'They are in sight, eh! Then we will attack them at once ere they are formed. Rare, rare! We'll beat them yet. Courage, dear brother. Scherirah will be here at dawn in good time, very good time: very, very good time.'

'I like the thought'

'The men are in good heart. At break of dawn, charge with thirty thousand cavalry upon their forming ranks. I'll take the right, Asriel the left. It shall be a family affair, dear Abner. How is Miriam?'

'I heard this morn, quite well. She sends you her love and prayers. The Queen is here?'

'She came this eve. Quite well.'

'She must excuse all courtesy.'

'Say nothing. She is a soldier's wife. She loves thee well, dear Abner.'

'I know that. I hope my sword may guard her children's throne.'

'Well, give thy orders. Instant battle, eh?'

'Indeed I think so.'

'I'll send couriers to hurry Scherirah. All looks well. Reserve the guard.'

'Ay, ay! Farewell, dear Sire. When we meet again, I trust your enemies may be your slaves!'

At the first streak of dawn the Hebrew cavalry, with the exception of the Guard, charged the advancing columns of the Karasmians with irresistible force, and cut them in pieces. Alp Arslan rallied his troops, and at length succeeded in forming his main body in good order. Alroy and Asriel led on their divisions, and the battle now became general. It raged for several hours, and was on both sides well maintained. The slaughter of the Karasmians was great, but their stern character and superior numbers counterbalanced for a time all the impetuosity of the Hebrews and all the energy of their leaders. This day Alroy threw into the shade all his former exploits. Twelve times he charged at the head of the Sacred Guard, and more than once penetrated to the very pavilion of Alp Arslan.

In vain he endeavoured singly, and hand to hand, to meet that famous chieftain. Both monarchs fought in the ranks, and yet Fate decided that their scimitars should never cross. Four hours before noon, it was evident to Alroy, that, unless Scherirah arrived, he could not prevail against the vast superiority of numbers. He was obliged early to call his reserve into the field, and although the number of the slain on the side of Arslan exceeded any in the former victories of the Hebrews, still the Karasmians maintained an immense front, which was constantly supplied by fresh troops. Confident in his numbers, and aware of the weakness of his antagonists, Arslan contented himself with acting on the defensive, and wearying his assailants by resisting their terrible and repeated charge.

For a moment, Alroy at the head of the Sacred Guard had withdrawn from the combat. Abner and Asriel still maintained the fight, and the Caliph was at the same time preparing for new efforts, and watching with anxiety for the arrival of Scherirah. In the fifth hour, from an eminence he marked with exultation the advancing banners of his expected succours. Confident now that the day was won, he announced the exhilarating intelligence to his soldiers; and, while they were excited by the animating tidings, led them once more to the charge. It was irresistible; Scherirah seemed to have arrived only for the pursuit, only in time to complete the victory. What then was the horror, the consternation of Alroy, when Benaiah, dashing up to him, informed him that the long-expected succours consisted of the united forces of Scherirah and Abidan, and had attacked him in the rear. Human genius could afford no resource. The exhausted Hebrews, whose energies had been tasked to the utmost, were surrounded. The Karasmians made a general and simultaneous advance. In a few minutes the Hebrew army was thrown into confusion. The stoutest warriors threw away their swords in despair. Every one thought only of self-preservation. Even Abner fled towards Hamadan. Asriel was slain. Alroy, finding it was all over, rushed to his pavilion at the head of about three hundred of the guards, seized the fainting Schirene, threw her before him on his saddle, and cutting his way through all obstacles, dashed into the desert.

For eight-and-forty hours they never stopped. Their band was soon reduced one-third. On the morning of the third day they dismounted and refreshed themselves at a well. Half only regained their saddles. Schirene never spoke. On they rushed again, each hour losing some exhausted co-mate. At length, on the fifth day, about eighty strong, they arrived at a grove of palm-trees. Here they dismounted. And Alroy took Schirene in his arms, and the shade seemed to revive her. She opened her eyes, and pressed his hand and smiled. He gathered her some dates, and she drank some water.

'Our toils will soon be over, sweetest,' he whispered to her; 'I have lost everything but thee.'

Again they mounted, and, proceeding at a less rapid pace, they arrived towards evening at the ruined city, whither Alroy all this time had been directing his course. Dashing down the great street, they at length entered the old amphitheatre. They dismounted. Alroy made a couch with their united cloaks for Schirene. Some collected fuel, great store of which was found, and kindled large fires. Others, while it was yet light, chased the gazelles, and were sufficiently fortunate to provide their banquet, or fetched water from the well known to their leader. In an hour's time, clustering round their fires in groups, and sharing their rude fare, you might have deemed them, instead of the discomfited and luxurious guards of a mighty monarch, the accustomed tenants of this wild abode.

'Come, my lads,' said Alroy, as he rubbed his hands over the ascending flame, 'at any rate, this is better than the desert.'

After all his exertions, Alroy fell into profound and dreamless sleep. When he awoke, the sun had been long up. Schirene was still slumbering. He embraced her, and she opened her eyes and smiled.

'You are now a bandit's bride,' he said. 'How like you our new life?'

'Well! with thee.'

'Rest here, my sweetest: I must rouse our men, and see how fortune speeds.' So saying, and tripping lightly over many a sleeping form, he touched Benaiah.

'So! my brave captain of the guard, still napping! Come! stir, stir.'

Benaiah jumped up with a cheerful face. 'I am ever ready, Sire.'

'I know it; but remember I am no more a king, only a co-mate. Away with me, and let us form some order.'

The companions quitted the amphitheatre and reconnoitred the adjoining buildings. They found many stores, the remains of old days, mats, tents, and fuel, drinking-bowls, and other homely furniture. They fixed upon a building for their stable, and others for the accommodation of their band. They summoned their companions to the open place, the scene of Hassan Subah's fate, where Alroy addressed them and explained to them his plans. They were divided into companies; each man had his allotted duty. Some were placed on guard at different parts; some were sent out to the chase, or to collect dates from the Oasis; others led the horses to the contiguous pasture, or remained to attend to their domestic arrangements. The amphitheatre was cleared out. A rude but convenient pavilion was formed for Schirene. They covered its ground with mats, and each emulated the other in his endeavours to study her accommodation. Her kind words and inspiring smiles animated at the same time their zeal and their invention.

They soon became accustomed to their rough but adventurous life. Its novelty pleased them, and the perpetual excitement of urgent necessity left them no time to mourn over their terrible vicissitudes. While Alroy lived, hope indeed never deserted their sanguine bosoms. And such was the influence of his genius, that the most desponding felt that to be discomfited with him, was preferable to conquest with another. They were a faithful and devoted band, and merry faces were not wanting when at night they assembled in the amphitheatre for their common meal.

No sooner had Alroy completed his arrangements than he sent forth spies in all directions to procure intelligence, and especially to communicate, if possible, with Ithamar and Medad, provided that they still survived and maintained themselves in any force.

A fortnight passed away without the approach of any stranger; at the end of which, there arrived four personages at their haunt, not very welcome to their chief, who, however, concealed his chagrin at their appearance. These were Kisloch the Kourd, and Calidas the Indian, and their inseparable companions, the Guebre and the Negro.

'Noble Captain,' said Kisloch, 'we trust that you will permit us to enlist in the band. This is not the first time we have served under your orders in this spot. Old co-mates, i'faith, who have seen the best and the worst. We suspected where you might be found, although, thanks to the ever felicitous invention of man, it is generally received that you died in battle. I hope your Majesty is well,' added Kisloch, bowing to Schirene.

'You are welcome, friends,' replied Alroy; 'I know your worth. You have seen, as you say, the best and the worst, and will, I trust, see better. Died in battle, eh! that's good.'

"Tis so received,' said Calidas.

'And what news of our friends?'

'Not over good, but strange.'

'How so?'

'Hamadan is taken.'

'I am prepared; tell me all.'

'Old Bostenay and the Lady Miriam are borne prisoners to Bagdad.'

'Prisoners?'

'But so; all will be well with them, I trow. The Lord Honain is in high favour with the conqueror, and will doubtless protect them.'

'Honain in favour?'

'Even so. He made terms for the city, and right good ones.'

'Hah! he was ever dexterous. Well! if he save my sister, I care not for his favour.'

'There is no doubt. All may yet be well, Sir.'

'Let us act, not hope. Where's Abner?'

'Dead.'

'How?'

'In battle.'

'Art sure?'

'I saw him fall, and fought beside him.'

'A soldier's death is all our fortune now. I am glad he was not captured. Where's Medad, Ithamar?'

'Fled into Egypt.'

'We have no force whatever, then?'

'None but your guards here.'

'They are strong enough to plunder a caravan. Honain, you say, in favour?'

'Very high. He'll make good terms for us.'

'This is strange news.'

'Very, but true.'

'Well! you are welcome! Share our fare; 'tis rough, and somewhat scanty; but we have feasted, and may feast again. Fled into Egypt, eh?'

'Ay! Sir.'

'Schirene, shouldst like to see the Nile?'

'I have heard of crocodiles.'

If the presence of Kisloch and his companions were not very pleasing to Alroy, with the rest of the band they soon became great favourites. Their local knowledge, and their experience of desert life, made them valuable allies, and their boisterous jocularity and unceasing merriment were not unwelcome in the present monotonous existence of the fugitives. As for Alroy himself, he meditated an escape to Egypt. He determined to seize the first opportunity of procuring some camels, and then, dispersing his band, with the exception of Benaiah and a few faithful retainers, he trusted that, disguised as merchants, they might succeed in crossing Syria, and entering Africa by Palestine. With these plans and prospects, he became each day more cheerful and more sanguine as to the future. He had in his possession some valuable jewels, which he calculated upon disposing of at Cairo for a sum sufficient for all his purposes; and having exhausted all the passions of life while yet a youth, he looked forward to the tranquil termination of his existence in some poetic solitude with his beautiful companion.

One evening, as they returned from the Oasis, Alroy guiding the camel that bore Schirene, and ever and anon looking up in her inspiring face, her sanguine spirit would have indulged in a delightful future.

'Thus shall we pass the desert, sweet,' said Schirene. 'Can this be toil?'

'There is no toil with love,' replied Alroy.

'And we were made for love, and not for empire,' rejoined Schirene.

'The past is a dream,' said Alroy. 'So sages teach us; but, until we act, their wisdom is but wind. I feel it now. Have we ever lived in aught but deserts, and fed on aught but dates? Methinks 'tis very natural. But that I am tempted by the security of distant lands, I could remain here a free and happy outlaw. Time, custom, and necessity form our natures. When I first met Scherirah in these ruins, I shrank with horror from degraded man; and now I sigh to be his heir. We must not think!'

'No, love, we'll only hope,' replied Schirene; and they passed through the gates.

The night was beautiful, the air was still warm and sweet. Schirene gazed upon the luminous heavens. 'We thought not of these skies when we were at Bagdad,' she exclaimed; 'and yet, my life, what was the brightness of our palaces compared to these? All is left to us that man should covet, freedom, beauty, and youth. I do believe, ere long, Alroy, we shall look back upon the wondrous past as on another and a lower world. Would that this were Egypt! 'Tis my only wish.'

'And it shall soon be gratified. All will soon be arranged. A few brief days, and then Schirene will mount her camel for a longer ride than just to gather dates. You'll make a sorry traveller, I fear!'

'Not I; I'll tire you all.'

They reached the circus, and seated themselves round the blazing fire. Seldom had Alroy, since his fall, appeared more cheerful. Schirene sang an Arab air to the band, who joined in joyous chorus. It was late ere they sought repose; and they retired to their rest, sanguine and contented.

A few hours afterwards, at the break of dawn, Alroy was roused from his slumbers by a rude pressure on his breast. He started; a ferocious soldier was kneeling over him; he would have spurned him; he found his hand manacled. He would have risen; his feet were bound. He looked round for Schirene, and called her name; he was answered only by a shriek. The amphitheatre was filled with

Karasmian troops. His own men were surprised and overpowered. Kisloch and the Guebre had been on guard. He was raised from the ground, and flung upon a camel, which was instantly trotted out of the circus. On every side he beheld a wild scene of disorder and dismay. He was speechless from passion and despair. The camel was dragged into the desert. A body of cavalry instantly surrounded it, and they set off at a rapid pace. The whole seemed the work of an instant.

How many days had passed Alroy knew not. He had taken no account of time. Night and day were to him the same. He was in a stupor. But the sweetness of the air and the greenness of the earth at length partially roused his attention. He was just conscious that they had quitted the desert. Before him was a noble river; he beheld the Euphrates from the very spot he had first viewed it in his pilgrimage. The strong association of ideas called back his memory. A tear stole down his cheek; the bitter drop stole to his parched lips; he asked the nearest horseman for water. The guard gave him a wetted sponge, with which he contrived with difficulty to wipe his lips, and then he let it fall to the ground. The Karasmian struck him.

They arrived at the river. The prisoner was taken from the camel and placed in a covered boat. After some hours they stopped and disembarked at a small village. Alroy was placed upon an ass with his back to its head. His clothes were soiled and tattered. The children pelted him with mud. An old woman, with a fanatic curse, placed a crown of paper on his brow. With difficulty his brutal guards prevented their victim from being torn to pieces. And in such fashion, towards noon of the fourteenth day, David Alroy again entered Bagdad.

The intelligence of the capture of Alroy spread through the agitated city. The Moolahs bustled about as if they had received a fresh demonstration of the authenticity of the prophetic mission. All the Dervishes began begging. The men discussed affairs in the coffee-houses, and the women chatted at the fountains.[79]

'They may say what they like, but I wish him well,' said a fair Arab, as she arranged her veil. 'He may be an impostor, but he was a very handsome one.'

'All the women are for him, that's the truth,' responded a companion; 'but then we can do him no good.'

'We can tear their eyes out,' said a third.

'And what do you think of Alp Arslan, truly?' inquired a fourth.

'I wish he were a pitcher, and then I could break his neck,' said a fifth.

'Only think of the Princess!' said a sixth.

'Well! she has had a glorious time of it,' said a seventh.

'Nothing was too good for her,' said an eighth.

'I like true love,' said a ninth.

'Well! I hope he will be too much for them all yet,' said a tenth.

'I should not wonder,' said an eleventh.

'He can't,' said a twelfth, 'he has lost his sceptre.'

'You don't say so?' said a thirteenth.

'It is too true,' said a fourteenth.

'Do you think he was a wizard?' said a fifteenth. 'I vow, if there be not a fellow looking at us behind those trees.'

'Impudent scoundrel!' said a sixteenth. 'I wish it were Alroy. Let us all scream, and put down our veils.'

And the group ran away.

Two stout soldiers were playing chess[80] in a coffee-house.

'May I slay my mother,' said one, 'but I cannot make a move. I fought under him at Nehauend; and though I took the amnesty, I have half a mind now to seize my sword and stab the first Turk that enters.'

''Twere but sheer justice,' said his companion. 'By my father's blessing, he was the man for a charge. They may say what they like, but compared with him, Alp Arslan is a white-livered Giaour.'

'Here is confusion to him and to thy last move. There's the dirhem, I can play no more. May I slay my mother, though, but I did not think he would let himself be taken.'

'By the blessing of my father, nor I; but then he was asleep.'

'That makes a difference. He was betrayed.'

'All brave men are. They say Kisloch and his set pocket their fifty thousand by the job.'

'May each dirhem prove a plague-spot!'

'Amen! Dost remember Abner?'

'May I slay my mother if I ever forget him. He spoke to his men like so many lambs. What has become of the Lady Miriam?'

'She is here.'

'That will cut Alroy.'

'He was ever fond of her. Dost remember she gained Adoram's life?'

'Oh! she could do anything next to the Queen.'

'Before her, I say, before her. He has refused the Queen, he never refused the Lady Miriam.'

'Because she asked less.'

'Dost know it seemed to me that things never went on so well after Jabaster's death?'

'So say I. There was a something, eh?'

'A sort of a peculiar, as it were, kind of something, eh?'

'You have well described it. Every man felt the same. I have often mentioned it to my comrades. Say what you like, said I, but slay my mother if ever since the old man strangled himself, things did not seem, as it were, in their natural propinquity. 'Twas the phrase I used.'

'A choice one. Unless there is a natural propinquity, the best-arranged matters will fall out. However, the ass sees farther than his rider, and so it was with Alroy, the best commander I ever served under, all the same.'

'Let us go forth and see how affairs run.'

'Ay, do. If we hear any one abuse Alroy, we'll cleave his skull.'

'That will we. There are a good many of our stout fellows about; we might do something yet.'

'Who knows?'

A subterranean dungeon of the citadel of Bagdad held in its gloomy limits the late lord of Asia. The captive did not sigh, or weep, or wail. He did not speak. He did not even think. For several days he remained in a state of stupor. On the morning of the fourth day, he almost unconsciously partook of the wretched provision which his gaolers brought him. Their torches, round which the bats whirled and flapped their wings, and twinkled their small eyes, threw a ghastly glare over the nearer walls of the dungeon, the extremity of which defied the vision of the prisoner; and, when the gaolers retired, Alroy was in complete darkness.

The image of the past came back to him. He tried in vain to penetrate the surrounding gloom. His hands were manacled, his legs also were loaded with chains. The notion that his life might perhaps have been cruelly spared in order that he might linger on in this horrible state of conscious annihilation filled him with frenzy. He would have dashed his fetters against his brow, but the chain restrained him. He flung himself upon the damp and rugged ground. His fall disturbed a thousand obscene things. He heard the quick glide of a serpent, the creeping retreat of the clustering scorpions, and the swift escape of the dashing rats. His mighty calamities seemed slight when compared with these petty miseries. His great soul could not support him under these noisome and degrading incidents. He sprang, in disgust, upon his feet, and stood fearful of moving, lest every step should introduce him to some new abomination. At length, exhausted nature was unable any longer to sustain him. He groped his way to the rude seat, cut in the rocky wall, which was his only accommodation. He put forth his hand. It touched the slimy fur of some wild animal, that instantly sprang away, its fiery eyes sparkling in the dark. Alroy recoiled with a sensation of woe-begone dismay. His shaken nerves could not sustain him under this base danger, and these foul and novel trials. He could not refrain from an exclamation of despair; and, when he remembered that he was now far beyond the reach of all human solace and sympathy, even all human aid, for a moment his mind seemed to desert him; and he wrung his hands in forlorn and almost idiotic woe. An awful thing it is, the failure of the energies of a master-mind. He who places implicit confidence in his genius will find himself some day utterly defeated and deserted. 'Tis bitter! Every paltry hind seems but to breathe to mock you. Slow, indeed, is such a mind to credit that the never-failing resource can at least be wanting. But so it is. Like a dried-up fountain, the perennial flow and bright fertility have ceased, and ceased for ever. Then comes the madness of retrospection.

Draw a curtain! draw a curtain! and fling it over this agonising anatomy.

The days of childhood, his sweet sister's voice and smiling love, their innocent pastimes, and the kind solicitude of faithful servants, all the soft detail of mild domestic life: these were the sights and memories that flitted in wild play before the burning vision of Alroy, and rose upon his tortured mind. Empire and glory, his sacred nation, his imperial bride; these, these were nothing. Their worth had vanished with the creative soul that called them into action. The pure sympathies of nature alone remained, and all his thought and grief, all his intelligence, all his emotion, were centred in his sister.

It was the seventh morning. A guard entered at an unaccustomed hour, and, sticking a torch into a niche in the wall, announced that a person was without who had permission to speak to the prisoner. They were the first human accents that had met the ear of Alroy during his captivity, which seemed to him an age, a long dark period, that cancelled all things. He shuddered at the harsh tones. He tried to answer, but his unaccustomed lips refused their office. He raised his heavy arms, and endeavoured to signify his consciousness of what had been uttered. Yet, indeed, he had not listened to the message without emotion. He looked forward to the grate with strange curiosity; and, as he looked, he trembled. The visitor entered, muffled in a dark caftan. The guard disappeared; and the caftan falling to the ground, revealed Honain.

'My beloved Alroy,' said the brother of Jabaster; and he advanced, and pressed him to his bosom. Had it been Miriam, Alroy might have at once expired; but the presence of this worldly man called back his worldliness. The revulsion of his feelings was wonderful. Pride, perhaps even hope, came to his aid; all the associations seemed to counsel exertion; for a moment he seemed the same Alroy.

'I rejoice to find at least thee safe, Honain.'

'I also, if my security may lead to thine.'

'Still whispering hope!'

'Despair is the conclusion of fools.'

'O Honain! 'tis a great trial. I can play my part, and yet methinks 'twere better we had not again met. How is Schirene?'

'Thinking of thee.'

''Tis something that she can think. My mind has gone. Where's Miriam?'

'Free.'

'That's something. Thou hast done that. Good, good Honain, be kind to that sweet child, if only for my sake. Thou art all she has left.'

'She hath thee.'

'Her desolation.'

'Live and be her refuge.'

'How's that? These walls! Escape? No, no; it is impossible.'

'I do not deem it so.'

'Indeed! I'll do anything. Speak! Can we bribe? can we cleave their skulls? can we——'

'Calm thyself, my friend. There is no need of bribes, no need of bloodshed. We must make terms.'

'Terms! We might have made them on the plain of Nehauend. Terms! Terms with a captive victim?'

'Why victim?'

'Is Arslan then so generous?'

'He is a beast, more savage than the boar that grinds its tusks within his country's forests.'

'Why speakest thou then of hope?'

'I spoke of certainty. I did not mention hope.'

'Dear Honain, my brain is weak; but I can bear strange things, or else I should not be here. I feel thy thoughtful friendship; but indeed there need no winding words to tell my fate. Pr'ythee speak out.'

'In a word, thy life is safe.'

'What! spared?'

'If it please thee.'

'Please me? Life is sweet. I feel its sweetness. I want but little. Freedom and solitude are all I ask. My life spared! I'll not believe it. Thou hast done this deed, thou mighty man, that masterest all souls. Thou hast not forgotten me; thou hast not forgotten the days gone by, thou hast not forgotten thine own Alroy! Who calls thee worldly is a slanderer. O Honain! thou art too faithful!'

'I have no thought but for thy service, Prince.'

'Call me not Prince, call me thine own Alroy. My life spared! 'Tis wonderful! When may I go? Let no one see me. Manage that, Honain. Thou canst manage all things. I am for Egypt. Thou hast been to Egypt, hast thou not, Honain?'

'A very wondrous land, 'twill please thee much.'

'When may I go? Tell me when I may go. When may I quit this dark and noisome cell? 'Tis worse than all their tortures, dear Honain. Air and light, and I really think my spirit never would break, but this horrible dungeon—— I scarce can look upon thy face, sweet friend. 'Tis serious.'

'Wouldst thou have me gay?'

'Yes! if we are free.'

'Alroy! thou art a great spirit, the greatest that I e'er knew, have ever read of. I never knew thy like, and never shall.'

'Tush, tush, sweet friend, I am a broken reed, but still I am free. This is no time for courtly phrases. Let's go, and go at once.'

'A moment, dear Alroy. I am no flatterer. What I said came from my heart, and doth concern us much and instantly. I was saying thou hast no common mind, Alroy; indeed thou hast a mind unlike all others. Listen, my Prince. Thou hast read mankind deeply and truly. Few have seen more than thyself, and none have so rare a spring of that intuitive knowledge of thy race, which is a gem to which experience is but a jeweller, and without which no action can befriend us.'

'Well, well!'

'A moment's calmness. Thou hast entered Bagdad in triumph, and thou hast entered the same city with every contumely which the base spirit of our race could cast upon its victim. 'Twas a great lesson.'

'I feel it so.'

'And teaches us how vile and valueless is the opinion of our fellow-men.'

'Alas! 'tis true.'

'I am glad to see thee in this wholesome temper. 'Tis full of wisdom.'

'The miserable are often wise.'

'But to believe is nothing unless we act. Speculation should only sharpen practice. The time hath come to prove thy lusty faith in this philosophy. I told thee we could make terms. I have made them. To-morrow it was doomed Alroy should die—and what a death! A death of infinite torture! Hast ever seen a man impaled?'[81]

'Hah!'

'To view it is alone a doom.'

'God of Heaven!'

'It is so horrible, that 'tis ever marked, that when this direful ceremony occurs, the average deaths in cities greatly increase. 'Tis from the turning of the blood in the spectators, who yet from some ungovernable madness cannot refrain from hurrying to the scene. I speak with some authority. I speak as a physician.'

'Speak no more, I cannot endure it.'

'To-morrow this doom awaited thee. As for Schirene———'

'Not for her, oh! surely not for her?'

'No, they were merciful. She is a Caliph's daughter. 'Tis not forgotten. The axe would close her life. Her fair neck would give slight trouble to the headsman's art. But for thy sister, but for Miriam, she is a witch, a Jewish witch! They would have burnt her alive!'

'I'll not believe it, no, no, I'll not believe it: damnable, bloody demons! When I had power I spared all, all but———ah, me! ah, me! why did I live?'

'Thou dost forget thyself; I speak of that which was to have been, not of that which is to be. I have stepped in and communed with the conqueror. I have made terms.'

'What are they, what can they be?'

'Easy. To a philosopher like Alroy an idle ceremony.'

'Be brief, be brief.'

'Thou seest thy career is a great scandal to the Moslemin. I mark their weakness, and I have worked upon it. Thy mere defeat or death will not blot out the stain upon their standard and their faith. The public mind is wild with fantasies since Alroy rose. Men's opinions flit to and fro with that fearful change that bodes no stable settlement of states. None know what to cling to, or where to place their trust. Creeds are doubted, authority disputed. They would gladly account for thy success by other than human means, yet must deny thy mission. There also is the fame of a fair and mighty Princess, a daughter of their Caliphs, which they would gladly clear. I mark all this, observe and work upon it. So, could we devise some means by which thy lingering followers could be for ever silenced, this great scandal fairly erased, and the public frame brought to a sounder and more tranquil pulse, why, they would concede much, much, very much.'

'Thy meaning, not thy means, are evident.'

'They are in thy power.'

'In mine? 'Tis a deep riddle. Pr'ythee solve it.'

'Thou wilt be summoned at to-morrow's noon before this Arslan. There in the presence of the assembled people who are now with him as much as they were with thee, thou wilt be accused of magic, and of intercourse with the infernal powers. Plead guilty.'

'Well! is there more?'

'Some trifle. They will then examine thee about the Princess. It is not difficult to confess that Alroy won the Caliph's daughter by an irresistible spell, and now 'tis broken.'

'So, so. Is that all?'

'The chief. Thou canst then address some phrases to the Hebrew prisoners, denying thy Divine mission, and so forth, to settle the public mind, observe, upon this point for ever.'

'Ay, ay, and then——?'

'No more, except for form. (Upon the completion of the conditions, mind, you will be conveyed to what land you please, with such amount of treasure as you choose.) There is no more, except, I say, for form, I would, if I were you ('twill be expected), I would just publicly affect to renounce our faith, and bow before their Prophet.'

'Hah! Art thou there? Is this thy freedom? Get thee behind me, tempter! Never, never, never! Not a jot, not a jot: I'll not yield a jot. Were my doom one everlasting torture, I'd spurn thy terms! Is this thy high contempt of our poor kind, to outrage my God! to prove myself the vilest of the vile, and baser than the basest? Rare philosophy! O Honain! would we had never met!'

'Or never parted. True. Had my word been taken, Alroy would ne'er have been betrayed.'

'No more; I pray thee, sir, no more. Leave me.'

'Were this a palace, I would. Harsh words are softened by a friendly ear, when spoken in affliction.'

'Say what they will, I am the Lord's anointed. As such I should have lived, as such at least I'll die.'

'And Miriam?'

'The Lord will not desert her: she ne'er deserted Him.'

'Schirene?'

'Schirene! why! for her sake alone I will die a hero. Shall it be said she loved a craven slave, a base impostor, a vile renegade, a villainous dealer in drugs and charms? Oh! no, no, no! if only for her sake, her sweet, sweet sake, my end shall be like my great life. As the sun I rose, like him I set. Still the world is warm with my bright fame, and my last hour shall not disgrace my noon, stormy indeed, but glorious!'

Honain took the torch from the niche, and advanced to the grate. It was not fastened: he drew it gently open, and led forward a veiled and female figure. The veiled and female figure threw herself at the feet of Alroy, who seemed lost to what was passing. A soft lip pressed his hand. He started, his chains clanked.

'Alroy!' softly murmured the kneeling female.

'What voice is that?' wildly exclaimed the Prince of the Captivity. 'It falls upon my ear like long-forgotten music. I'll not believe it. No! I'll not believe it. Art thou Schirene?'

'I am that wretched thing they called thy bride.'

'Oh! this indeed is torture! What impalement can equal this sharp moment? Look not on me, let not our eyes meet! They have met before, like to the confluence of two shining rivers blending in one great stream of rushing light. Bear off that torch, sir. Let impenetrable darkness cover our darker fortunes.'

'Alroy.'

'She speaks again. Is she mad, as I am, that thus she plays with agony?'

'Sire,' said Honain advancing, and laying his hand gently on the arm of the captive, 'I pray thee moderate this passion. Thou hast some faithful friends here, who would fain commune in calmness for thy lasting welfare.'

'Welfare! He mocks me.'

'I beseech, thee, Sire, be calm. If, indeed, I speak unto that great Alroy whom all men fear and still may fear, I pray remember, 'tis not in palaces or in the battle-field alone that the heroic soul can conquer and command. Scenes like these are the great proof of a superior soul. While we live, our body is a temple where our genius pours forth its godlike inspiration, and while the altar is not overthrown, the deity may still work marvels. Then rouse thyself, great Sire; bethink thee that, a Caliph or a captive, there is no man within this breathing world like to Alroy. Shall such a being fall without a struggle, like some poor felon, who has naught to trust to but the dull shuffling accident of Chance? I, too, am a prophet, and I feel thou still wilt conquer.'

'Give me my sceptre, then, give me the sceptre! I speak to the wrong brother! It was not thou, it was not thou that gavest it me.'

'Gain it once more. The Lord deserted David for a time; still he pardoned him, and still he died a king.'

'A woman worked his fall.'

'But thee a woman raises. This great Princess, has she not suffered too? Yet her spirit is still unbroken. List to her counsel: it is deep and fond.'

'So was our love.'

'And is, my Alroy!' exclaimed the Princess. 'Be calm, I pray thee! For my sake be calm; I am calm for thine. Thou hast listened to all Honain has told thee, that wise man, my Alroy, who never erred.

'Tis but a word he counsels, an empty word, a most unmeaning form. But speak it, and thou art free, and Alroy and Schirene may blend again their glorious careers and lives of sweet fruition. Dost thou not remember when, walking in the garden of our joy, and palled with empire, how often hast thou sighed for some sweet isle unknown to man, where thou mightst pass thy days with no companion but my faithful self, and no adventures but our constant loves? O my beloved, that life may still be thine! And dost thou falter? Dost call thyself forlorn with such fidelity, and deem thyself a wretch, when Paradise with all its beauteous gates but woos thy entrance? Oh! no, no, no, no! thou hast forgot Schirene: I fear me much, thy over-fond Schirene, who doats upon thy image in thy chains more than she did when those sweet hands of thine were bound with gems and played with her bright locks!'

'She speaks of another world. I do remember something. Who has sent this music to a dungeon? My spirit softens with her melting words. My eyes are moist. I weep! 'Tis pleasant. Sorrow is joy compared with my despair. I never thought to shed a tear again. My brain is cooler.'

'Weep, weep, I pray thee weep; but let me kiss away thy tears, my soul! Didst think thy Schirene had deserted thee? Ah! that was it that made my bird so sad. It shall be free, and fly in a sweet sky, and feed on flowers with its faithful mate. Ah me! I am once more happy with my boy. There was no misery but thy absence, sweet! Methinks this dungeon is our bright kiosk! Is that the sunbeam, or thy smile, my love, that makes the walls so joyful?'

'Did I smile? I'll not believe it.'

'Indeed you did. Ah! see he smiles again. Why this is freedom! There is no such thing as sorrow. Tis a lie to frighten fools!'

'Why, Honain, what's this? 'Twould seem I am really joyful. There's inspiration in her very breath. I am another being. Nay! waste not kisses on those ugly fetters.'

'Methinks they are gold.'

They were silent. Schirene drew Alroy to his rough seat, and gently placing herself on his knees, threw her arms round his neck, and buried her face in his breast. After a few minutes she raised her head, and whispered in his ear in irresistible accents of sweet exultation, 'We shall be free to-morrow!'

'To-morrow! is the trial so near?' exclaimed the captive, with an agitated voice and changing countenance. 'To-morrow!' He threw Schirene aside somewhat hastily, and sprang from his seat. 'To-morrow! would it were over! To-morrow! Methinks there is within that single word the fate of ages! Shall it be said to-morrow that Alroy—— Hah! what art thou that risest now before me? Dread, mighty spirit, thou hast come in time to save me from perdition. Take me to thy bosom, 'tis not stabbed. They did not stab thee. Thou seest me here communing with thy murderers. What then? I am innocent. Ask them, dread ghost, and call upon their fiendish souls to say I am pure. They would make me dark as themselves, but shall not.'

'Honain, Honain!' exclaimed the Princess in a terrible whisper as she flew to the Physician. 'He is wild again. Calm him, calm him. Mark! how he stands with his extended arms, and fixed vacant eyes, muttering most awful words! My spirit fails me. It is too fearful.'

The Physician advanced and stood by the side of Alroy, but in vain attempted to catch his attention. He ventured to touch his arm. The Prince started, turned round, and recognising him, exclaimed in a shrieking voice, 'Off, fratricide!'

Honain recoiled, pale and quivering. Schirene sprang to his arm. 'What said he, Honain? Thou dost not speak. I never saw thee pale before. Art thou, too, mad?'

'Would I were!'

'All men are growing wild. I am sure he said something. I pray thee tell me what was it?'

'Ask him.'

'I dare not. Tell me, tell me, Honain!'

'That I dare not.'

'Was it a word?'

'Ay! a word to wake the dead. Let us begone.'

'Without our end? Coward! I'll speak to him. My own Alroy,' sweetly whispered the Princess, as she advanced before him.

'What, has the fox left the tigress! Is't so, eh? Are there no judgments? Are the innocent only haunted? I am innocent! I did not strangle thee! He said rightly, "Beware, beware! they who did this may do even feller deeds." And here they are quick at their damned work. Thy body suffered, great Jabaster, but me they would strangle body and soul!'

The Princess shrieked, and fell into the arms of the advancing Honain, who bore her out of the dungeon.

After the fall of Hamadan, Bostenay and Miriam had been carried prisoners to Bagdad. Through the interference of Honain, their imprisonment had been exempted from the usual hardships, but they were still confined to their chambers in the citadel. Hitherto all the endeavours of Miriam to visit her brother had been fruitless. Honain was the only person to whom she could apply for assistance, and he, in answer to her importunities, only regretted his want of power to aid her. In vain had she attempted, by the offer of some remaining jewels, to secure the co-operation of her guards, with whom her loveliness and the softness of her manners had already ingratiated her. She had not succeeded even in communicating with Alroy. But after the unsuccessful mission of Honain to the dungeon, the late Vizier visited the sister of the captive, and, breaking to her with delicate skill the intelligence of the impending catastrophe, he announced that he had at length succeeded in obtaining for her the desired permission to visit her brother; and, while she shuddered at the proximity of an event for which she had long attempted to prepare herself, Honain, with some modifications, whispered the means by which he flattered himself that it might yet be averted. Miriam listened to him in silence, nor could he, with all his consummate art, succeed in extracting from her the slightest indication of her own opinion as to their expediency. They parted, Honain as sanguine as the wicked ever are.

As Miriam dreaded, both for herself and for Alroy, the shock of an unexpected meeting, she availed herself of the influence of Honain to send Caleb to her brother, to prepare him for her presence, and to consult him as to the desirable moment. Caleb found his late master lying exhausted on the floor of his dungeon. At first he would not speak or even raise his head, nor did he for a long time apparently recognise the faithful retainer of his uncle. But at length he grew milder, and when he fully comprehended who the messenger was, and the object of his mission, he at first seemed altogether disinclined to see his sister, but in the end postponed their meeting for the present, and, pleading great exhaustion, fixed for that sad interview the first hour of dawn.

The venerable Bostenay had scarcely ever spoken since the fall of his nephew; indeed it was but too evident that his faculties, even if they had not entirely deserted him, were at least greatly impaired. He never quitted his couch; he took no notice of what occurred. He evinced no curiosity, scarcely any feeling. If indeed he occasionally did mutter an observation, it was generally of an irritable character, nor truly did he appear satisfied if anyone approached him, save Miriam, from whom alone he would accept the scanty viands which he ever appeared disinclined to touch. But his devoted niece, amid all her harrowing affliction, could ever spare to the protector of her youth a placid countenance, a watchful eye, a gentle voice, and a ready hand. Her religion and her virtue, the strength of her faith, and the inspiration of her innocence, supported this pure and hapless lady amid all her undeserved and unparalleled sorrows.

It was long past midnight; the young widow of Abner reposed upon a couch in a soft slumber. The amiable Beruna and the beautiful Bathsheba, the curtains drawn, watched the progress of the night.

'Shall I wake her?' said the beautiful Bathsheba. 'Methinks the stars are paler! She bade me rouse her long before the dawn.'

'Her sleep is too benign! Let us not wake her,' replied the amiable Beruna. 'We rouse her only to sorrow.'

'May her dreams at least be happy;' rejoined the beautiful Bathsheba. 'She sleeps tranquilly, as a flower.'

'The veil has fallen from her head,' said the amiable Beruna. 'I will replace it lightly on her brow. Is that well, my Bathsheba?'

'It is well, sweet Beruna. Her face shrouded by the shawl is like a pearl in its shell. See! she moves!'

'Bathsheba!'

'I am here, sweet lady.'

'Is it near dawn?'

'Not yet, sweet lady; it is yet night. It is long past the noon of night, sweet lady; methinks I scent the rising breath of morn; but still 'tis night, and the young moon shines like a sickle in the heavenly field, amid the starry harvest.'

'Beruna, gentle girl, give me thy arm. I'll rise.'

The maidens advanced, and gently raising their mistress, supported her to the window.

'Since our calamities,' said Miriam, 'I have never enjoyed such tranquil slumber. My dreams were slight, but soothing. I saw him, but he smiled. Have I slept long, sweet girls? Ye are very watchful.'

'Dear lady, let me bring thy shawl. The air is fresh——'

'But sweet; I thank thee, no. My brow is not so cool as to need a covering. 'Tis a fair night!'

Miriam gazed upon the wide prospect of the moonlit capital. The elevated position of the citadel afforded an extensive view of the mighty groups of buildings-each in itself a city, broken only by some vast and hooded cupola, the tall, slender, white minarets of the mosques, or the black and spiral form of some lonely cypress—through which the rushing Tigris, flooded with light, sent forth its broad and brilliant torrent. All was silent; not a single boat floated on the fleet river, not a solitary voice broke the stillness of slumbering millions. She gazed and, as she gazed, she could not refrain from contrasting the present scene, which seemed the sepulchre of all the passions of our race, with the unrivalled excitement of that stirring spectacle which Bagdad exhibited on the celebration of the marriage of Alroy. How different then, too, was her position from her present, and how happy! The only sister of a devoted brother, the lord and conqueror of Asia, the bride of his most victorious captain, one worthy of all her virtues, and whose youthful valour had encircled her brow with a diadem. To Miriam, exalted station had brought neither cares nor crimes. It had, as it were, only rendered her charity universal, and her benevolence omnipotent. She could not accuse herself, this blessed woman—she could not accuse herself, even in this searching hour of self-knowledge—she could not accuse herself, with all her meekness, and modesty, and humility, of having for a moment forgotten her dependence on her God, or her duty to her neighbour.

But when her thoughts recurred to that being from whom they were indeed scarcely ever absent; and when she remembered him, and all his life, and all the thousand incidents of his youth, mysteries to the world, and known only to her, but which were indeed the prescience of his fame, and thought of all his surpassing qualities and all his sweet affection, his unrivalled glory and his impending fate, the tears, in silent agony, forced their way down her pale and pensive cheek. She bowed her head upon Bathsheba's shoulder, and sweet Beruna pressed her quivering hand.

The moon set, the stars grew white and ghastly, and vanished one by one. Over the distant plain of the Tigris, the scene of the marriage pomp, the dark purple horizon shivered into a rich streak of white and orange. The solemn strain of the Muezzin sounded from the minarets. Some one knocked at the door. It was Caleb.

'I am ready,' said Miriam; and for a moment she covered her face with her right hand. 'Think of me, sweet maidens; pray for me!'

Leaning on Caleb, and lighted by a gaoler, bearing torches, Miriam descended the damp and broken stairs that led to the dungeon. She faltered as she arrived at the grate. She stopped, and leant against the cold and gloomy wall. The gaoler and Caleb preceded her. She heard the voice of Alroy. It was firm and sweet. Its accents reassured her. Caleb came forth with a torch, and held it to her feet; and, as he bent down, he said, 'My lord bade me beg you to be of good heart, for he is.'

The gaoler, having stuck his torch in the niche, withdrew. Miriam desired Caleb to stay without. Then, summoning up all her energies, she entered the dreadful abode. Alroy was standing to receive her. The light fell full upon his countenance. It smiled. Miriam could no longer restrain herself. She ran forward, and pressed him to her heart.

'O, my best, my long beloved,' whispered Alroy; 'such a meeting indeed leads captivity captive!'

But the sister could not speak. She leant her head upon his shoulder, and closed her eyes, that she might not weep.

'Courage, dear heart; courage, courage!' whispered the captive. 'Indeed I am happy!'

'My brother, my brother!'

'Had we met yesterday, you would have found me perhaps a little vexed. But to-day I am myself again. Since I crossed the Tigris, I know not that I have felt such self-content. I have had sweet dreams, dear Miriam, full of solace. And, more than dreams, the Lord has pardoned me, I truly think.'

'O, my brother! your words are full of comfort; for, indeed, I too have dreamed, and dreamed of consolation. My spirit, since our fall, has never been more tranquil.'

'Indeed I am happy.'

'Say so again, my David; let me hear again these words of solace!'

'Indeed, 'tis very true, my faithful friend. It is not spoken in kind mockery to make you joyous. For know, last eve, whether the Lord repented of his wrath, or whether some dreadful trials, of which I will not speak, and wish not to remember, had made atonement for my manifold sins, but so it was, that, about the time my angel Miriam sent her soothing message, a feeling of repose came over me, such as I long have coveted. Anon, I fell into a slumber, deep and sweet, and, instead of those wild and whirling images that of late have darted from my brain when it should rest, glimpses of empire and conspiracy, snatches of fierce wars and mocking loves, I stood beside our native fountain's brink, and gathered flowers with my earliest friend. As I placed the fragrant captives in your flowing locks, there came Jabaster, that great, injured man, no longer stern and awful, but with benignant looks, and full of love. And he said, "David, the Lord hath marked thy faithfulness, in spite of the darkness of thy dungeon." So he vanished. He spoke, my sister, of some strange temptations by heavenly aid withstood. No more of that. I awoke. And lo! I heard my name still called. Full of my morning dream, I thought it was you, and I answered, "Dear sister, art thou here?" But no one answered; and then, reflecting, my memory recognised those thrilling tones that summoned Alroy in Jabaster's cave.' 'The Daughter of the Voice?' 'Even that sacred messenger. I am full of faith. The Lord hath pardoned me. Be sure of that.'

'I cannot doubt it, David. You have done great things for Israel; no one in these latter days has risen like you. If you have fallen, you were young, and strangely tempted.'

'Yet Israel, Israel! Did I not feel a worthier leader will yet arise, my heart would crack. I have betrayed my country!'

'Oh no, no, no! You have shown what we can do and shall do. Your memory alone is inspiration. A great career, although baulked of its end, is still a landmark of human energy. Failure, when sublime, is not without its purpose. Great deeds are great legacies, and work with wondrous usury. By what Man has done, we learn what Man can do; and gauge the power and prospects of our race.'

'Alas! there is no one to guard my name. 'Twill be reviled; or worse, 'twill be forgotten.'

'Never! the memory of great actions never dies. The sun of glory, though awhile obscured, will shine at last. And so, sweet brother, perchance some poet, in some distant age, within whose veins our sacred blood may flow, his fancy fired with the national theme, may strike his harp to Alroy's wild career, and consecrate a name too long forgotten?'

'May love make thee a prophetess!' exclaimed Alroy, as he bent down his head and embraced her. 'Do not tarry,' he whispered. ''Tis better that we should part in this firm mood.'

She sprang from him, she clasped her hands. 'We will not part,' she exclaimed, with energy; 'I will die with thee.'

'Blessed girl, be calm! Do not unman me.'

'I am calm. See! I do not weep. Not a tear, not a tear. They are all in my heart.'

'Go, go, my Miriam, angel of light. Tarry no longer; I pray thee go. I would not think of the past. Let all my mind be centred in the present. Thy presence calls back our bygone days, and softens me too much. My duty to my uncle. Go, dear one, go!'

'And leave thee, leave thee to——Oh! my David, thou hast seen, thou hast heard——Honain?'

'No more; let not that accursed name profane those holy lips. Raise not the demon in me.'

'I am silent. Yet 'tis madness! Oh! my brother, thou hast a fearful trial.'

'The God of Israel is my refuge. He saved our fathers in the fiery furnace. He will save me.'

'I am full of faith. I pray thee let me stay.'

'I would be silent; I would be alone. I cannot speak, Miriam. I ask one favour, the last and dearest, from her who has never had a thought but for my wishes; blessed being, leave me.'

'I go. O Alroy, farewell! Let me kiss you. Again, once more! Let me kneel and bless you. Brother, beloved brother, great and glorious brother, I am worthy of you: I will not weep. I am prouder in this dread moment of your love than all your foes can be of their hard triumph!'

Beruna and Bathsheba received their mistress when she returned to her chamber. They marked her desolate air. She was silent, pale, and cold. They bore her to her couch, whereon she sat with a most listless and unmeaning look; her quivering lips parted, her eyes fixed upon the ground in vacant abstraction, and her arms languidly folded before her. Beruna stole behind her, and supported her back with pillows, and Bathsheba, unnoticed, wiped the slight foam from her mouth. Thus Miriam remained for several hours, her faithful maidens in vain watching for any indication of her self-consciousness.

Suddenly a trumpet sounded.

'What is that?' exclaimed Miriam, in a shrill voice, and looking up with a distracted glance.

Neither of them answered, since they were aware that it betokened the going forth of Alroy to his trial.

Miriam remained in the same posture, and with the same expression of wild inquiry. Another trumpet sounded, and after that a shout of the people. Then she raised up her arms to heaven, and bowed her head, and died.

'Has the second trumpet sounded?'

'To be sure: run, run for a good place. Where is Abdallah?'

'Selling sherbet in the square. We shall find him. Has Alroy come forth?'

'Yes! he goes the other way. We shall be too late. Only think of Abdallah selling sherbet!'

'Father, let me go?'

'You will be in the way; you are too young; you will see nothing. Little boys should stay at home.'

'No, they should not. I will go. You can put me on your shoulders.'

'Where is Ibrahim? Where is Ali? We must all keep together. We shall have to fight for it. I wish Abdallah were here. Only think of his selling sherbet!'

'Keep straight forward. That is right. It is no use going that way. The bazaar is shut. There is Fakreddin, there is Osman Effendi. He has got a new page.'

'So he has, I declare; and a very pretty boy too.'

'Father, will they impale Alroy alive?'

'I am sure I do not know. Never ask questions, my dear. Little boys never should.'

'Yes, they should. I hope they will impale him alive. I shall be so disappointed if they do not.'

'Keep to the left. Dash through the Butchers' bazaar: that is open. All right, all right. Did you push me, sir?'

'Suppose I did push you, sir, what then, sir?'

'Come along, don't quarrel. That is a Karasmian. They think they are to do what they like. We are five to one, to be sure, but still there is nothing like peace and quiet. I wish Abdallah were here with his stout shoulders. Only think of his selling sherbet!'

The Square of the Grand Mosque, the same spot where Jabaster met Abidan by appointment, was the destined scene of the pretended trial of Alroy. Thither by break of day the sight-loving thousands of the capital had repaired. In the centre of the square, a large circle was described by a crimson cord, and guarded by Karasmian soldiers. Around this the swelling multitude pressed like the gathering waves of ocean, but, whenever the tide set in with too great an impulse, the savage Karasmians appeased the ungovernable element by raising their battle-axes, and brutally breaking the crowns and belabouring the shoulders of their nearest victims. As the morning advanced, the terraces of the surrounding houses, covered with awnings, were crowded with spectators. All Bagdad was astir. Since the marriage of Alroy, there had never been such a merry morn as the day of his impalement.

At one end of the circle was erected a magnificent throne. Half way between the throne and the other end of the circle, but further back, stood a company of negro eunuchs, hideous to behold, who, clothed in white, and armed with various instruments of torture, surrounded the enormous stakes, tall, thin, and sharp, that were prepared for the final ceremony.

The flourish of trumpets, the clash of cymbals, and the wild beat of the tambour, announced the arrival of Alp Arslan from the Serail. An avenue to the circle had been preserved through the multitude. The royal procession might be traced as it wound through the populace, by the sparkling and undulating line of plumes of honour, and the dazzling forms of the waving streamers, on which were inscribed the names of Allah and the Prophet. Suddenly, amid the bursts of music, and the shouts of the spectators, many of whom on the terraces humbled themselves on their knees, Alp Arslan mounted the throne, around which ranged themselves his chief captains, and a deputation of the Mullahs, and Imams, and Cadis, and other principal personages of the city.

The King of Karasmé was tall in stature, and somewhat meagre in form. He was fair, or rather sandy-coloured, with a red beard, and blue eyes, and a flat nose. The moment he was seated, a trumpet was heard in the distance from an opposite quarter, and it was soon understood throughout the assembly that the great captive was about to appear.

A band of Karasmian guards first entered the circle, and ranged themselves round the cord, with their backs to the spectators. After them came fifty of the principal Hebrew prisoners, with their hands bound behind them, but evidently more for form than security. To these succeeded a small covered wagon drawn by mules, and surrounded by guards, from which was led forth, his legs relieved from their manacles, but his hands still in heavy chains, David Alroy!

A universal buzz of blended sympathy, and wonder, and fear, and triumph arose, throughout the whole assembly. Each man involuntarily stirred. The vast populace moved to and fro in agitation. His garments soiled and tattered, his head bare, and his long locks drawn off his forehead, pale and thin, but still unsubdued, the late conqueror and Caliph of Bagdad threw around a calm and imperial glance upon those who were but recently his slaves.

The trumpets again sounded, order was called, and a crier announced that his Highness Alp Arslan, the mighty Sovereign of Karasmé, their Lord, Protector, and King, and avenger of Allah and the Prophet, against all rebellious and evil-minded Jews and Giaours, was about to speak. There was a deep and universal silence, and then sounded a voice high as the eagle's in a storm.

'David Alroy!' said his conqueror, 'you are brought hither this day neither for trial nor for judgment. Captured in arms against your rightful sovereign, you are of course prepared, like other rebels, for your doom. Such a crime alone deserves the most avenging punishments. What then do you merit, who are loaded with a thousand infamies, who have blasphemed Allah and the Prophet, and, by the practice of magic arts and the aid of the infernal powers, have broken the peace of kingdoms, occasioned infinite bloodshed, outraged all law, religion, and decency, misled the minds of your deluded votaries, and especially by a direct compact with Eblis, by horrible spells and infamous incantations, captivated the senses of an illustrious Princess, heretofore famous for the practice of every virtue, and a descendant of the Prophet himself.

'Behold these stakes of palm-wood, sharper than a lance! The most terrible retribution that human ingenuity has devised for the guilty awaits you. But your crimes baffle all human vengeance. Look forward for your satisfactory reward to those infernal powers by whose dark co-operation you have occasioned such disasters. Your punishment is public, that all men may know that the guilty never escape, and that, if your heart be visited by the slightest degree of compunction for your numerous victims, you may this day, by the frank confession of the irresistible means by which you seduced them, exonerate your victims from the painful and ignominious end with which, through your influence they are now threatened. Mark, O assembled people, the infinite mercy of the Vicegerent of Allah! He allows the wretched man to confess his infamy, and to save by his confession, his unfortunate victims. I have said it. Glory to Allah!'

And the people shouted, 'He has said it, he has said it! Glory to Allah! He is great, he is great! and Mahomed is his prophet!'

'Am I to speak?' enquired Alroy, when the tumult had subsided. The melody of his voice commanded universal attention.

Alp Arslan nodded his head in approbation.

'King of Karasmé! I stand here accused of many crimes. Now hear my answers. 'Tis said I am a rebel. My answer is, I am a Prince as thou art, of a sacred race, and far more ancient. I owe fealty to no one but to my God, and if I have broken that I am yet to learn that Alp Arslan is the avenger of His power. As for thy God and Prophet, I know not them, though they acknowledge mine. 'Tis well understood in every polity, my people stand apart from other nations, and ever will, in spite of suffering. So much for blasphemy; I am true to a deep faith of ancient days, which even the sacred writings of thy race still reverence. For the arts magical I practised, and the communion with infernal powers 'tis said I held, know, King, I raised the standard of my faith by the direct commandment of my God, the great Creator of the universe. What need of magic, then? What need of paltering with petty fiends, when backed by His omnipotence? My magic was His inspiration. Need I prove why, with such aid, my people crowded round me? The time will come when from out our ancient seed, a worthier chief will rise, not to be quelled even by thee, Sire.

'For that unhappy Princess of whom something was said (with no great mercy, as it seemed to me), that lady is my wife, my willing wife; the daughter of a Caliph, still my wife, although your stakes may make her soon a widow. I stand not here to account for female fancies. Believe me, Sire, she gave her beauty to my raptured arms with no persuasions but such as became a soldier and a king. It may seem strange to thee upon thy throne that the flower of Asia should be plucked by one so vile as I am. Remember, the accidents of Fortune are most strange. I was not always what I am. We have met before. There was a day, and that too not long since, when, but for the treachery of some knaves I mark here,

Fortune seemed half inclined to reverse our fates. Had I conquered, I trust I should have shown more mercy.'

The King of Karasmé was the most passionate of men. He had made a speech according to the advice and instructions of his councillors, who had assured him that the tone he adopted would induce Alroy to confess all that he required, and especially to vindicate the reputation of the Princess Schirene, who had already contrived to persuade Alp Arslan that she was the most injured of her sex. The King of Karasmé stamped thrice on the platform of his throne, and exclaimed with great fire, 'By my beard, ye have deceived me! The dog has confessed nothing!'

All the councillors and chief captains, and the Mullahs, and the Imams, and the Cadis, and the principal personages of the city were in consternation. They immediately consulted together, and, after much disputation, agreed that, before they proceeded to extremities, it was expedient to prove what the prisoner would not confess. A venerable Sheikh, clothed in flowing robes of green, with a long white beard, and a turban like the tower of Babel, then rose. His sacred reputation procured silence while he himself delivered a long prayer, supplicating Allah and the Prophet to confound all blaspheming Jews and Giaours, and to pour forth words of truth from the mouths of religious men. And then the venerable Sheikh summoned all witnesses against David Alroy. Immediately advanced Kisloch the Kourd, to whom, being placed in an eminent position, the Cadi of Bagdad drawing forth a scroll from his velvet bag, read a deposition, wherein the worthy Kisloch stated that he first became acquainted with the prisoner, David Alroy, in some ruins in the desert, the haunt of banditti, of whom Alroy was the chief; that he, Kisloch, was a reputable merchant, and that his caravan had been plundered by these robbers, and he himself captured; that, on the second night of his imprisonment, Alroy appeared to him in the likeness of a lion, and on the third, of a bull with fiery eyes; that he was in the habit of constantly transforming himself; that he frequently raised spirits; that, at length, on one terrible night, Eblis himself came in great procession, and presented Alroy with the sceptre of Solomon Ben Daoud; and that the next day Alroy raised his standard, and soon after massacred Hassan Subah and his Seljuks, by the visible aid of many terrible demons.

Calidas the Indian, the Guebre, and the Negro, and a few congenial spirits, were not eclipsed in the satisfactory character of their evidence by the luminous testimony of Kisloch the Kourd. The irresistible career of the Hebrew conqueror was undeniably accounted for, and the honour of Moslem arms and the purity of Moslem faith were established in their pristine glory and all their unsullied reputation. David Alroy was proved to be a child of Eblis, a sorcerer, and a dealer in charms and magical poisons. The people listened with horror and with indignation. They would have burst through the guards and torn him in pieces, had not they been afraid of the Karasmian battle-axes. So they consoled themselves with the prospect of his approaching tortures.

The Cadi of Bagdad bowed himself before the King of Karasmé, and whispered at a respectful distance in the royal ear. The trumpets sounded, the criers enjoined silence, and the royal lips again moved.

'Hear, O ye people, and be wise. The chief Cadi is about to read the deposition of the royal Princess Schirene, chief victim of the sorcerer.'

And the deposition was read, which stated that David Alroy possessed, and wore next to his heart, a talisman, given him by Eblis, the virtue of which was so great that, if once it were pressed to the heart of any woman, she was no longer mistress of her will. Such had been the unhappy fate of the daughter of the Commander of the Faithful.

'Is it so written?' enquired the captive.

'It is so written,' replied the Cadi, 'and bears the imperial signature of the Princess.'

'It is a forgery.'

The King of Karasmé started from his throne, and in his rage nearly descended its steps. His face was like scarlet, his beard was like a flame. A favourite minister ventured gently to restrain the royal robe.

'Kill the dog on the spot,' muttered the King of Karasmé.

'The Princess is herself here,' said the Cadi, 'to bear witness to the spells of which she was a victim, but from which, by the power of Allah and the Prophet, she is now released.'

Alroy started!

'Advance, royal Princess,' said the Cadi, 'and, if the deposition thou hast heard be indeed true, condescend to hold up the imperial hand that adorned it with thy signature.'

A band of eunuchs near the throne gave way; a female figure veiled to her feet appeared. She held up her hand amid the breathless agitation of the whole assembly; the ranks of the eunuchs again closed; a shriek was heard, and the veiled figure disappeared.

'I am ready for thy tortures, King,' said Alroy, in a tone of deep depression. His firmness appeared to have deserted him. His eyes were cast upon the ground. Apparently he was buried in profound thought, or had delivered himself up to despair.

'Prepare the stakes,' said Alp Arslan.

An involuntary, but universal, shudder might be distinguished through the whole assembly.

A slave advanced and offered Alroy a scroll. He recognised the Nubian who belonged to Honain. His former minister informed him that he was at hand, that the terms he offered in the dungeon might even yet be granted; that if Alroy would, as he doubted not, as he entreated him, accept them, he was to place the scroll in his bosom, but that if he were still inexorable, still madly determined on a horrible and ignominious end, he was to tear the scroll and throw it in to the arena. Instantly Alroy took the scroll, and with great energy tore it into a thousand pieces. A puff of wind carried the fragments far and wide. The mob fought for these last memorials of David Alroy, and this little incident occasioned a great confusion.

In the meantime the negroes prepared the instruments of torture and of death.

'The obstinacy of this Jewish dog makes me mad,' said the King of Karasmé to his courtiers. 'I will hold some parley with him before he dies.' The favourite minister entreated his sovereign to be content; but the royal beard grew so red, and the royal eyes flashed forth such terrible sparks of fire, that even the favourite minister at length gave way.

The trumpet sounded, the criers called silence, and the voice of Alp Arslan was again heard.

'Thou dog, dost see what is preparing for thee? Dost know what awaits thee in the halls of thy master Eblis? Can a Jew be influenced even by false pride? Is not life sweet? Is it not better to be my slipper-bearer than to be impaled?'

'Magnanimous Alp Arslan,' replied Alroy in a tone of undisguised contempt; 'thinkest thou that any torture can be equal to the recollection that I have been conquered by thee?'

'By my beard, he mocks me!' exclaimed the Karasmian monarch, 'he defies me! Touch not my robe. I will parley with him. Ye see no farther than a hooded hawk, ye sons of a blind mother. This is a sorcerer; he hath yet some master spell; he will yet save himself. He will fly into the air, or sink into the earth. He laughs at our tortures.' The King of Karasmé precipitately descended the steps of his throne, followed by his favourite minister, and his councillors, and chief captains, and the Cadis, and the Mullahs, and the Imams, and the principal personages of the city.

'Sorcerer!' exclaimed Alp Arslan, 'insolent sorcerer! base son of a base mother! dog of dogs! dost thou defy us? Does thy master Eblis whisper hope? Dost thou laugh at our punishments? Wilt thou fly into the air? wilt thou sink into the earth? eh, eh? Is it so, is it so?' The breathless monarch ceased, from the exhaustion of passion. He tore his beard out by the roots, he stamped with uncontrollable rage.

'Thou art wiser than thy councillors, royal Arslan; I do defy thee. My master, although not Eblis, has not deserted me. I laugh at thy punishments. Thy tortures I despise. I shall both sink into the earth and mount into the air. Art thou answered?'

'By my beard,' exclaimed the enraged Arslan, 'I am answered. Let Eblis save thee if he can;' and the King of Karasmé, the most famous master of the sabre in Asia, drew his blade like lightning from its sheath, and took off the head of Alroy at a stroke. It fell, and, as it fell, a smile of triumphant derision seemed to play upon the dying features of the hero, and to ask of his enemies, 'Where now are all your tortures?'[82]

NOTES TO ALROY.

[1] [Footnote 1:—*We shall yet see an ass mount a ladder.*—Hebrew proverb.]

[2] [Footnote 2:—Our walls are hung with flowers you love. It is the custom of the Hebrews in many of their festivals, especially in the feast of the Tabernacle, to hang the walls of their chambers with garlands of flowers.]

[3] [Footnote 3:—*The traditionary tomb of Esther and Mordecai.* 'I accompanied the priest through the town over much ruin and rubbish to an enclosed piece of ground, rather more elevated than any in its immediate vicinity. In the centre was the Jewish tomb-a square building of brick, of a mosque-like form, with a rather elongated dome at the top. The door is in the ancient sepulchral fashion of the country, very small, consisting of a single stone of great thickness, and turning on its own pivots from one side. Its key is always in possession of the eldest of the Jews resident at Hamadan. Within the tomb are two sarcophagi, made of a very dark wood, carved with great intricacy of pattern and richness of twisted ornament, with a line of inscription in Hebrew,' &c.—*Sir R. K. Porter's Travels in Persia, vol. ii. p. 107.*]

[4] [Footnote 4:—*A marble fountain, the richly-carved cupola supported by twisted columns.* The vast magnificence and elaborate fancy of the tombs and fountains is a remarkable feature of Oriental architecture. The Eastern nations devote to these structures the richest and the most durable materials. While the palaces of Asiatic monarchs are in general built only of wood, painted in fresco, the rarest marbles are dedicated to the sepulchre and the spring, which are often richly gilt, and adorned even with precious stones.]

[5] [Footnote 5:—*The chorus of our maidens.* It is still the custom for the women in the East to repair at sunset in company to the fountain for their supply of water. In Egypt, you may observe at twilight the women descending the banks of the Nile in procession from every town and village. Their graceful drapery, their long veils not concealing their flashing eyes, and the classical forms of their vases, render this a most picturesque and agreeable spectacle.]

[6] [Footnote 6:—I describe the salty deserts of Persia, a locality which my tale required; but I have ventured to introduce here, and in the subsequent pages, the principal characteristics of the great Arabian deserts: the mirage, the simoom, the gazelle, the oasis.]

[7] [Footnote 7:—*Jackals and marten-cat.* At nightfall, especially in Asia Minor, the lonely horseman will often meet the jackals on their evening prowl. Their moaning is often heard during the night. I remember, when becalmed off Troy, the most singular screams were heard at intervals throughout the night, from a forest on the opposite shore, which a Greek sailor assured me proceeded from a marten-cat, which had probably found the carcass of some horse.]

[8] [Footnote 8: Elburz, or Elborus, the highest range of the Caucasus.]

[9] [Footnote 9:—*A circular and brazen table, sculptured with strange characters and mysterious figures; near it was a couch on which lay several volumes.* A cabalistic table, perhaps a zodiac. The books were doubtless *Sepher Happeliah*, the Book of Wonders; *Sepher Hakkaneh*, the Book of the Pen; and *Sepher Habbahir*, the Book of Light. This last unfolds the most sublime mysteries.]

[10] [Footnote 10:—*Answered the Cabalist.* 'Simeon ben Jochai, who flourished in the second century, and was a disciple of Akibha, is called by the Jews the Prince of the Cabalists. After the suppression of the sedition in which his master had been so unsuccessful, he concealed himself in a cave, where, according to the Jewish historians,

he received revelations, which he after-wards delivered to his disciples, and which they carefully preserved in the book called Sohar. His master, Akibha, who lived soon after the destruction of Jerusalem, was the author of the famous book Jezirah, quoted by the Jews as of Divine authority. When Akibha was far advanced in life, appeared the famous impostor Barchochebas, who, under the character of the Messiah, promised to deliver his countrymen from the power of the Emperor Adrian. Akibha espoused his cause, and afforded him the protection and support of his name, and an army of two hundred thousand men repaired to his standard. The Romans at first slighted the insurrection; but when they found the insurgents spread slaughter and rapine wherever they came, they sent out a military force against them. At. first, the issue of the contest was doubtful. The Messiah himself was not taken until the end of four years.'—Enfield, *Philosophy of the Jews*, vol. ii.

'Two methods of instruction were in use among the Jews; the one public, or *exoteric*; the other secret, or esoteric. The exoteric doctrine was that which was openly taught the people from the law of Moses and the traditions of the fathers. The esoteric was that which treated of the mysteries of the Divine nature, and other sublime subjects, and was known by the name of the Cabala. The latter was, after the manner of the Pythagorean and Egyptian mysteries, taught only to certain persons, who were bound, under the most solemn anathema, not to divulge it. Concerning the miraculous origin and preservation of the Cabala, the Jews relate many marvellous tales. They derive these mysteries from Adam, and assert that, while the first man was in Paradise, the angel Rasiel brought him a book from heaven, which contained the doctrines of heavenly wisdom, and that, when Adam received this book, angels came down to him to learn its contents, but that he refused to admit them to the knowledge of sacred things entrusted to him alone; that, after the Fall, this book was taken back into heaven; that, after many prayers and tears, God restored it to Adam, from whom it passed to Seth. In the degenerate age before the flood this book was lost, and the mysteries it contained almost forgotten; but they were restored by special revelation to Abraham, who committed them to writing in the book *Jezirah.*'—*Vide Enfield, vol. ii. p. 219.*

'The Hebrew word *Cabala,*' says Dom Calmet, 'signifies tradition, and the Rabbins, who are named Cabalists, apply themselves principally to the combination of certain words, numbers, and letters, by the means of which they boasted they could reveal the future, and penetrate the sense of the most difficult passages of Scripture. This science does not appear to have any fixed principles, but depends upon certain ancient traditions, whence its name Cabala. The Cabalists have a great number of names which they style sacred, by means of which they raise spirits, and affect to obtain supernatural intelligence.'—See Calmet, Art. *Cabala.*

'We spake before,' says Lightfoot, 'of the commonness of Magick among them, one singular means whereby they kept their own in delusion, and whereby they affronted ours. The general expectation of the nation of Messias coming when he did had this double and contrary effect, that it forwarded those that belonged to God to believe and receive the Gospel; and those that did not, it gave encouragement to some to take upon them they were Christ or some great prophet, and to others it gave some persuasion to be deluded by them. These deceivers dealt most of them with Magick, and that cheat ended not when Jerusalem ended, though one would have thought that had been a fair term of not further expecting Messias; but since the people were willing to be deceived by such expectation, there rose up deluders still that were willing to deceive them.'—Lightfoot, vol. ii. p. 371.

For many curious details of the Cabalistic Magic, Vide Basnage, vol. v. p. 384, &c.]

[11] [Footnote 11:—*Read the stars no longer.* 'The modern Jews,' says Basnage, 'have a great idea of the influence of the stars.' Vol. iv. p. 454. But astrology was most prevalent among the Babylonian Rabbins, of whom Jabaster was one. Living in the ancient land of the Chaldeans, these sacred sages imbibed a taste for the mystic lore of their predecessors. The stars moved, and formed letters and lines, when consulted by any of the highly-initiated of the Cabalists. This they styled the Celestial Alphabet.]

[12] [Footnote 12:—*The Daughter of the Voice.* 'Both the Talmudick and the latter Rabbins,' says Lightfoot, 'make frequent mention of *Bath Kol, or Filia Vocis,* or an echoing voice which served under the Second Temple for their utmost refuge of revelation. For when Urim and Thummim, the oracle, was ceased, and prophecy was decayed and gone, they had, as they say, certain strange and extraordinary voices upon certain extraordinary occasions, which were their warnings and advertisements in some special matters. Infinite instances of this might be adduced, if they might be believed. Now here it may be questioned why they called it *Bath Kol, the daughter of a voice,* and not a voice itself? If the strictness of the Hebrew word Bath be to be stood upon, which always it is not, it may be answered, that it is called The Daughter of a Voice in relation to the oracles of Urim and Thummim. For whereas that was a voice given from off the mercy-seat, within the vail, and this, upon the decay of that oracle, came as it were in its place, it might not unfitly or improperly be called a *daughter,* or successor of that voice.'—Lightfoot, vol. i. pp. 485, 486. Consult also the learned Doctor, vol. ii. pp. 128, 129: 'It was used for a testimony from heaven, but was indeed performed by magic art.']

[13] [Footnote 13:—*The walls and turrets of an extensive city.* In Persia, and the countries of the Tigris and Euphrates, the traveller sometimes arrives at deserted cities of great magnificence and antiquity. Such, for instance, is the city of Anneh. I suppose Alroy to have entered one of the deserted capitals of the Seleucidae. They are in general the haunt of bandits.]

[14] [Footnote 14:—*Punctured his arm.* From a story told by an Arab.]

[15] [Footnote 15:—*The pilgrim could no longer sustain himself.* An endeavor to paint the simoom.]

[16] [Footnote 16:—*By the holy stone.* The Caaba.—The Caaba is the same to the Mahomedan as the Holy Sepulchre to the Christian. It is the most unseemly, but the most sacred, part of the mosque at Mecca, and is a small, square stone building.]

[17] [Footnote 17:—*I am a Hakim;* i.e. Physician, an almost sacred character in the East. As all Englishmen travel with medicine-chests, the Turks are not be wondered at for considering us physicians.]

[18] [Footnote 18:—*Threw their wanton jerreeds in the air.* The Persians are more famous for throwing the jerreed than any other nation. A Persian gentleman, while riding quietly by your side, will suddenly dash off at full gallop, then suddenly check his horse, and take a long aim with his lance with admirable precision. I should doubt, however, whether he could hurl a lance a greater distance or with greater force and effect than a Nubian, who will fix a mark at sixty yards with his javelin.]

[19] [Footnote 19:—*Some pounded coffee.* The origin of the use of coffee is obscure; but there is great reason to believe that it had not been introduced in the time of Alroy. When we consider that the life of an Oriental at the present day mainly consists in drinking coffee and smoking tobacco, we cannot refrain from asking ourselves, 'What did he do before either of these comparatively modern inventions was discovered?' For a long time, I was inclined to suspect that tobacco might have been in use in Asia before it

was introduced into Europe; but a passage in old Sandys, in which he mentions the wretched tobacco smoke in Turkey, and accounts for it by that country being supplied with 'the dregs of our markets,' demonstrates that, in his time, there was no native growth in Asia. Yet the choicest tobaccos are now grown on the coast of Syria, the real Levant. But did the Asiatics smoke any other plant or substance before tobacco? In Syria, at the present day, they smoke a plant called *timbac*, the Chinese smoke opium; the artificial preparations for the hookah are known to all Indians. I believe, however, that these are all refinements, and for this reason, that in the classic writers, who were as well acquainted with the Oriental nations as ourselves, we find no allusion to the practice of smoking. The anachronism of the pipe I have not therefore ventured to commit, and that of coffee will, I trust, be pardoned.]

[20] [Footnote 20:—*Wilder gestures of the dancing girls*. These dancing girls abound throughout Asia. The most famous are the Almeh of Egypt, and the Nautch of India. These last are a caste, the first only a profession.]

[21] [Footnote 21:—*For thee the bastinado*. The bastinado is the common punishment of the East, and an effective and dreaded one. It is administered on the soles of the feet, the instrument a long cane or palm-branch. Public executions are very-rare.]

[22] [Footnote 22:—*A door of tortoise-shell and mother-of-pearl*. This elegant mode of inlay is common in Oriental palaces, and may be observed also in Alhambra, at Granada.]

[23] [Footnote 23:—*A vaulted, circular, and highly embossed roof, of purple, scarlet, and gold*. In the very first style of Saracenic architecture. See the Hall of the Ambassadors in Alhambra, and many other chambers in that exquisite creation.]

[24] [Footnote 24:—*Nubian eunuchs dressed in rich habits of scarlet and gold*. Thus the guard of Nubian eunuchs of the present Pacha of Egypt, Mehemet Ali, or rather Caliph, a title which he wishes to assume. They ride upon white horses.]

[25] [Footnote 25:—*A quadrangular court of roses*. So in Alhambra, 'The Court of Myrtles,' leading to the Court of Columns, wherein is the famous Fountain of Lions.]

[26] [Footnote 26:—*An Abyssinian giant*. A giant is still a common appendage to an Oriental court even at the present day. See a very amusing story in the picturesque 'Persian Sketches' of that famous elchee, Sir John Malcolm.]

[27] [Footnote 27:—*Surrounded by figures of every rare quadruped*. 'The hall of audience,' says Gibbon, from Cardonne, speaking of the magnificence of the Saracens of Cordova, 'was encrusted with gold and pearls, and a great basin in the centre was surrounded with the curious and costly figures of birds and quadrupeds.'-*Decline and Fall*, vol. x. p. 39.]

[28] [Footnote 28:—*A tree of gold and silver*. 'Among the other spectacles of rare and stupendous luxury was a tree of gold and silver, spreading into eighteen large branches, on which, and on the lesser boughs, sat a variety of birds made of the same precious metals, as well as the leaves of the tree. While the machinery effected spontaneous motions, the several birds warbled their natural harmony.'-*Gibbon*, vol. x. p. 38, from Abulfeda, describing the court of the Caliphs of Bagdad in the decline of their power.]

[29] [Footnote 29:—*Four hundred men led as many white bloodhounds, with collars of gold and rubies*. I have somewhere read of an Indian or Persian monarch whose coursing was conducted in this gorgeous style: if I remember right, it was Mahmoud the Gaznevide.]

[30] [Footnote 30:—*A steed marked on its forehead with a star*. The sacred steed of Solorhon.]

[31] [Footnote 31:—*Instead of water, each basin was replenished with the purest quicksilver*. 'In a lofty pavilion of the gardens, one of those basins and fountains so delightful in a sultry climate, was replenished, not with water, but with the purest quicksilver.'—*Gibbon*, vol. x, from Cardonne.]

[32] [Footnote 32:-*Playing with a rosary of pearls and emeralds*. Moslems of rank are never without the rosary, sometimes of amber and rare woods, sometimes of jewels. The most esteemed is of that peculiar substance called Mecca wood.]

[33] [Footnote 33:—*The diamond hilt of a small poniard*. The insignia of a royal female.]

[34] [Footnote 34:—*You have been at Paris*. Paris was known to the Orientals at this time as a city of considerable luxury and importance. The Embassy from Haroun Alraschid to Charlemagne, at an earlier date, is of course recollected.]

[35] [Footnote 35:—*At length beheld the lost capital of his fathers*. The finest view of Jerusalem is from the Mount of Olives. It is little altered since the period when David Alroy is supposed to have gazed upon it, but it is enriched by the splendid Mosque of Omar, built by the Moslem conquerors on the supposed site of the temple, and which, with its gardens, and arcades, and courts, and fountains, may fairly be described as the most imposing of Moslem fanes. I endeavoured to enter it at the hazard of my life. I was detected, and surrounded by a crowd of turbaned fanatics, and escaped with difficulty; but I saw enough to feel that minute inspection would not belie the general character I formed of it from the Mount of Olives. I caught a glorious glimpse of splendid courts, and light aify gates of Saracenic triumph, flights of noble steps, long arcades, and interior gardens, where silver fountains spouted their tall streams amid the taller cypresses.]

[36] [Footnote 36:—*Entered Jerusalem by the gate of Zion*. The gate of Zion still remains, and from it you descend into the valley of Siloah.]

[37] [Footnote 37: - *King Pirgandicus*. According to a Talmudical story, however, of which I find a note, this monarch was not a Hebrew but a Gentile, and a very wicked one. He once invited eleven famous doctors of the holy nation to supper. They were received in the most magnificent style, and were then invited, under pain of death, either to eat pork, to accept a pagan mistress, or to drink wine consecrated to idols. After long consultation, the doctors, in great tribulation, agreed to save their heads by accepting the last alternative, since the first and second were forbidden by Moses, and the last only by the Rabbins. The King assented, the doctors drank the impure wine, and, as it was exceedingly good, drank freely. The wine, as will sometimes happen, created a terrible appetite; the table was covered with dishes, and the doctors, heated by the grape, were not sufficiently careful of what they partook. In short, the wicked King Pirgandicus contrived that they should sup off pork, and being carried from the table quite tipsy, each of the eleven had the mortification of finding himself next morning in the arms of a pagan mistress. In the course of the year all the eleven died sudden deaths, and this visitation occurred to them, not because they had violated the law of Moses, but because they believed that the precepts of the Rabbins could be outraged with more impunity than the Word of God.]

[38] [Footnote 38:—*And conquered Julius Cæsar*. This classic hero often figures in the erratic pages of the Talmud.]

[39] [Footnote 39:—*The Tombs of the Kings*. The present pilgrim to Jerusalem will have less trouble than Alroy in discovering the Tombs of the Kings, though he probably would not as easily obtain the sceptre of Solomon. The tombs that bear this title are of the time of the Asmonean princes, and of a more ambitious character than any other of the remains. An open court, about fifty feet in breadth, and extremely deep, is excavated out of the rock. One side is formed by a portico, the frieze of which is sculptured in a good Syro-Greek style. There is no grand portal; you crawl into the tombs by a small opening on one of the sides. There are a few small chambers with niches, recesses, and sarcophagi, some sculptured in the same flowing style as the frieze. This is the most

important monument at Jerusalem; and Dr. Clarke, who has lavished wonder and admiration on the tombs of Zachariah and Absalom, has declared the Tombs of the Kings to be one of the marvellous productions of antiquity.]

[40] [Footnote 40:—'*Rabbi Hillel* was one of the most celebrated among the Jewish Doctors, both for birth, learning, rule, and children. He was of the seed of David by his mother's side, being of the posterity of Shephatiah, the son of Abital, David's wife. He was brought up in Babel, from whence he came up to Jerusalem at forty years old, and there studied the law forty years more under Shemaiah and Abtalion, and after them he was President of the Sanhedrim forty years more. The beginning of his Presidency is generally conceded upon to have been just one hundred 'years before the Temple was destroyed; by which account he began eight-and-twenty years before our Saviour was born, and died when he was about twelve years old. He is renowned for his fourscore scholars.'—*Lightfoot*, vol. ii. p. 2008.
The great rival of Hillel was Shammai. Their controversies, and the fierceness of their partisans, are a principal feature of Rabbinical history. They were the same as the Scotists and Thomists. At last the Bath Kol interfered, and decided for Hillel, but in a spirit of conciliatory dexterity. The Bath Kol came forth and spake thus: 'The words both of the one party and the other are the words of the living God, but the certain decision of the matter is according to the decrees of the school of Hillel. And henceforth, whoever shall transgress the decrees of the school of Hillel is punishable with death.']

[41] [Footnote 41:—*A number of small, square, low chambers.* These excavated cemeteries, which abound in Palestine and Egypt, were often converted into places of worship by the Jews and early Christians. Sandys thus describes the Synagogue at Jerusalem in his time.]

[42] [Footnote 42:—*Their heads mystically covered.* The Hebrews cover their heads during their prayers with a sacred shawl.]

[43] [Footnote 43:—*Expounded the law to the congregation of the people.* The custom, I believe, even to the present day, among the Hebrews, a remnant of their old academies, once so famous.]

[44] [Footnote 44:—*The Valley of Jehoshaphat and the Tomb of Absalom.* In the Vale of Jehoshaphat, among many other tombs, are two of considerable size, and which, although of a corrupt Grecian architecture, are dignified by the titles of the tombs of Zachariah and Absalom.]

[45] [Footnote 45:—*The scanty rill of Siloah.* The sublime Siloah is now a muddy rill; you descend by steps to the fountain which is its source, and which is covered with an arch. Here the blind man received his sight; and, singular enough, to this very day the healing reputation of its waters prevails, and summons to its brink all those neighbouring Arabs who suffer from the ophthalmic affections not uncommon in this part of the world.]

[46] [Footnote 46:—*Several isolated tombs of considerable size.* There are no remains of ancient Jerusalem, or the ancient Jews. Some tombs there are which may be ascribed to the Asmonean princes; but all the monuments of David, Solomon, and their long posterity, have utterly disappeared.]

[47] [Footnote 47:—*Are cut strange characters and unearthly forms.* As at Benihassan, and many other of the sculptured catacombs of Egypt.]

[48] [Footnote 48:—*A crowd of bats rushed forward and extinguished his torch.* In entering the Temple of Dendara, our torches were extinguished by a crowd of bats.]

[49] [Footnote 49:—*The gallery was of great extent, with a gradual declination.* So in the great Egyptian tombs.]

[50] [Footnote 50: *The Afrite, for it was one of those dread beings.* Beings of a monstrous form, the most terrible of all the orders of the Dives.]

[51] [Footnote 51:—*An avenue of colossal lions of red granite.* An avenue of Sphinxes more than a mile in length connected the quarters of Luxoor and Carnak in Egyptian Thebes. Its fragments remain. Many other avenues of Sphinxes and lion-headed Kings may be observed in various parts of Upper Egypt.]

[52] [Footnote 52:—*A stupendous portal, cut out of the solid rock, four hundred feet in height, and supported by clusters of colossal Caryatides.* See the great rock temple of Ipsambul in Lower Nubia. The sitting colossi are nearly seventy feet in height. But there is a Torso of a statue of Rameses the Second at Thebes, vulgarly called the great Memnon, which measures upwards of sixty feet round the shoulders.]

[53] [Footnote 53:—*Fifty steps of ivory, and each step guarded by golden lions.* See 1st Kings, chap. x. 18-20.]

[54] [Footnote 54:—*Crossed the desert on a swift dromedary.* The difference between a camel and a dromedary is the difference between a hack and a thorough-bred horse. There is no other.]

[55] [Footnote 55:—*That celestial alphabet known to the true Cabalist.* See Note 11.]

[56] [Footnote 56:—*The last of the Seljuks had expired.* The Orientals are famous for their massacres: that of the Mamlouks by the present Pacha of Egypt, and of the Janissaries of the Sultan, are notorious. But one of the most terrible, and effected under the most difficult and dangerous circumstances, was the massacre of the Albanian Beys by the Grand Vizir, in the autumn of 1830. I was in Albania at the time.]

[57] [Footnote 57:—*The minarets were illumined.* So, I remember, at Constantinople, at the commencement of 1831 at the departure of the Mecca caravan, and also at the annual fast of Ramadan.]

[58] [Footnote 58:—*One asking alms with a wire run through his cheek.* Not uncommon. These Dervishes frequent the bazaars.]

[59] [Footnote 59:—*One hundred thousand warriors were now assembled.* In countries where the whole population is armed, a vast military force is soon assembled. Barchochebas was speedily at the head of two hundred thousand fighting men, and held the Romans long in check under one of their most powerful emperors.]

[60] [Footnote 60:—*Some high-capped Tatar with despatches.* I have availed myself of a familiar character in Oriental life, but the use of a Tatar as a courier in the time of Alroy is, I fear, an anachronism.]

[61] [Footnote 61:—*Each day some warlike Atabek, at the head of his armed train, poured into the capital of the caliphs.* I was at Yanina, the capital of Albania, when the Grand Vizir summoned the chieftains of the country, and I was struck by their magnificent arrays each day pouring into the city.]

[62] [Footnote 62:—*It is the Sabbath etc.* 'They began their Sabbath from sunset, and the same time of day they ended it.'—Talm. Hierosolym. in *Sheveith*, fol. 33, col. I. The eve of the Sabbath, or the day before, was called the day of the preparation for the Sabbath.—Luke xxiii. 54.

'And from the time of the evening sacrifice and forward, they began to fit themselves for the Sabbath, and to cease from their works, so as not to go to the barber, not to sit in judgment, &c.; nay, thenceforward they would not set things on working, which, being set a-work, would complete their business of themselves, unless it would be completed before the Sabbath came—*as wool was not put to dye, unless it could take colour while it was yet day! &c.*—Talm. in Sab., par. I; Lightfoot, vol. i. p. 218.

'Towards sunsetting, when the Sabbath was now approaching, they lighted up the Sabbath lamp. Men and women were bound to have a lamp lighted up in their houses on the Sabbath, though they were never so poor—nay, though they were forced to go a-begging for oil for this purpose; and the lighting up of this lamp was a part of making the Sabbath a delight; and women were especially commanded to look to this business.'—Maimonides in Sab. par. 36.]

[63] [Footnote 63:—*The presence of the robes of honour.* These are ever carried in procession, and their number denotes the rank and quality of the chief, or of the individual to whom they are offered.]

[64] [Footnote 64:—*Pressed it to his lips, and placed it in his vest.* The elegant mode in which the Orientals receive presents.]

[65] [Footnote 65:—A cap of transparent pink porcelain, studded with pearls. Thus a great Turk, who afforded me hospitality, was accustomed to drink his coffee.]

[66] [Footnote 66:—*Slippers powdered with pearls.* The slippers in the East form a very fanciful portion of the costume. It is not uncommon to see them thus adorned and beautifully embroidered. In precious embroidery and enamelling the Turkish artists are unrivalled.]

[67] [Footnote 67:—*The policy of the son of Kareah. Vide* Jeremiah, chap. xlii.]

[68] [Footnote 68:—*The inviting gestures and the voluptuous grace of the dancing girls of Egypt.* A sculptor might find fine studies in the Egyptian Almeh.]

[69] [Footnote 69:—*Six choice steeds sumptuously caparisoned.* Led horses always precede a great man. I think there were usually twelve before the Sultan when he went to Mosque, which he did in public every Friday.]

[70] [Footnote 70:—*Six Damascus sabres of unrivalled temper.* But sabres are not to be found at Damascus, any more than cheeses at Stilton, or oranges at Malta. The art of watering the blade is, however, practised, I believe, in Persia. A fine Damascus blade will fetch fifty or even one hundred guineas English.]

[71] [Footnote 71:—*Roses from Rocnabad.* A river in Persia famous for its bowery banks of roses.]

[72] [Footnote 72:—*Screens made of the feather of a roc.* The screens and fans in the East, made of the plumage of rare birds with jewelled handles, are very gorgeous.]

[73] [Footnote 73:—*A tremulous aigrette of brilliants.* Worn only by persons of the highest rank. The Sultan presented Lord Nelson after the battle of the Nile with an aigrette of diamonds.]

[74] [Footnote 74:—*To send him the whole of the next course.* These compliments from the tables of the great are not uncommon in the East. When at the head-quarters of the Grand Vizir at Yanina, his Highness sent to myself and my travelling companions a course from his table, singers and dancing girls.]

[75] [Footnote 75:—*The golden wine of Mount Lebanon.* A most delicious wine, from its colour, brilliancy, and rare flavour, justly meriting this title, is made on Lebanon; but it will not, unfortunately, bear exportation, and even materially suffers in the voyage from the coast to Alexandria.]

[76] [Footnote 76:—*And the company of gardeners.* These gardeners of the Serail form a very efficient body of police.]

[77] [Footnote 77:—Alroy retired to the bath. The bath is a principal scene of Oriental life. Here the Asiatics pass a great portion of their day. The bath consists of a long suite

of chambers of various temperatures, in which the different processes of the elaborate ceremony are performed.]

[78] [Footnote 78:—*We are the watchers of the moon.* The feast of the New Moon is one of the most important festivals of the Hebrews. 'Our year,' says the learned author of the 'Rites and Ceremonies,' 'is divided into twelve lunar months, some of which consist of twenty-nine, others of thirty days, which difference is occasioned by the various appearance of the new moon, in point of time: for if it appeared on the 30th day, the 29th was the last day of the precedent month; but if it did not appear till the 31st day, the 30th was the last day, and the 31st the first of the subsequent month; and that was an intercalary moon, of all which take the following account.

'Our nation heretofore, not only observing the rules of some fixed calculation, also celebrated the feast of the New Moon, according to the phasis or first appearance of the moon, which was done in compliance with God's command, as our received traditions inform us.

'Hence it came to pass that the first appearance was not to be determined only by rules of art, but also by the testimony of such persons as deposed before the Sanhedrim, or Great Senate, that they had seen the New Moon. So a committee of three were appointed from among the said Sanhedrim to receive the deposition of the parties aforesaid, who, after having calculated what time the moon might possibly appear, despatched some persons *into high and mountainous places, to observe and give their evidence accordingly, concerning the first appearance of the moon.*

'As soon as the new moon was either consecrated or appointed to be observed, notice was given by the Sanhedrim to the rest of the nation what day had been fixed for the New Moon, or first day of the month, because that was to be the rule and measure according to which they were obliged to keep their feasts and fasts in every month respectively.

'This notice was given to them in time of peace, *by firing of beacons, set up for that purpose,* which was looked upon as the readiest way of communication, but, in time of war, when all places were full of enemies, who made use of beacons to amuse our nation with, it was thought fit to discontinue it.']

[79] [Footnote 79:—*The women chatted at the fountain.* The bath and the fountain are the favourite scenes of feminine conversation.]

[80] [Footnote 80:—*Playing chess.* On the walls of the palace of Amenoph the Second, called Medeenet Abuh, at Egyptian Thebes, the King is represented playing chess with the Queen. This monarch reigned long before the Trojan war.]

[81] [Footnote 81:—*Impaled.* A friend of mine witnessed this horrible punishment in Upper Egypt. The victim was a man who had secretly murdered nine persons. He held an official post, and invited travellers and pilgrims to his house, whom he regularly disposed of and plundered. I regret that I have mislaid his MS. account of the ceremony.]

[82] [Footnote 82:—In the *Germen Davidis of Gants*, translated into Latin by Vorstius, Lug. 1654, is an extract from a Hebrew MS. containing an account of Alroy. I subjoin a translation of a passage respecting his death.

R. Maimonides deposes: That the Sultan asked him whether he were the Messiah, and that he answered him, "I am"; and that then the monarch inquired of him what sign he had. To this he replied that they might cut off his head and that he would return to life. Then the King commanded that his head should be cut off, and he died, having said previously to the monarch that the latter should not lack in his life the most grievous torments.

Seven years before the incident quoted above, the Israelites had serious troubles on account of a son of Belial who called himself the Messiah, so that the tetrarch and the princes were justly incensed against the Jews, to such an extent, indeed, that they sent to the latter to inquire whether they desired the reign of the Messiah. The name of this accursed troubler was David El-David, *alias* Alroy, who hailed from the city of Omadia, where were gathered about a thousand rich, honest, happy and decently-living families, whose tabernacle was the principal resort of those that dwelt in the neighbourhood of the river Sabbathion; and around them were gathered more than a hundred minor tabernacles.

This city was on the border of the region of Media, and the dialect used there was the Targum. Thence to the region of Golan is a journey of fifty days. It is under the rule of Persia, to which it pays a heavy tribute every fifteen years, and one golden talent in addition. Moreover, this man David El-David was educated under the Prince of the Chaldean captivity, in the care of the eminent Scholiarch, in the city of Bagdad, who was preeminently wise in the Talmud and in all foreign sciences, as well as in all books of divination, magic, and Chaldean lore; This David El-David, out of the boldness and arrogance of his heart, lifted his hand against the ruling powers, and collected those Jews who dwelt in the neighbourhood of Mount Chophtan, seducing them to follow him into battle against all the neighbouring peoples. He showed them signs-of what value they knew not: there were men, indeed, who supported him on account of his magic art and of certain things to be done; others said that his great power came from the hand of God. Those who flocked to him called him the Messiah, lauding and extolling him.

In another epoch of Persian history a certain Jew arose, calling himself the Messiah, and prospered greatly. A large part of the Israelitish population believed in him. But when the King indeed heard of all this pretender's power, and that he proposed to join battle with him, he sent to the Jews who lived thereabouts and notified them that unless they deserted this man, and came oui; from all association with him, they certainly should be slain, every one of them, with the sword, and afterward the children and the women should perish. Then the whole population of Israel assembled, and argued with this man, and threw themselves down before him on the ground, strongly supplicating him, with clamour and tears, to depart from them. Why, indeed, should he put them and others in danger? Had not the King already sworn that they should perish by the sword, and wherefore should he bring affliction upon all the Jewish inhabitants of Persia? Responding, he said: "I have come to serve you, and ye will not have me. Whom do ye fear? Who dares stand in front of me, and what doth this Persian King that he dare not oppose me and my sword?" The Jews asked him what sign he had that he was the Messiah. He answered: "My mission prospers: the Messiah needs no other sign." They answered that many had acted likewise, and that none had reached success. Then he drove them forth from his face with superb indignation.]

Echo Library

www.echo-library.com

Echo Library uses advanced digital print-on-demand technology to build and preserve an exciting world class collection of rare and out-of-print books, making them readily available for everyone to enjoy.

Situated just yards from Teddington Lock on the River Thames, Echo Library was founded in 2005 by Tom Cherrington, a specialist dealer in rare and antiquarian books with a passion for literature.

Please visit our website for a complete catalogue of our books, which includes foreign language titles.

The Right to Read

Echo Library actively supports the Royal National Institute of the Blind's Right to Read initiative by publishing a comprehensive range of large print and clear print titles.

Large Print titles are in 16 point Tiresias font as recommended by the RNIB.

Clear Print titles are in 13 point Tiresias font and designed for those who find standard print difficult to read.

Customer Service

If there is a serious error in the text or layout please send details to feedback@echo-library.com and we will supply a corrected copy. If there is a printing fault or the book is damaged please refer to your supplier.

Printed in the United States
126102LV00010B/128/A